# Effective Preaching

## Bringing People into an Encounter with God

Edited by

**Michael E. Connors, CSC**

*Nihil Obstat*
Rev. Mr. Daniel G. Welter, JD
Chancellor
Archdiocese of Chicago
October 5, 2018

*Imprimatur*
Most Rev. Ronald A. Hicks
Vicar General
Archdiocese of Chicago
October 5, 2018

The *Nihil Obstat* and *Imprimatur* are declarations that the material is free from doctrinal or moral error and thus is granted permission to publish in accordance with c. 827. No legal responsibility is assumed by the grant of this permission. No implication is contained herein that those who have granted the *Nihil Obstat* and *Imprimatur* agree with the content, opinions, or statements expressed.

Selected material in chapter 5 excerpted from *Of Poets, Prophets, and Preachers* by Joseph J. Juknialis, copyright © 2016, World Library Publications, wlpmusic.com. Used with permission.

EFFECTIVE PREACHING: BRINGING PEOPLE INTO AN ENCOUNTER WITH GOD © 2019 Archdiocese of Chicago: Liturgy Training Publications, 3949 South Racine Avenue, Chicago, IL 60609; 800-933-1800; fax: 800-933-7094; email: orders@ltp.org; website: www.LTP.org. All rights reserved.

This book was edited by Kevin Thornton. Christian Rocha was the production editor, Anna Manhart was the cover designer, and Kari Nicholls was the interior designer and production artist.

Cover: The Lord of the Parables © Jorge Cocco Santángelo https://jorgecocco.com/
Sk-Modernist title font © Sean Kane Design www.SeanKaneDesign.com

23 22 21 20 19 1 2 3 4 5

Printed in the United States of America

Library of Congress Control Number: 2018966224

ISBN 978-1-61671-486-4

EFP

# CONTENTS

INTRODUCTION v

■ CHAPTER 1
Preaching in the Mother Tongue—
Calming and Ordering the Chaos inside Our Listeners 1
Ronald Rolheiser, OMI

■ CHAPTER 2
To What Effect? Qualities of Effective Catholic Preaching 13
Michael E. Connors, CSC

■ CHAPTER 3
Does It Resound? Congregational Exegesis
in Conversation with Negotiation Science 29
Ann M. Garrido

■ CHAPTER 4
Emmaus Revisited: The Convergence of the
Word Proclaimed and the Eucharist Celebrated 43
Bishop Sylvester Ryan

■ CHAPTER 5
Preaching Hope in a Postmodern World 53
Joseph J. Juknialis

■ CHAPTER 6
The Ladder of Homiletics:
Seven Steps to Effective Preaching 63
Guerric DeBona, OSB

■ CHAPTER 7
Making a Scene in the Pulpit! 75
Alyce M. McKenzie

■ CHAPTER 8
Story/Point/Passage: Ten Rules of Thumb for Homilists 89
John Shea

■ CHAPTER 9
Plotting a Path for People to Follow 99
Richard L. Eslinger

■ CHAPTER 10
"Murder Your Darlings": How to Edit for Effective Preaching 111
Deborah Wilhelm

■ CHAPTER 11
Focus and Function: Kindling the Fire 123
Edward J. Griswold

■ CHAPTER 12
Entertain or Else! The Preacher as Performer in Attending to Augustine's "Delight" 133
David J. Shea

■ CHAPTER 13
Igniting the Flame of Intentional Listeners 145
Sharon Schuhmann and Rev. Jeff Nicolas

■ CHAPTER 14
The Holy Spirit and Listener Receptivity: Preaching That Soaks in Like Good Butter on Warm Toast 155
Karla Bellinger

■ CHAPTER 15
If You're Not Real, I'm Not Coming 165
Peter McCormick, CSC

■ CHAPTER 16
If Our Hearts Are on Fire, What Are Our Bodies Doing? 175
Suzanne Nawrocki

■ CHAPTER 17
Fired Up—Burned Out 185
Richard Stern

■ CHAPTER 18
Spirituality: Preaching's Catalyst 197
Fred A. Baumer and Patricia Hughes Baumer

ABOUT THE CONTRIBUTORS 209

INDEX 211

# INTRODUCTION

> *Let us renew our confidence in preaching, based on the conviction that it is God who seeks to reach out to others through the preacher, and that he displays his power through human words.*
>
> —Pope Francis, *Evangelii gaudium*, 136

IS THERE A CRISIS IN CONFIDENCE IN CATHOLIC PREACHING? Many factors would seem to indicate that there is. Traveling around the Church in North America, one rarely hears praise of the preaching issuing forth from our sanctuaries. On the contrary, nearly everyone—lay and clergy, people of all ecclesiological stripes and diverse theological interests—seems to agree that Catholic preaching in general is impoverished, uninspiring, aimless, and just plain dull. It has become altogether commonplace to make Catholic preaching the object of cynicism and derision. Stories of Catholics gravitating to evangelical or Pentecostal churches in search of livelier and more meaningful preaching abound, as do stories of former attendees who drift off into secular pursuits and leisure pastimes. Fatigued priests and deacons themselves, many of them preaching at multiple liturgies on a weekend, in multiple worship sites comprising a single parish, report chronic battles with pulpit discouragement. When results from preaching are not immediate nor obvious, we are tempted to say to ourselves, "What's the point, anyway? No one is listening. I can't compete with television, the internet, Facebook, Twitter, or YouTube." Increasingly we preachers and those who long for "a word from the Lord" can feel sidelined.

Unquestionably, we have urgent needs in the practice of preaching. Yet I myself am inclined to think that the situation is not as grim as the critics would have us believe. I know scores of Catholic preachers—priests and deacons, as well as some lay ministers—who toil week after week, listening to the Word, constructing a message of meaning, faithfulness, and hope for their congregations. In recent years, I've had the privilege of speaking with many of them, and have been universally impressed by their reverence for preaching, their lively sense that they want preaching to matter, and their earnest desire to do better in the pulpit. Many of them are inadequately trained in homiletics—indeed, sadly, too many Catholic preachers do not even know the rudimentary basics of what our tradition and magisterium have to say about the purpose and point of preaching. Their formation has failed to introduce them into the exciting adventure of listening for the voice of God speaking to people today. Nonetheless, many perform this ministry with dignity and diligence, and they produce homilies of sound quality, which are often quietly received and respectfully, even warmly, appreciated in the pews. What they lack in homiletic skill or delivery polish, these preachers make up for in sincerity and humility. As I try to impress upon my preaching students, you don't have to be a Fulton Sheen, a St. Paul, or a Billy Graham to be an effective preacher. You just have to be an authentic seeker, a genuine disciple of Jesus with some gift for discernment and the courage to overcome your fear and speak.

Perhaps our current situation is not so much characterized by a crisis of confidence in preaching, as it is by a long-term and still nascent process of rediscovery of the power of the Word. Before the Second Vatican Council, we collectively had allowed the importance of the proclaimed Scriptures and the preached word to fall into serious neglect. *Sacrosanctum concilium* and the other council documents roused us to renewal, but that renewal is barely more than fifty years on. It should not surprise us that a reinvigoration of preaching has thus far been spotty and incomplete. The recovery of our preaching instincts will continue for decades to come as we once again plumb the theological riches of our homiletic tradition. Voices from the pews, pleading for more attention to the homily's vital importance, are beginning to be heard. And the Church is beginning to respond, most especially through its preacher-in-chief, the Bishop of Rome, whose writing and personal preaching example are challenging and inspiring all of us on a near-daily basis.

Much of what I do as director of the John S. Marten Program in Homiletics and Liturgics at the University of Notre Dame is to impress upon whoever will listen the worth of preaching and the value of careful investment of time and energy in its preparation and delivery. As Fr. Ron Knott claimed several years ago, "Catholic pulpits are indeed buried treasures waiting to be claimed."[1] Preaching still matters for the life of the Christian community—of this I remain fully convinced. Pope Francis evidently believes it too. So do the 225 priests, deacons, homileticians, students, and pew Catholics who attended our 2017 conference, "'To Set the Earth on Fire': Effective Catholic Preaching," which gave rise to this book. There was no shortage of energy, joy, and hope as we gathered at this, the fourth major preaching conference at Notre Dame in this decade. Through prayer, rich conversation with peers, and dialogue with presenters, participants returned home encouraged, challenged, and given some creative stimulation and support in their preaching ministries.

The contributors to this volume are a diverse lot who nonetheless eagerly share with us their wisdom and love for preaching. You will find in these pages a wealth of insight and encouragement, ranging from the broadest vision to the most concretely practical. You will not find perfect consonance of thought, as far as what actually constitutes excellent or effective preaching. No surprise there—after all, surprisingly little has been written on what homiletic effectiveness means, especially in the Catholic world. Yet I think you will be pleasantly surprised by points of convergence and unexpected moments of harmony. I hope that for each reader this process will come as thought provoking and hopeful, inspiring you to a new appreciation of your own immersion in the preached word.

If this book, like the conference, succeeds just a little in rekindling the fire of Catholic preaching, it will have done its work. To put it another way, may we all come a little closer to the warmth and illumination Jesus himself had in mind when he said, "I have come to set the earth on fire, and how I wish it were already blazing!" (Luke 12:49).

Michael E. Connors, CSC
Notre Dame, Indiana
Feast of St. Barnabas, Apostle, 2018

1. J. Ronald Knott, "Claiming Your Pulpit for Spiritual Leadership – Part I," *The Priest*, January 31, 2011: https://www.osv.com/OSVNewsweekly/Perspectives/Editorials/Article/TabId/798/ArtMID/13633/ArticleID/2079/Claiming-Your-Pulpit-for-Spiritual-Leadership—Part-I.aspx.

■ CHAPTER 1

# Preaching in the Mother Tongue—Calming and Ordering the Chaos inside Our Listeners

Ronald Rolheiser, OMI

*How does one preach in the mother tongue of one's listeners? What is one's mother tongue? What religious words speak truly to touch our souls?*

## A Gathering Hymn

As a young man, the gifted Irish writer John Moriarty drifted from the Roman Catholicism of his youth. But one day, as he shares in his writings, he came to the realization that Roman Catholicism was his "mother tongue," something that was in him like a brand in his soul, and he returned to the faith of his youth. While initially the sense that Roman Catholicism was his mother tongue was just a gut feeling, eventually he began to understand more and more what it meant. One incident in particular helped him understand and articulate how Roman Catholicism was his mother tongue. It happened as he was present at the deathbed of a dying woman.

At the time, Moriarty was living in a cottage in rural Ireland. One evening he got word that a woman, Celia, was dying. Along with his neighbors he went to her house to be with her family and her neighbors as Celia died. Here is how he describes what happened then:

> We were at a loss what to do or to say. Soon, Annie Coneely, the oldest woman in the neighborhood, came in and she took over. Going straight to the bed, she cradled Celia's head in her arm and she recited the act of contrition into her ear. Telling us to say the rosary so that Celia could hear it in the voices of neighbors that she would recognize, she continued to cradle the dying woman's head, touching it and stroking it, all the time talking and praying. It was a wonder watching her. As perhaps only an old woman out of an old culture could, she midwifed Celia, whom we all called Granny, out into eternity.

Later, Moriarty will put this lesson to work when he himself is attending to a dying friend, Michéal, Celia's son:

> Remembering this, I one day crossed the floor to Michéal's hospital bed. Bending down into the hot smell of gangrene, I talked to him, seeking to give him the memories he could, surely with some confidence, walk out into eternity with.
>
> > Growing up in the old thatched house, gone now, with Celia your mother, you went to the local school. You became an altar boy and even now you remember the great words, *Introibo ad altare Dei; Kyrie eleison; Christe eleison; Dominus vobiscum, et cum spiritu tuo; sursum corda; habemus ad Dominum; sanctus, sanctus, sanctus, Dominus Deus Sabaoth, pleni sunt caeli et terra gloria tua; Pater noster qui es in caelis; pax vobiscum; ite, missa est; Deo gratias*. As a young lad you worked in the forestry and at eighteen years of age you built a new house for yourself and your mother. You married Kathleen Ward from Leitrim. Two girls, Mary Teresa and Noeleen, were born to ye. Thanks to ye they are fine young women now. I showed up in the neighborhood and I was one day over in your house talking to ye. You and Kathleen got up and went out. I stayed on, talking to the girls. As I was leaving, I met you and Kathleen coming back in the door. Kathleen continued on into the kitchen and you turned to walk over the road with me. As we walked past the ice house, you picked a stone off the road, you threw it across the wall into your field and you said, 'Now John, from where that stone landed to the far wall, that's yours, 'tis a site for a house for you.' Remembering all this, Michéal, walk on, listen to me. I'm saying the old great words for you, *Introibo ad altare Dei; Kyrie eleison; Christe eleison; Dominus vobiscum, et cum spiritu tuo; sursum corda; habemus ad Dominum; sanctus, sanctus, sanctus . . . Deo gratias.*
>
> That done, I asked the neighbors who were sitting there to go and talk to him. Shy men, men not normally talkative, did go over and they talked saying, Michéal, this is Jimmy, or this is Maureen, or this is Frank. One by one, men and women, we all talked to him. Looking on, I sensed that we the next generation, stupefied an hour ago, had somehow learned to keep house with the dying and, within that house, to walk with the dying.[1]

1. John Moriarty, *Serious Sounds* (Dublin: Lilliput Press Ltd., 2007), 52–54.

## Some Initial Reflections about Language

> *Myths are the most open, most exploratory, most suggestively subtle, yet precise, stories allowing the soul the widest imagination for its complexes. (James Hillman)*[2]

There are various languages within a language and some of these speak more deeply than others.

Thirty years ago, the American educator Allan Bloom wrote a book entitled *The Closing of the American Mind.*[3] This was his thesis: In our secularized world today our language is becoming ever more empirical, one-dimensional, and devoid of depth and this is closing our minds by stripping us of the deeper meanings inside our own experience. For Bloom, how we name an experience determines to a large extent its meaning.

Twenty years earlier, in a rather provocative essay, *The Triumph of the Therapeutic,* Philip Rieff[4] had already suggested something similar. For Rieff, we live our lives under a certain "symbolic hedge," namely, a language and set of symbols within which we interpret our experience. And that hedge can be high or low and consequently so too will be the meaning we derive from any experience. Experience can be rich or shallow, depending upon the language by which we interpret it.

Take this example: A man has a backache and sees his doctor. The doctor tells him that he's suffering from *arthritis*. This brings the man some initial calm. But he isn't satisfied and sees a psychologist. The psychologist tells him that his symptoms are not just physical but that he is also suffering from *midlife crisis*. This names his pain at a deeper level and affords him a richer understanding of his pain. But he's still dissatisfied and sees a spiritual director. The spiritual director, while not denying him arthritis and midlife crisis, tells him that he should understand this pain as his *Gethsemane*, as his cross to carry.

Notice all three diagnoses speak of the same pain but that each places that pain under a different symbolic hedge. Language speaks at different levels and only a certain language speaks at the level of the soul. Recently we have been helped to understand this through the work of Carl Jung and a number of his disciples, notably James Hillman and Thomas Moore, who

---

2. James Hillman, given in an oral presentation at the Scottish Rite Temple, San Francisco, CA, March 11, 1990. See: *Men and the Life of Desire, Oral Traditions Archives*, Box 51155, Pacific Grove, CA, 93950.

3. Allan Bloom, *The Closing of the American Mind: How Higher Education Has Failed Democracy and Impoverished the Souls of Today's Students* (New York: Simon & Schuster, 1987).

4. Philip Rieff, *The Triumph of the Therapeutic: Uses of Faith after Freud* (Chicago: University of Chicago Press, 1987; first published 1966).

have helped us to understand more explicitly the language of the soul and how that language helps us touch the deep archetypes within us.

We see the language of soul, among other places, in some of our great myths and fairy tales, many of them centuries old. Their seeming simplicity can fool you. They may be simple, but they're not simplistic. To offer one example, the story of *Cinderella:* The first thing to notice in this story is that the name, *Cinderella,* is not a real name but a composite of two words: *cinder,* meaning ashes, and *puella,* meaning the eternal girl. This is not a simple fairy tale about a lonely, beaten-down young girl. It's a myth that highlights a deep structure within the human soul, namely, that before our souls are ready to wear the glass slipper, to be the belle of the ball, to marry the prince, and to live happily ever after, we must first spend some necessary time sitting in the ashes, suffering humiliation, and being purified by a time in the dust. Notice how this story speaks in its own way of our spirituality of Lent, a season of penance, wherein we mark ourselves with ashes in order to enter a desert of our own making. Cinderella is a story that shines a tiny light into the depth of our souls. Many of our famous myths do that, though nothing shines a light into the soul as deeply as does Scripture, the Bible. Its language and symbols name our experience in a way that both honors the soul and helps us plumb the genuine depth inside our own experiences.

For example, we can be confused, or we can be *inside the belly of the whale*. We can be helpless before an addiction, or we can be *possessed by a demon*. We can vacillate in our prayer lives between fervor and dark nights, or we can vacillate between *being with Jesus in Galilee or with him in Jerusalem*. We can be paralyzed as we stand before a globalization that's overwhelming, or we can be *standing with Jesus on the borders of Samaria in a new conversation with a Syro-Phoenician woman*. We can be struggling with fidelity and with keeping our commitments in relationships, or we can be *standing with Joshua before God, receiving instructions to kill off the Canaanites if we are to sustain ourselves in the Promised Land*. We can be suffering from arthritis, or we can be *sweating blood in the garden of Gethsemane*.

The language we use makes a huge, huge difference in how we appropriate meaning. And the language and symbols of Scripture are the deepest language of the soul that we have, and in them we can recognize our mother tongue.

One further comment on religious language: Religious language is also not just of one kind. It has a number of different functions. There are three distinct, though interpenetrating, functions to religious language—and this, of course, is true for our preaching:

- *There is a religious language of the ascent,* a language that challenges us towards idealistic striving, to push ourselves always towards what's higher, language that tells us to never be content, to never get complacent, to never look back, to be ever more selfless, to take up your cross daily, to hold up martyrdom as our supreme goal, to always look and strive upward.

- *There is a religious language of maintenance, steadiness, balance, and buoyance.* This is a language that challenges us to keep our feet on the ground, to hold on, to not give in to weariness, to not despair, to do proper self-care, to not bite off more than we can chew, to not overtax ourselves, to not just view life as a test but as a time within which God also wants us to flourish, and to not enter the darkness imprudently. This language, even while religious, contains always a robust pragmatism, common sense, and a religious and ascetic caution.

- *There is a religious language of the descent,* a language that challenges us to learn from sitting in the ashes, to accept humiliation and learn from it, to accept that diminishment and death also bring greatness and salvation, to see the necessary connection between Good Friday and Easter Sunday, and to have us go voluntarily at times into the desert as Jesus did. This language eschews comfort and easy safety.

All three of these are part of our mother tongue and good preaching knows and utilizes all three, picking with prudence the timely moment for each.

## The Search for a Vocabulary for the Faith

Too much of our religious language today is not functioning as mother tongue—nor, indeed, as sacred poetry that can inspire. What we see commonly today in our preaching is a religious language that, depending on the preacher, falls into one, or a mixture, of five genres:

- Literal and rote repetition of the biblical vocabulary, the creeds, our Christian dogmas, the catechism, and our moral positions.

- "Chicken soup for the soul": inspirational stories, but with no real meaningful connection to Scripture.

- The language of self-development: again with no real reference to Scripture.

- Language that attempts to be relevant by an appeal to what's popular in the language and the contemporary currents in the culture.
- Language that believes there is salvation in "technology alone," *Sola Technologia*: an approach that believes that the primary task of preaching today is through electronic media and is more focused on that medium than on the message.

Not that any of these are bad in themselves, and indeed, they all have their usefulness, but they need to be ancillary, not central, to how we understand preaching. And I say this sympathetically, for it is not easy to find a vocabulary for the faith that speaks as our mother tongue.

## The Search for Our Mother Tongue within Our Preaching

> After a mother has smiled for a long time at her child, the child will begin to smile back; she has awakened love in its heart and in awakening love, she awakes also recognition. In the same way, God awakes himself before us as love. Love radiates from God and instills the light of love in our hearts. (Hans Urs von Balthasar)[5]

What is a mother tongue? It is interesting to note that nowhere do we ever speak of a father tongue. One's country can be one's fatherland, but no language is ever one's father tongue. We get our first language from our mothers. They awaken communication in us and they, first and foremost, draw language out of us, even before we can consciously speak. And we go through life carrying a deep, residual, inchoate, unconscious memory, a psychic and emotional imprint, of that first communicative encounter between our mothers and ourselves. Forever afterwards we are able to recognize what happened between our mothers and ourselves as our mother tongue.

How does this work? Perhaps a good entry into understanding what constitutes a mother tongue can be a deeper examination of an image that Jesus leaves with us in John's Gospel. Speaking of how we are to recognize God's voice inside the many other voices that surround us, Jesus said this:

> Amen, amen, I say to you, whoever does not enter a sheepfold through the gate but climbs over elsewhere is a thief and a robber. But whoever enters through the gate is the shepherd of the sheep. The gatekeeper opens it for him, and the sheep hear his voice, as he calls his own sheep by name and

5. Hans Urs Von Balthasar, *Love Alone Is Credible* (San Francisco: Ignatius Press, 2004), 76.

> leads them out. When he has driven out all his own, he walks ahead of them, and the sheep follow him, because they recognize his voice. But they will not follow a stranger; they will run away from him, because they do not recognize the voice of strangers. (John 10:1–5)

To understand what Jesus is saying here it is helpful to place it against the background of two things, *sheep farming* and *babysitting.*

*Sheep farming.* During Jesus' time shepherds often grazed their flocks in open places, public lands, rather than in individual privately owned pastures. But it was necessary each night to round up the sheep and bring them into an enclosure for the night. And because the shepherds wanted companionship, safety, and each other's help in guarding the sheep they would put the sheep in a common enclosure where the shepherds would take turns keeping guard as the others slept. However, in the morning each shepherd would lead his own flock away to separate for the day. They had a simple method for doing this. Each sheep had a name and each was trained to recognize the voice of its own shepherd. The shepherd then would simply walk away from the enclosure and call each sheep by its name and each sheep, recognizing its name pronounced by its shepherd, would follow the shepherd out.

Then, like now, there were some conniving, dishonest shepherds who would rise early in the morning and try to draw away some of another shepherd's sheep by imitating his voice and fooling a sheep or two to follow him. If a sheep got fooled and followed the voice of the wrong shepherd it probably got sold and slaughtered that same day. Thus it was vital for each sheep to recognize the voice of its own shepherd. If it did, and followed him, it meant pasture, food, and safety. If it got fooled and followed the wrong voice it often meant death. Each sheep had to know its mother tongue!

*Babysitting.* Anyone who has ever had an experience of babysitting a very young baby in the absence of its mother knows that inevitably the moment will come when the baby will no longer be soothed by the voice of the babysitter but will begin to cry for its mother. No matter how much the babysitter tries to imitate the voice, tone, and words of the mother, the baby will not find calm, quiet, and rest. Only on hearing again the voice of its mother, upon her return, will the baby find calm and be soothed in its mother tongue. Analyzing this example, we might ask ourselves: What does the mother's voice do that other, imitative voices cannot do at that moment?

In archetypal language, we might say that the mother's voice does four things and, at that moment, is the only voice that can provide those four things:

- *The mother's voice dispels chaos.* It makes everything safe again. It provides a sense of safety; it makes the darkness safe, familiar, and warm, and chaos is dispelled.
- *The mother's voice comforts.* The very sound of the mother's voice has the effect of embracing the baby's anxieties and stilling them.
- *The mother's voice evokes ideals.* This, of course, is pretty rudimentary in a mother quieting a baby, but even there, by dispelling the chaos, erasing the fear, and comforting the baby's anxieties, she is drawing the baby outward, inviting it to have courage to enter the outside world and take its place there. And in the months and years that follow in the baby's young life, the mother, more than anyone else, has the power to challenge that young life towards every kind of healthy ideal.
- *The mother's voice blesses.* It is the mother's voice, more than anyone else's, that can in those early years, even before the baby is self-conscious, let the baby know that it is loved, wanted, and precious. The baby must hear, however consciously or unconsciously, from its mother the words that Jesus heard from his Father at his baptism: "You are my beloved Son; with you I am well pleased" (Mark 1:11; Luke 3:22), This knowledge, that it is precious and loved, does for the human baby what a cow does for her baby calf immediately after it is born, that is, it turns around and licks the constricting afterbirth off of every inch of the calf's body, thus setting it free to walk on its own legs. That is an archetypal image of primal blessing and it is one of the things a mother's voice does for a baby.

Our mother's voice is imprinted in each of us so that throughout the rest of our lives we are forever, consciously and unconsciously, searching for a voice, or voices, that touch us at that level, namely, that dispels our deepest chaos, comforts us at our deepest level, evokes the highest ideals in us, and lets us know that we are precious, are loved, and are God's beloved.

And that is also how we recognize the voice of the Good Shepherd among the myriad of seductive and threatening voices that surround us and, today, speak to us from a thousand electronic screens. How do we recognize the voice of God within all these voices? We recognize it inside that voice that offers us the deepest safety, the deepest comfort, the highest ideals, and the ultimate assurance of unconditional love.

Admittedly this isn't always easy to recognize and we will be fooled many times by voices that seemingly promise those things but in the end leave us disappointed and empty. However, like fishing, where you are sometimes fooled by something on your hook that is not a live fish but you are never fooled when you actually have a live fish on the line, we are never fooled when we hear the true voice of the Good Shepherd. We recognize our mother tongue.

## Preaching in the Mother Tongue

The Word of God is not something that we pass down from generation to generation like a baton in a relay race. It is, as Jesus tells us, a batch of yeast that gets thrown into a batch of dough and which slowly, in a hidden manner, transforms the dough. Let me attempt to highlight that with two stories.

While doing my doctorate I was living in a seminary along with about sixty seminarians. At the seminary at that time we were blessed with a wonderful, gracious, faith-filled woman who was an executive secretary working in one of the offices. During my last year there, this wonderful woman succumbed to cancer and died. Her brother-in-law, a priest, presided at her funeral and preached (to my mind) an exceptional homily. The Gospel he chose for the funeral was the passage in Matthew's Gospel where Jesus speaks the Beatitudes. In his homily, he went on to show how in her life this woman had given concrete flesh to those teachings. Moreover he did this in a way that celebrated the life of this woman, comforted her family, and celebrated our common faith. The homily let us drink more deeply of both this woman's faith and our own faith as it highlighted the reality of God in our lives through the prism of this woman's life, the prism of our faith, and the prism of the Beatitudes.

On the bus returning to the seminary after the funeral, I overheard a number of seminarians lament to each other how terrible the homily had been. Unable to contain my frustration, I turned and asked them what was wrong with the homily. Their answer: "He never used the word of God! He gave a eulogy!" They were young and in first fervor so their narrowness in understanding the Word of God was forgivable. But they were wrong, very wrong. The priest delivering this homily used the Word of God skillfully, wonderfully, and accurately. He began and ended his homily with the words: "And the Word was made flesh and it dwelt among us!" The woman we were burying, like Jesus himself, had given real flesh to God and to God's Word. Those of us who knew her recognized in her voice and in her life our mother tongue, the voice of the Good Shepherd.

My second story adds a further dimension to this: Some years ago a priest colleague of mine was sent to work with the Cree First Nation in Canada. He spent the first year in preparation, learning the Cree language and his teacher was no less than the chief himself. One day he asked the chief this question: "What are some good stories from your tribe and tradition that I can use in my preaching?" The chief's answer surprised him: "The stories you need when you preach to our tribe don't exist yet. They have to be created as you live with us and minister to us. For many in our community it will be the first time that they hear the Gospel preached in their mother tongue. We have to see what that will do to them and what kind of stories that will generate in their lives."

Putting these two stories together we see that the task of preaching is not simply a matter of passing on a sacred baton, a set of truths and dogmas, a rote repetition of the Bible, or even just finding inspirational faith stories that we can use to inspire people. Each of these, of course, has its place, but our deeper task is to try to read what is happening when the yeast mixes with the dough and how that dough itself then becomes the word made flesh. When we are able to do that, our preaching will be in the mother tongue and our voice will be that of the Good Shepherd.

## So What Must Our Preaching Incarnate and Radiate?

In brief, we will be preaching the mother tongue when, in listening to us, people, consciously and unconsciously, will feel safe, comforted, challenged, and blessed at their deepest level, that is, at that level where everyday concerns, worries, pains, successes, and joys cannot touch us. And this will necessitate that our preaching be free from our own temperamental leanings as well as from our own ideological preferences. When we preach in the mother tongue there is no liberal or conservative, no right or left, only sacred words that soothe, comfort, challenge, and bless.

Moreover, our words will radiate too the power of powerlessness, the supreme power of the resurrection, the centrality of forgiveness and gratitude, and the vision given to us by hope. And our words will also be a complete keyboard upon which it is possible to play every kind of song, whether of suffering, bitterness, and anger, or of celebration, joy, and warmth.

How will we know when this happens? We will know it when people begin to follow us out of our present enclosures towards true, free, and open pasture.

## A Contemporary Example of Religious Language as Mother Tongue: Henri Nouwen

In our own generation, perhaps no one has been as effective a spiritual teacher and writer as Henri Nouwen. His books have sold millions of copies and he is a spiritual mentor to countless people. And his fruitfulness continues to grow, not decline, long after his death. His books and his preaching had a rare quality, that is, they spoke to everyone in the same way, irrespective of education, economic background, profession, age, or denomination. His words had a simplicity and transparency that was singular. But this was no accident or simply natural talent. He worked at it. He worked at his language with deliberation, long and hard, often rewriting something more than five times over in an effort to make it simpler.

His use of language, I believe, can help every preacher dig more deeply towards the mother tongue. His formula for preaching and writing, a fine tightrope that is not easy to walk, was this: Try, in the language and images you use, as well as in your very body language when you are preaching, to be: The following formula from his preaching and writing about the words, images, and body language to use make for a fine tightrope that is not easy to walk:

- Be radically simple—without being simplistic.
- Carry deep sentiment—without being sentimental.
- Be self-revealing—without being exhibitionist.
- Be deeply personal—yet profoundly universal.
- Be clearly Christian—but without the inner table talk of the worshipping congregation or the rote repetition of biblical language and metaphor.
- Be devotional—without being pious.
- Be clearly committed, speaking from a defined place—yet never hard, judgmental, exclusive, or doctrinaire.
- Be contemporary—but devoid of cliché, fad, hype, or "cool."
- Be highly moral—without the alienating rhetoric of political correctness.
- Be invitational—yet respecting freedom and not proselytizing.

- Be unconventional—yet always respecting where people are at in their development.
- Be deconstructionist—yet always offering the tools with which to build.
- Use the language of critical thought—yet ever with the positive aesthetic of the Gospel artist.
- Use a language that radiates the joy of the Resurrection—even as it leads ever deeper into the Paschal Mystery.
- Use the language of energy and color—but as initiated by wisdom and tempered by grey.
- Use a language deeply sensitive to human weakness—even as it challenges that weakness and invites to what is more sublime.
- Use the language of compassion—yet never compensatory.[6]

This is not an easy formula to emulate. It takes a lot of concentration to remain balanced on this very thin tightrope. But Nouwen's formula for preaching and writing, I believe, shows us what the language of the soul can look like and how religious language, more than any other language, can be our mother tongue.

6. See Wil Hernandez, *Mere Spirituality: The Spiritual Life according to Henri Nouwen*, with a foreword by Ronald Rolheiser (Woodstock, VT: Sky Light Paths Publishing, 2015).

■ CHAPTER 2

# To What Effect? Qualities of Effective Catholic Preaching

Michael E. Connors, CSC

Sooner or later, tired, overworked preachers who face seemingly passive congregations week after week find themselves muttering, "What does it matter, anyway?" Let's look again at why it does matter and what we're trying to do in preaching. Then let's look at some things that seem to characterize preaching that matters.

## Part 1: To What Effect?

I'd like to begin by introducing you to my friend John Cross. John and I entered the candidate program of the Congregation of Holy Cross at the same time, and we soon became good friends. John was one of those amazingly gifted but high-strung people, the likes of which we're only likely to meet a few times in the course of our lives. He was fun, and terribly funny, and had a heart for the suffering of others as big as all outdoors. The next August we went to the novitiate in Cascade, Colorado, in the mountains just west of Colorado Springs. It was not an easy year—but then, in some ways, it's not supposed to be easy. Tragedy struck our little formation community on the afternoon of December 29. John was returning to the novitiate, walking along the side of the busy road that ran by our property, US 24. It was a bright, chilly afternoon, with long, sharp shadows. As they rounded a curve in that road, just a hundred yards from our house, a family from Minnesota entered one of those long shadows, hit a patch of black ice, slid to the side of the road, and struck John, tossing him twenty feet into a ditch. John was rushed to the hospital, where he lingered until early the next morning, but the outcome was never really in doubt. To complicate matters, this terrible accident occurred almost simultaneously with the arrival of my parents for a long-planned visit. As you can imagine, I was grief stricken, confused, angry. Nothing remotely like this had ever happened to me before. Within a few days, I also got terribly sick (strep throat, probably).

However, this story is really not about John, nor about me and my grief. It really is about the homily I heard preached a few days later at the memorial Mass we held for John before his body returned for burial at Notre Dame. The homilist was one of my Holy Cross confreres who lived with us at the novitiate, Fr. Milt Adamson, CSC. I remember two things to this day from the homily he delivered in the Sacred Heart Basilica. One is quite simply the clear and powerful impression that he spoke as a fellow mourner, one who knew and loved John as I did. He spoke tenderly of John's life and goodness. He exuded authentic feeling and compassion for all of us who were grieving, and he was open about his own searing sense of loss. And the second thing I remember is a fragment of the central message I heard, and what I heard went like this: "We gather today in deep pain, and we want to know why. We are enraged that John has been taken from us. We want to know how God could take him from us now, at the age of twenty-six years. But," he continued, "eventually, the question, 'How can it be that a good God would take John from us so soon?' will be transformed into the question, 'How can it be that God is so good as to give John to us, even for a time?'"

Now, the amazing thing is that I heard anything at all at that Mass, for I was in a thick fog, so sick, so heartsick, and so numb that I could barely function. I left that church completely unmoved by the homily that day. But somewhere in my mind and heart those words lodged themselves, and over the next weeks and months they became just a tiny pinpoint of light in a dark tunnel, until finally, gradually, half-reluctantly, I was able to walk out of my tunnel into the light of day again. That homily was January of 1980. I have treasured its gift to me for all these years. Perhaps the first question Fr. Milt spoke of never completely disappears and yields to the second. But slowly, inexplicably, what that homily offered did change me.

How many homilies can you remember from thirty-seven years ago? Or even from last year? Not many, I'll bet. And memorability is itself neutral—bad preaching can lodge itself in our memories, too. So maybe the better question is, how many homilies can you recall that actually made a difference in your life for the better? And why? What was it about those preaching moments that made them "work," made them effective?

We here in the Marten Program have been pondering exactly this question. What distinguishes truly effective preaching, excellent preaching, from preaching that is merely adequate, or worse? You might think that there is an extensive literature around this. There is an extensive homiletic literature out there, for sure. But we have found relatively little, especially in the Catholic world, that wrestles with that question: what makes for really good preaching?

The question could be glibly instrumentalized. We could turn directly to some quick and easy utilitarian answers, a list of practical suggestions that I could market to you. But before we get to that practical level—which does indeed interest me—I think we first have to linger over what we even mean by effectiveness. What is the "effect" we want our "effectiveness" to have on the hearer? "To what effect?" The way we understand preaching's goal will have a profound impact on the kinds of qualities we prize in preaching, and hence, on the strategies and techniques we employ.

I would wager that all of us who preach regularly have been tempted to a kind of despair about it. We put forth our best efforts, but little or nothing seems to change in our hearers. Overwhelmingly they seem passive, even sullen. We feel we are not reaching them, not making a difference. Soon we find ourselves no longer investing our best effort, but cutting corners. We may even say to ourselves, "What does it matter anyway?" So I ask you, what is the point of preaching at all? What are we trying to do with all this jabber? In addition, why has the Christian tradition almost consistently clung to the conviction that preaching is important?

Let me state a conviction that you probably already share: preaching *does* matter—or, at least, it *can* matter—yes, even in the age of YouTube, PowerPoint, video games, and slick websites. It's true that preaching faces some new obstacles in today's information-saturated world. However, done well, I believe it still has life-shaping power. My conviction rests on an even more fundamental conviction, and that is that *the Gospel matters*. A conscious, intentional relationship with Jesus Christ and with the God of Jesus Christ matters, and not only abstractly in some life beyond death, but here and now. The salvific power of the Good News is not reserved only to life in a place we dream about called "heaven." It shapes the way we live here on earth, what we put our trust in, what sorts of hopes we treasure not only for ourselves but for our world. If this is not true, we're wasting our time.

Each year when I meet a new crop of Preaching I students, I pose two questions to them. The first is: "What is the Good News?" I say to them, "I don't want the Catechism answer. I don't want a quote from the Bible, nor a theologian's answer. I want *your* answer, in your own words. There is no one right answer," I tell the students, "although I do believe there are some wrong or incomplete answers. But the point is *you have to have an answer,* an answer lodged in your guts. What difference does being a disciple of Jesus Christ make?"[1] Then there is the second question: "Assuming you have a

1. See Timothy Radcliffe, OP, *What Is the Point of Being a Christian?* (London: Burns & Oates, 2005).

personal answer to the first, an answer imbued with some sense of urgent purpose, the second question is this: *Why do you have to preach it?*" I say, "I can't give you that answer, either. But you have to have one, and it has to be yours. If you don't feel a certain not-fully-explainable sense in your very bones that you must do this, then I'd question why you are following this path leading you toward public ministry." Ideally, I tell them, I'd like to have them begin their formation in preaching by going away with me for an all-day retreat, during which we would reflect together prayerfully on those two questions, perhaps with the aid of Barbara Brown Taylor's *The Preaching Life*[2]—a beautiful book, if you don't know it.

So I believe preaching's effectiveness is first and most seriously compromised by confusion over its real purpose, and most fundamentally that confusion can be about what the Gospel even is, or means. If we are indeed in "the generation after hell," as one commentator claims, then the Gospel isn't just about saving souls from eternal damnation—but was it ever really just about that? Then what is it about?

At the next level up from that foundation, as it were, there is, I believe, still more confusion about preaching's purpose. Here is the level where we ask, "What does the Church need and want from preaching?" Some of the confusion here results from ignorance, owing to inadequate homiletic education in our formation programs for priesthood, the diaconate, and lay ecclesial ministry, and our collective failure to instill in candidates the habit of lifelong learning. And some of it results from lack of clarity on the Church's part, that is to say, ecclesial statements about preaching that cannot be easily harmonized. When combined with a dearth of good homiletic example by Church leadership—the kind of examples that attest that preaching is important and indeed among the highest callings of those deputized to do it—then these seemingly diverging official documents easily lend themselves to conflicting notions of purpose. I want to look briefly at a few of those statements, and add my own attempt to pull them together into some kind of rough coherence.

Let's start with the Second Vatican Council. *Sacrosanctum concilium: The Constitution on the Sacred Liturgy*, as we know, restored the homily to an essential place in the liturgy. However, what the document says about the purpose of the homily is quite spare:

> 52. By means of the homily, the mysteries of the faith and the guiding principles of the christian life are expounded from the sacred text during

2. Brown Tayler, *The Preaching Life* (Lanham, MD: Cowley Publications, 1993).

> the course of the liturgical year. The homily is strongly recommended since it forms part of the liturgy itself. . . . It should not be omitted except for a serious reason.[3]

The wording of these lines, which aim at distilling "principles" and "expounding," seem to give a pedantic cast to the homily—it's a catechetical, teaching moment. Still, it will be readily agreed, I'm sure, that the "mysteries of faith" to be "expounded" are much more than mastery of the catechism. The context of the paragraph situates preaching as an integral part of worship, thus drawing the hearer to "participate"[4] in the mysteries proclaimed and celebrated.

The *General Instruction of the Roman Missal* maintains this pedagogical orientation when it says:

> 65. The Homily is part of the Liturgy and is highly recommended, for it is necessary for the nurturing of the Christian life. It should be an explanation of some aspect of the readings from Sacred Scripture or of another text from the Ordinary or the Proper of the Mass of the day and should take into account both the mystery being celebrated and the particular needs of the listeners.[5]

The emphasis here is clearly on "explanation" of the biblical text, with the concrete needs of the assembly acknowledged, but in a secondary role. In both of these statements, preaching is seen as predominantly one-directional, from the pulpit to the pews. Today we have at least a whole generation of Catholic clergy formed basically in this understanding of preaching's aim. I call it the "Getting the Gospel *Said*" model.

The second, somewhat contrasting understanding I call the "Getting the Gospel *Heard*" model.[6] It is a more fully dialogical understanding of what is taking place in preaching. The Bishops' Committee on Priestly Life and Ministry, in their landmark 1982 statement *Fulfilled in Your Hearing: The Homily in the Sunday Assembly*, took a more expansive view, saying, "The

---

3. Austin Flannery, ed., *Vatican Council II: Constitutions, Decrees, Declarations*, rev. ed. (Collegeville, MN: Liturgical Press, 1996).

4. *The Rite of Christian Initiation of Adults*, 75.1.

5. The language of this paragraph is essentially unchanged from the previous (1975) edition of the GIRM, which reads:

> 41. The homily is an integral part of the liturgy and is strongly recommended: it is necessary for the nurturing of the Christian life. It should develop some point of the readings or of another text from the Ordinary or from the Proper of the Mass of the day, and take into account the mystery being celebrated and the needs proper to the listeners.

6. As Fred B. Craddock said, "The goal is not to get something said but to get something heard." *Preaching* (Nashville: Abingdon Press, 1985), 167.

homily is not so much *on* the Scriptures, as *from* and *through* them."[7] In *Fulfilled*'s point of view, the interpretation of the scriptural text is necessary but not sufficient, because the response of the hearers in faith is the aim. The bishops claim, "The preacher then has a formidable task: to speak from the Scriptures . . . to a gathered congregation *in such a way that those assembled will be able to worship God in spirit and truth, and then go forth to love and serve the Lord.*"[8] Later they will sum up the real homiletic goal as to provide "a *scriptural interpretation of human existence* which enables a community to recognize God's active presence, to respond to that presence in faith through liturgical word and gesture, and beyond the liturgical assembly, through a life lived in conformity with the gospel."[9] Thus, the contours and circumstances of the hearer's real life situation form one of the partners in the homiletic dialogue. In good preaching, the homilist aims to assist us not just to understand the text better, but to understand ourselves better. The light of the biblical word illumines us and the world we inhabit, and invites a response of faith and action.

An even clearer statement of purpose came from perhaps an unlikely source, the Pontifical Biblical Commission (PBC) in their 1994 statement *The Interpretation of the Bible in the Church*. The PBC spoke of the need to go beyond a mere historical reading of the sacred texts, to an "actualization" of the texts as they are "reread in the light of new circumstances and applied to the contemporary situation of the people of God."[10] The PBC continued, "*The presentation of the Gospels should be done in such a way as to elicit an encounter with Christ,* who provides the key to the whole biblical revelation and communicates the call of God that summons each one to respond."[11]

Preaching "to elicit an encounter with Christ." What can this mean? And how might we do it? Pope Benedict XVI put it well when he said, "Being Christian is not the result of an ethical choice or a lofty idea, but *the encounter with an event, a person, which gives life a new horizon and a decisive direction.*"[12] Overall, however, the homiletic literature, both Catholic and Protestant, is surprisingly mum about this goal, which, for my money, is just about the most exciting motivation one could possibly have for the risk of

7. US Conference of Catholic Bishops, *Fulfilled in Your Hearing: The Homily in the Sunday Assembly* (Washington, DC: USCCB Publishing, 1982), 17.

8. Ibid., 19. Emphasis mine.

9. Ibid., 29. Emphasis mine.

10. Pontifical Biblical Commission, *The Interpretation of the Bible in the Church*, (Boston: St. Paul Books and Media, 1994), IV.A.

11. Ibid., IV.C.3. Emphasis mine.

12. *Deus caritas est*, 7. Emphasis mine.

getting into the pulpit! Fr. Peter John Cameron, OP, wrote a beautiful chapter on preaching as encounter in his fine book *Why Preach? Encountering Christ in God's Word.*[13] Echoing Benedict XVI, Cameron says, "The essence of Christianity is not an *idea* but a *Person*. Encounter is God's very *method* of salvation."[14] But Cameron is quite sober about preaching's urgency, as he says, "Preaching exists in the Church to be a life-saving presence that reaches out to those in peril and that rescues them from their despair, their demise."[15]

It seems to me that there is actually a development of thought going on over the postconciliar period, a development which is now ripening in the ministry of Pope Francis, both in his writing and in his powerful homiletic example. Remarkably, in *Evangelii gaudium: The Joy of the Gospel* the word "encounter" appears dozens of times. The encounter with a living Christ, which brings with it that mysterious experience we call joy, is indeed the premise of that document. Of many possible passages for our reflection in that beautiful document—a document which has been such a gift to the Church, and especially to those of us who teach preaching or care about it in any way—let me just call your attention to paragraphs 139–142. Here the pope envisions preaching as maternal conversation, a conversation in which both the Church and her children have something to say. Both are speakers; both are listeners. It is within this conversation of liturgical preaching, Francis says, that a deeper conversation is taking place, "the dialogue between the Lord and his people."[16] That dialogue or encounter will be "encouraged by the closeness of the preacher, the warmth of his tone of voice, the unpretentiousness of his manner of speaking, the joy of his gestures."[17] The pope continues, "The Lord truly enjoys talking with his people; the preacher should strive to communicate that same enjoyment to his listeners."[18] Thus, the homily will "set hearts on fire" because it is a form of "heart-to-heart communication."[19] Through it the hearer will sense that "each word of Scripture is a gift before it is a demand."[20]

For Pope Francis, then, preaching is about facilitating an intimate encounter between people and the living, risen Christ. Our own experience

---

13. Peter John Cameron, OP, *Why Preach? Encountering Christ in God's Word* (San Francisco: Ignatius Press, 2009).

14. Ibid., 52. Emphases in original.

15. Ibid., 48.

16. *Evangelii gaudium*, 140.

17. Ibid.

18. Ibid., 141.

19. Ibid.,142.

20. Ibid.

as preachers seems to verify this. In the back of church, after we have preached, the best possible feedback we could receive would be for people to say, "Father, your homily really moved me . . . You brought me closer to God . . . " or "Your homily gave me another way to look at things . . . I see my life, my possibilities, our world's possibilities differently or more clearly . . . " or "You know, Father, I heard what you said from the pulpit last week and I went home and made up with my wife . . . " or "I decided to help with our parish soup kitchen or a tutoring program or a job training effort . . . " We long to hear these kinds of things. It's what drew many of us into ministry in the first place. It's the sort of thing I would say and have said to Fr. Milt Adamson about his preaching at John Cross' memorial Mass: "Your preaching saved me. You helped me find my way through the darkness and into the arms of a living, loving Jesus Christ. The power of your words was delayed, in this case, but prolonged, deep, and life changing. I see now that a loving Lord was wrapping his arms around me."

Let me conclude this section with my own attempt to sum up. Why preach? *We preach for encounter*; that is to say, *we preach to bring people closer to God, to guide, to facilitate or make more possible the encounter of our hearers with a living God. Meeting the living God changes us—we call this* metanoia *(conversion or transformation)—and on the basis of that transformation, which is an ongoing, lifelong process, we become disciples who live differently.*

## Part 2: Qualities of Effective Preaching

How do we get there? What are some qualities of preaching that actually seem to make that sort of encounter more likely to happen? Here are some things that stand out for me.[21]

*1. Every homily must be (the) Good News.* Every time we preach we must raise up for our people—and for ourselves—the sweetness which intimate relationship with Christ holds for us. Every homily should hold out life and hope for human living both here and beyond. Explicitly or not, the *telos* or goal of every time we preach is the Kingdom or Reign of God, which is both

---

21. Some of the material in the following pages has appeared in a four-part series I wrote for the online publication *Church Life Journal* (Institute for Church Life, University of Notre Dame) in 2016–17. Those pieces can be found at the following.

Part 1: http://churchlife.nd.edu/2016/09/28/effective-catholic-preaching-part-1/ (Sept. 28, 2016).

Part 2: http://churchlife.nd.edu/2016/10/12/effective-catholic-preaching-part-2/ (Oct. 12, 2016).

Part 3: http://churchlife.nd.edu/2016/11/09/effective-catholic-preaching-part-three/ (Nov. 9, 2016).

Part 4: http://churchlife.nd.edu/2017/01/25/effective-catholic-preaching-part-4/ (Jan. 25, 2017).

already and not yet. We point to what God is already doing among us, and wants to do. All of the points that follow are essentially corollaries to this point.

*2. Every homily should make only one point.* This is, in the first place, true to the unity of the Good News, which is the unity of the Trinity itself. And, in the second place, if you want your homily to "stick"—i.e., to be memorable, then the single most important strategy for memorability is to be sure the homily is unified,[22] that it sings a single song which the hearer is still humming as he or she gets in the car and drives away from church. Make the message clear, while looking at it from multiple angles, embedding it in various dimensions of the hearer.

*3. That single point or theme must be something with enough seriousness, enough gravitas, if you will, that it is worth remembering.* It has to mean something to the living of life. It must offer to uplift, elevate, or change one's perspective on life. This means it will challenge. People don't come to church to be entertained or just to be lightly soothed. In their heart of hearts, they want to be challenged. They long for meaning. They ache for a way to connect with God. Don't give in to the temptation to make preaching light and airy. Avoid the trite, the formulaic, and the superficial like the plague. "Go deeper" —this was one of the surprising discoveries of my colleague Karla Bellinger in her study of the way youth and young adults respond to preaching.[23]

*4. The unity of the homily may not be a discursive point or theme at all, but rather, a narrative or image which affords the hearer a new way to see her or his life, her or his world.* We tend to overemphasize the discursive when, in fact, lives change, the world changes, because the human imagination changes, people imagine their lives, their place in the world, or their possibilities differently. A big part of preaching is fertilizing the imagination, helping it to break out of the narrow confines we have imposed on it. Just think of the Incarnation, or of resurrection from the dead—truly mind-expanding realities. I will return to this point in a few moments.

*5. We have to stop moralizing people.* Pope Francis warned us against this in *Evangelii gaudium.*[24] Moralizing is a short circuit. It condescendingly offers moral challenge without the Good News which makes that moral challenge desirable or even possible. There are moralisms of the right (usually

---

22. See, *inter alia,* Chip Heath and Dan Heath, *Made to Stick: Why Some Ideas Survive and Others Die* (New York: Random House, 2008).

23. Karla Belinger, *Connecting Pulpit and Pew: Breaking Open the Conversation about Catholic Preaching* (Collegeville, MN: Liturgical Press, 2014).

24. *Evangelii gaudium,* 142.

about sexual morality) and of the left (usually about social justice). They not only don't work, they are actually toxic to the soul, and they do long-term damage to people. I am *not* suggesting that preaching should not contain moral challenge. On the contrary, preach a homily with robust enough Good News, and you have the basis for some very strong moral challenge. The Good News inherently invites, indeed demands, response. But remember that moral response only flows from an experience of the divine, an experience real and powerful enough to evoke faith, and it is the gift of that encounter that will supply the energy to live faith in action. As Henri de Lubac stated, the mystical must precede the moral.[25]

*6. The preacher has to convey personal authenticity, investment, and urgency.* To be a minister of Jesus Christ should mean, among other things, to be deeply immersed in a spirituality of deflection. It's not about us, but about Christ. As John the Baptist said, "He must increase; I must decrease."[26] Our job is to call attention to Christ, not to ourselves. We've all had enough of preachers who lap up the limelight and enjoy the adulation of their flocks just to stroke their egos and fill the personal insecurity within. We are not out to make personal disciples, but disciples of Jesus.

However, this does not mean that the preacher ought to entirely disappear from view—as if that were even possible. Our listeners want to know that what we're saying matters to us. The messenger is part of the message, inevitably. After all, all of the Resurrection accounts pose themselves as personal witness or testimony, and implicitly invite us to become witnesses ourselves. People already sense it when we are speaking of spiritual matters from personal experience, and they sense the emptiness when we are not. We don't have to have mastered the message we're sending. We do not have to be completely safe from the charge of hypocrisy, thank God, because none of us can be. (If we think we are, we're either fooling ourselves about ourselves, or proclaiming a message in which the bar is too low.) It simply means that the listener will be reassured to know that we are preaching to ourselves first, that we too are challenged, that we too are on the journey of conversion. I do not hold with those homiletic voices which say that the preacher ought never talk about himself or herself, never use personal stories. I would simply say: don't be cute, don't be cynical or sarcastic, and don't overdo it. If you use a personal story, be sure that the connection to the larger Good News is unmistakably clear. Don't talk about yourself Sunday after Sunday. Don't

---

25. Henri de Lubac, *Medieval Exegesis*, vol. 2, *The Four Senses of Scripture* (Grand Rapids: Eerdmans, 2000), 31.

26. John 3:30.

make yourself the hero of your own story. And please don't talk about your travels or the other sorts of privileges that go with your clerical status, the sorts of things that many of your hearers cannot possibly partake of themselves. The one thing that listeners find it almost impossible to forgive in us is the lack of humility. Real humility cannot be feigned. Yet even the simplest believer sitting in the back pew knows that, whatever all of this religious stuff may be about, it's about humility.

*7. Every homily must appeal to all three dimensions of the human person: mind, heart, and will.* This was essentially the advice that none other than St. Augustine gave to his preachers and catechists in *De doctrina christiana* (On Christian Doctrine/Teaching), when he described the goals of preaching as to teach, to delight, and to persuade or move to action. Augustine got this tripartite understanding of the human person from Cicero, who got it from Aristotle. It's still a very serviceable understanding of the listener. Conscientiously appeal to all three, and in roughly equal measure. Most of us favor one over the others, or neglect one at the expense of the others. Hold yourself to strict account on this. Mix up the order too. Note that by appealing to the mind, I mean to include both right and left brains, both cognition and imagination. The appeal to the heart is not a superficial emotionality, but an invitation to fall in love with the very source of love. Remember that the heart needs to be educated, too. And the appeal to the will engages the body and moves the feet into service and mission. Good preaching both draws upon and inspires us to the good, the true, and the beautiful. Trust the insight of classical aesthetics, which assures us that the human person inherently recognizes and is attracted to these things. Treat the hearer seated before you with respect, as a fundamentally well-disposed, intelligent adult. As Fred Craddock advised, "the listeners want room to say no to the sermon but a genuine invitation to say yes."[27]

*8. Effective preaching has a quasi-narrative quality.* You are taking the hearer on a journey of discovery from point A to point B. As Craddock observed, your own path of discovery may provide a clue as to how to provide a path for the listeners.[28] Pay attention to the route you choose. Make sure there is a thread for the hearer to follow. Homiletic structure or form is important, and the simpler the better. Make too many moves (as David

27. Craddock, *Preaching*, 89.

28. Craddock argued for this most strenuously in his landmark book, As One Without Authority (4th ed., St. Louis: Chalice Press, 2001; 1st edition, Phillips, 1974). For example, on p. 48 he says, "Why not on Sunday morning retrace the inductive trip [the preacher] took earlier and see if the hearers come to the same conclusion?"

Buttrick describes moves[29]) and you will lose your listeners. Construct transitions with great care. Pause from time to time to let stragglers catch up. Double back to catch those who lost the thread. Make use of suspense. Yes, your message is more than likely one that most of your hearers have heard before. But, if it is worthwhile, it is one they need to hear again for the first time, and they don't know how you are going to get to the point of arrival. Good preaching has movement and dynamism. Give special attention to your conclusion, especially that last line, the one your hearer will take with him or her into the parking lot. Leave it just open-ended enough that it constitutes "homework" for the hearer beyond church; it should implant a desire within the listener to keep on reflecting, keep on unfolding and discovering. As we saw from *Fulfilled in Your Hearing*, and affirmed by Pope Francis,[30] you aim to invite a response at the Eucharistic Table and beyond the church doors.

*9. Dare to speak to a concrete hearer and a concrete community.* Generic preaching falls flat. Know your people, as much as you can, and speak to them personally. As Pope Francis says, "The preacher must know the heart of his community."[31] This doesn't mean calling out names from the ambo, of course, but it does mean we allow the content and shape of our preaching to be influenced by who the people before us are, their concerns, their joys, their worries, their culture. Let them know that you mean to speak to them, today, here and now. You are embracing real human beings with your words, and embracing real history, just as God has done. Recognize and embrace the experience of both men and women, young and old. Remember that inculturation means both affirmation and challenge, carefully discerned in "reading the signs of the times and interpreting them in the light of the Gospel," as Vatican II put it.[32] Preaching is a work of discernment. As you prepare, you must ask yourself: what do *these* people at *this* time and place need to hear from *this* text?

*10. Preach in a way that offers or points the way to authentic human encounter, relationship, and community.* I find myself preaching about relationship and community much more often than I used to. For one thing, it's such a need in our atomized society. For another, the Scriptures from which we preach are unabashedly communitarian documents. Catholic Christianity has guarded this communal, ecclesial dimension closely, and rightly so.

29. See *Homiletic: Moves and Structures* (Philadelphia: Fortress Press, 1987), esp. 23–53.

30. "[The liturgical] context demands that preaching should guide the assembly, and the preacher, to a life-changing communion with Christ in the Eucharist" (*Evangelii Gaudium*, 138).

31. *Evangelii gaudium*, 137.

32. *Gaudium et spes*, 4.

Because we are about encounter with God, God also supplies us with meaningful human relationships and forges of disparate individuals a living community. We matter to one another. We long for relationships of depth and quality, and in the Body of Christ, we find them.

*11. We need to learn to preach in the language of spirituality.* Preaching is an exercise of the larger ministry of spiritual leadership, a subject we want to explore more fully two years hence at our next conference. Our tradition has a wealth of wisdom about how to bring people to the encounter with God. We need to learn from that tradition. It's no accident that many of the saints of our tradition were great preachers, confessors, spiritual directors, and masters of the spiritual life. They knew how to lead people to God. It's true that, in one sense, there are many languages of spirituality. But we can identify some common elements and threads—not so we can just mindlessly repeat them, but so that we can learn to speak in our own contemporary idiom about a God who is alive and well and still calling people from death to life, still appealing to us to come and follow. Here are three essential points to speaking the language of spirituality: 1) That language consistently speaks both about God and to God as a living, personal, acting Being. It is relationship language, most at home in prayer. This is why our Catholic statements on the homily are so insistent that the liturgical homily is worship—not an interruption in worship, but part of it. The language has a directness and intimacy to it. 2) The language of spirituality remains closely tied to the sacramental imagination. One of its chief modes, in other words, is mystagogy, a savoring reflection on the sacraments and other rites we celebrate, extracting from them the precious oil of contact with God. The sacred rites we celebrate "preach" more eloquently than any of us can ever hope to. Use the homily to unleash their full power. Mystagogical preaching was very common in the early Church, and for good reason. It prolongs the liturgy in the memory, heart, and will of the faithful for the purpose of lodging the participant in the enfolding arms of the One worshiped. 3) Preaching in the language of spirituality respects and nurtures both the kataphatic and apophatic dimensions of spiritual life. There is an essential, necessary complementarity between words and wordlessness in the Christian life. Preaching is a speech act which belongs mostly to the kataphatic dimension. However, good preaching arises from having dwelled in deep and prayerful quiet, a quiet which teaches us that God is always beyond our best and most articulate words. When we give a pause in the homily, and especially when we end the homily and fall silent, it is an invitation for the whole community to enter a silence filled by God alone.[33]

*12. Preach a big God, One who is both transcendent and immanent.* Don't shrink from paradox. Paradox is mystery's other name, and it is delightful and inviting. A God who is too exclusively near to us, close and familiar, could be a domesticated God, shorn of the freedom which is God's alone. By the same token, a God who is too distant, like the watchmaker of the deists, is not the God of Judeo-Christian revelation. The amazing mystery we proclaim and invite people into is that the Almighty and Wholly Other One has come intimately close to us, especially through Jesus Christ.

*13. Preach in a way that is true to the Incarnation.* "Grace builds on nature," as Aquinas said. The Incarnation is not only absolutely unique in the person of Jesus Christ; it is the clue to how God usually works with creatures. God works through the goodness of creation, embodiment, materiality, history. The Incarnation is God's resounding affirmation of the goodness and dignity of human life. In the way we preach, it must be evident that we do not despise what God has so honored. As I preach, I often recall the words of the Jesuit poet Gerard Manley Hopkins: "The world is charged with the grandeur of God. . . . There lives the dearest freshness deep down things. . . ."[34] Help your hearers to see that grandeur, to feel and touch and taste that freshness clinging to life and to the world.

*14. Preaching should always be paschal—i.e., a liberating word from the paradox of death and resurrection.* We tell the story of the Paschal Mystery—Christ's suffering, death, and Resurrection—at every Mass. Don't tire of preaching the Paschal Mystery, no matter what liturgical season it is. It is *the* story, the master story of all stories. It is not just extrinsic, that is to say, to be found only in the death and Resurrection of Christ, as unique and unrepeatable as that story is. It is a story told by creation itself, and lived by each and every one of us: death yields to new life, and therein is our hope. Our listeners have known, and are now living, many death experiences. Through our preaching we stand in solidarity with them, accompany them, and hold out the promise that God continues to abide by the pattern of God's Son, offering some new grace, some new experience of God's fidelity to the covenant.

*15. Because of the Incarnation and the Paschal Mystery, our preaching embraces all of human experience and brings it into conversation with the*

---

33. For more on this, see James Keating's article, "Contemplative Homiletics," *Seminary Journal* 16:2 (2010), 63–69.

34. From "God's Grandeur" (1877).

*Good News.* Good preaching has a feet-on-the-ground, I-know-whereof-I-speak quality, even while it invites us to go beyond our own limited field of vision. Human experience can be a challenge to faith, and this should be honestly admitted in our preaching. Human experience is also the context in which we meet the unseen God, and we must assist our hearers to see that God and "name the grace"[35] infused into experience. In particular, our preaching must be candid about the experience of evil, whether as personal sin or the sin of others or the systemic sin in our world. Our hearers know these experiences of evil well, too. The God of our faith is engaged in a prolonged confrontation with evil, and we must help our hearers to find this God who takes their side against the forces of darkness and death. We are not doomed to be mere victims of evil—preaching joins us to God's power to rout the force of evil. In the life of Jesus, we see preaching, healing, and casting out evil as complementary parts of his ministry, and inextricably related to one another. So for us, our preaching must seek to heal and deliver.

*16. We must preach in a way that is dialogical, because it really is a dialogue.* Good preaching has a conversational quality—it's not a casual conversation, of course, but a conversation about things that matter greatly. We must preach in a way that is approachable, that arises from and returns to genuine mutuality with the listener that invites the hearer to speak back to us, whether in the back of church after Mass, or over coffee and donuts in the church basement, or in the Sacrament of Reconciliation or pastoral counseling or elsewhere. When our voice falls silent in the pulpit, the conversation is not over, but just begun. We have to find ways to honor the listener's need to speak back. On the practical level, I'm more and more convinced that one of the most potent strategies for improving preaching in the Church today is to find some mechanisms by which to allow the pew folk to provide us with feedback. The preaching ministry, unlike most other ministries, suffers from too much isolation, both before and after we do it. As one way of breaking down that excessive isolation, *Fulfilled in Your Hearing* years ago suggested the formation of homily preparation groups—a beautiful and undervalued suggestion, I think. At the same time, we could educate our listeners about what our tradition says about what preaching is and aims for. If we did that, they would not only be more active listeners, they would give us the kind of feedback that would make us continue to strive to be better preachers, too. But we clergy will have to get over our fear of giving them a voice. The truth

35. See M. Catherine Hilkert, *Naming Grace: Preaching and the Sacramental Imagination* (New York: Continuum, 1997).

is that they really are listening, or at least want to listen. And we need them to help us. Moreover, we have much to learn about listener receptivity. What makes some preaching land well on the hearer? What makes people pay attention and receive? Many things impact this process, and we need to understand the various places and life situations from which our hearers arrive in church on Sunday morning.[36] A fundamental shift needs to occur for us, from viewing the homily solely from the preacher's point of view, to seeing it from the point of view of the listener.

*17. We must preach in a way that animates, calls forth and focuses the proclamation of the Good News by all the baptized.* This is the large, unmet challenge of Vatican II, that all of the baptized are empowered to be heralds of the Good News, witnesses of the power of Christ, disciples. Liturgical preaching is not meant to be an end in itself. Our goal is to help the faithful encounter Christ in such a way that they are made bold to go forth and announce God's presence, God's goodness in their daily lives in the secular world. This is the very meaning of Baptism, which makes us God's own and deputizes us for service and witness in the world. It is only as our preaching inspires hearers to take up the cross and follow the way of discipleship that we can be certain that we're doing what we've been asked to do. Our preaching needs to be outward directed, assisting the hearer to make the connections. We preach with the hope to inspire our hearers to become—or become more deeply—intentional, committed, missionary disciples.

In short, our task is to light a fire by which our hearers are warmed and enlightened. As our bishops said in *Preaching the Mystery of Faith,* our task as preachers is to "set hearts on fire with praise and thanksgiving."[37] If all of that sounds like a formidable and complex task, it is! It's the most daring and the most humbling task I know. It's the most difficult . . . and most beautiful thing I know.

---

36. For more on listener receptivity, see Karla Bellinger's book *Connecting Pulpit and Pew,* op. cit.; see also her three-part series on homiletic effectiveness from the listener's point of view, which appeared in 2017 in *Church Life Journal,* listed below.

Part 1: http://churchlife.nd.edu/2017/01/26/effective-preaching-from-a-listener-part-1/ (Jan. 26, 2017).

Part 2: http://churchlife.nd.edu/2017/03/15/effective-preaching-from-a-listener-part-2/ (March 15, 2017).

Part 3: http://churchlife.nd.edu/2017/04/07/effective-preaching-from-a-listener-part-3/ (April 7, 2017).

37. US Conference of Catholic Bishops, *Preaching the Mystery of Faith* (Washington, DC: USCCB Publishing, 2013), 17.

CHAPTER 3

# Does It Resound? Congregational Exegesis in Conversation with Negotiation Science

Ann M. Garrido

A tree falls in a forest. If there is no one around to hear it, does it make a sound? This ever-so-familiar dilemma has been part of common parlance for quite some time now. The earliest variation of the question first appears in print in 1710, in the philosopher George Berkeley's tome *A Treatise Concerning the Principles of Human Knowledge*. The current phrasing, most easily recognized by the modern ear, first appears in the 1910 book *Physics* by Charles Riborg Mann and George Ransom Twiss. Philosophers and scientists continue to ruminate on the query, writing countless textbooks chapters and innumerable blog posts in response from the various angles of metaphysics, epistemology, the science of sound, quantum theory, rationalism, and immaterialism. In recent decades, environmentalists have weighed in on the implicit anthropocentric bias: "What?! Are you saying that squirrels don't count?" Comedians and cartoonists have frequently added their two cents. In 2011, the question was posed anew by a reader from Ukraine in the online queries section of the British newspaper *The Guardian* and—unlike so many reader questions that elicit no response whatsoever—this one rapidly solicited fifty-seven responses from around the world, several of which were so impassioned that they read as if a fist fight were about to break out online. Ordinary people reading the news over their oatmeal in the morning suddenly found themselves possessing remarkably strong opinions regarding a three-hundred-year-old entirely theoretical question about a tree falling in a forest. Which makes it all the more odd, perhaps, to find that one of the only subcategories of the human species seemingly *not* to have spent much time talking with each other about the implications of the dilemma for *their* lives is preachers. I say it is odd because—in contrast to the average reader of *The Guardian*—it is not an entirely theoretical question for those of us who preach. How we think about this dilemma shapes our real-life practice of our craft. If a preacher stands up and preaches, but no one is there to hear it, did the preacher make a sound? Did preaching actually happen? Do the squirrels in the rafters count?

I say *seemingly* have not spent much time because my assessment of this matter is merely anecdotal. Perhaps in other circles, the topic as it relates to preaching has surfaced often and I've simply not been part of those conversations. But from the conversations of which I *have* been a part, there is often a much greater weight placed on the *content* of the preacher's message than on *whether* and—if so—*how* it is heard.

One tiny case in point: Last fall I had eleven students in the Foundations of Homiletics course that I taught. These were bright students, deeply committed to quality preaching. Not one slacker in the bunch. The first assignment I gave was to "exegete" their "congregation" for the semester. In essence, I wanted them to get to know me and the other ten members of the class. I didn't expect resistance; a congregation of eleven is hardly an unwieldy congregation to exegete. Yet much grumbling and confusion ensued. "What does knowing your congregation have to do with being an excellent preacher? You just preach the truth." If I could sum up the general sentiment of the class, it might best be captured in a line from the sketch comedy show *The Royal Canadian Air Farce*: "If a tree falls in a forest and no one is there to hear it, *where are they?*"

We talked about that assumption a great deal over the course of the semester: the assumption that preaching is a one-man show, rather than a communal experience; the assumption that if people don't get the message, it must somehow be their fault. Preaching, I tried to convey, isn't just about talking; it's about being heard, and in order to be heard, you need to know something about *who* is doing the hearing and *how* they hear.

There were a couple moments in the semester when an "aha" seemed to be had. After one well-crafted preaching on the importance of "accepting Jesus as your Lord," one member of the class—pointing to his fellow seminarians and women religious sitting in the chapel, asked the preacher—"Which of us are you thinking hasn't already accepted Jesus?" But then, at the end of the semester, as a closing assignment, I had each student write out a personal preaching preparation process that he or she would commit to in the future. Characteristically, the students took the assignment seriously. They described detailed processes that included prayer and exegesis of Scripture and practicing in front of a mirror and taking time to craft their words—all excellent practices. But only one student included anything about the congregation, and it was that he would pray for them before getting up to preach. I was left sitting at my desk wondering: Did I as a teacher make a sound?

I hope it is clear that I loved these students and don't mean to pick on them. Rather, I am lifting up this experience to draw notice to the fact that many well-educated and well-meaning preachers fall short of "setting the world on fire" not because they don't have anything meaty to say, but because they pay so little attention to whether or not their congregation is vegan. If we are going to talk about effective Catholic preaching, we must be as curious about the role congregants play in the preaching act *as hearers* as we are about the role the preacher plays *as witness* or *herald*.

We might approach the question of what helps congregations to hear the preached message from many directions. In this book alone, multiple diverse and wonderful contributions are made. Acknowledging this richness, I want to narrow my own contribution to what preachers might learn about this topic to the perspective of negotiation science.

If that sounds to you like an odd thought partner for this conversation, allow me to say it is a bit of a surprise still for me as well. Ten years ago when I started to study in the field of negotiation, it was not for the sake of preaching, but rather because the other half of my job at Aquinas Institute was in administration (program direction, advising, committee chairing, etc.). As one might easily surmise, administration is a study in tension. Daily you are making decisions no one likes, pulled in a thousand directions, trying to persuade people to do stuff they do not want to do. It was for the sake of my own leadership development that I first began to read the literature of the Harvard Negotiation Project, and then began to do coursework and coaching in that arena, and eventually came to work part-time with a consulting firm founded by two members of the Harvard Negotiation Project.

Sometimes when people see on my resume that I divide my time between doing management training for places like Capitol One or United Airlines and teaching homiletics, it receives odd looks. Over the course of the past several years of living this bifurcated life, however, I've found frameworks from the world of negotiation seeping over more into my thinking about homiletics, especially the question of what helps or hinders hearing in a congregation. Preaching, I've come to see, is a form of negotiation—technically defined as a discussion aimed at reaching an agreement. Our words make an offer, but it is up to congregants whether to entertain this offer or not. And, negotiators have learned a great deal over time about what goes on in human brains and hearts while entertaining offers.

I want to share three concepts gleaned from the world of negotiation that I'm finding useful presently as a preacher in the hope that they may be useful to you also.

## Don't Assume People Are Listening Just Because They Are Silent

I want you to imagine yourself for a moment listening to two newscasters reading the morning news aloud to you, not as it typically takes place, where the newscasters take turns and the microphone shifts from one to the next, but rather imagine both newscasters reading at the exact same time. Two different stories—concurrently—and you are tasked with comprehending both in their entirety. What, as a hearer, would you do? Given the impossibility of fully listening to both, what would be your strategy for trying to grasp as much as possible? Toggle between the two to catch a word here and a word there? Tune one out to focus on the other? Give up?

The challenge presented by this scenario mirrors itself in every tough negotiation that we enter. Each of us in our own person possesses two voices: an external voice (what we say aloud) and an internal voice (the running commentary in our heads). Most of the time, when we are listening to someone else speak (with their external voice), our own internal voice remains relatively quiet. It says things like, "Oh, interesting." "Hmm." "Huh." The internal voice is able to listen and take information in. It is able to "receive a sound." But the nature of a difficult conversation is that the volume of the internal voice gets dialed up to full volume. The internal voice begins to say, "That's not right!" "He doesn't know what he's talking about." "Where did she come up with *that* as a fair price?" When the internal voice increases in volume, a hidden cacophony ensues: both parties often doing the best they are able to listen to what each is saying with their external voice, while at the same time dealing with their own screeching internal voices. As in the scenario imagined earlier, they toggle, catching only short snatches of what the other is saying. They end up listening only to one voice (and, let's admit, the internal voice has the home court advantage). Or, they give up listening altogether and mentally exit the conversation. Until the internal voice returns to a more neutral, receptive state, it does little good to continue talking.[1]

Consider the implications of this acknowledgment for the preaching act. Both the preacher and the congregant have internal and external voices.

---

1. The roots of this concept can be found in Douglas Stone, Bruce Patton, and Sheila Heen, *Difficult Conversations: How to Discuss What Matters Most* (New York: Penguin, 2010), 5–6.

There is an unusual dynamic in the communication that takes place in the preaching moment, however. Unlike most conversation, the norms for the preaching event dictate that one party does not use its external voice for the duration of the preaching. There are certainly ways that a person's internal voice can leak out—through their eyeballs, shifting in the pews, coughing. But, the silence of the other's external voice can create the illusion for the preacher that the other's internal voice is also silent; that by virtue of the fact that they are sitting in the pews, they are hearing what the preacher is saying. We know from our own experience that this is not true. Indeed the expectation that one remain silent—with the inability to ask follow up questions or ask the speaker to repeat something—creates prime conditions for the internal voice to only get louder. But we are lulled into thinking the other is hearing, nonetheless, when in fact congregants often experience the sensation described earlier—the frustration of trying to listen to two voices at once.

Hence one of the most important questions we as preachers can ask is: Once triggered, what is the best way to get the internal voice back to a quiet enough place where it can hear again? In ordinary conversation, one obvious strategy is to ask the other person to speak a bit, so that they can release some of what is in their internal voice and you can convey that the other's internal voice has been heard. But in preaching, the preacher will have to do some extra work. The preacher needs to help the other's internal voice feel it has been heard, even if the person has not been able to speak. The preacher needs—to the best of one's ability—to say aloud what is in the internal voices of the congregants.

Preachers will want to do that tentatively because, no matter how carefully a preacher exegetes their congregation, they never know for certain what is in congregants' internal voices, but the preacher can frame it as a guess:

- If I were you, right now I'd probably be saying to myself, "Love; schmove . . . he doesn't know my neighbor . . . "
- Maybe in your head right now, you are thinking . . .
- If I were in your spot, I imagine I'd be wondering . . .

Simple moves like these can help the congregants' internal voice to feel heard, so that it doesn't continue to argue silently with the preacher for the remainder of the preaching and miss everything else that is said.

## Beware the Core Emotional Interests

A second important question we should ask as preachers: What is it that gets the internal voice so riled in the first place? It is a question that long intrigued the founder of the Harvard Negotiation Project, Roger Fisher. For several decades, Fisher, coauthor of the classic negotiation text *Getting to Yes*,[2] was called upon by both businesses and governments worldwide for his expertise. By temperament, Fisher was a highly rational sort. He would listen carefully to all sides and then work on crafting a deal that could be called a win-win. He knew that what he presented was probably the best that both parties could get from one another and that it was in the interest of both parties to accept the agreement. But occasionally over the course of his long career, one or more of the parties would refuse to sign. They would let the deal fall through, even though it would have been the best thing for them financially, it would end the war, etc. And Fisher would be utterly perplexed. Why would people not take the offer? Fisher came to realize that reasonableness was not the primary motivation in many negotiations; something else was driving parties' behaviors.

In *Beyond Reason*, Fisher and coauthor Dan Shapiro identified emotional interests that regularly appear as drivers in negotiation. These are not emotions in themselves, but they are things that we as humans care about—across time and culture—that trigger emotions within us when they are stepped on. In short, they dial up the volume on the internal voice. Fisher and Shapiro name five.[3]

- *Autonomy*—We all desire to have a certain degree of control over our life. We want to be able to make decisions about things that affect us and influence the conditions that we live in.
- *Affiliation*—We all want a sense of belonging, of inclusion. We want to know that we are in the group rather than peripheral or outcast.
- *Appreciation*—We want others to notice what we do and show some gratitude for our contribution to the whole.
- *Status*—We want to be perceived in right relation to others based on what we value, be it age, education, place in the family, military rank,

2. Roger Fisher and William Ury, with Bruce Patton, ed., *Getting to Yes: Negotiating Agreement without Giving In* (New York: Penguin, 2011).

3. Roger Fisher and Daniel Shapiro, *Beyond Reason: Using Emotions as You Negotiate* (New York: Penguin, 2005).

years of experience, ordination, etc. We'd like the respect due us in this regard.

- *Role*—We want to have a "part in the play" that somehow contributes to the overall "performance." We want it to be something that we are good at, that we like, and that is valued by the group.

To this list, some have suggested adding a sixth:

- *Fairness*—We want to feel like we are being treated justly; that we are receiving our due.

This one seems so deeply hardwired into our biology that it may extend beyond the human species to include other primates, and possibly even other mammals. A famed 2003 study by researchers Sarah Brosnan and Frans de Waal tested the response of Capuchin monkeys when two monkeys were given a common task to complete but one monkey received a cucumber (an acceptable but less desirable treat) as a reward and the other monkey received a grape (a highly desirable treat). Initially the first monkey was content to repeat the task in trade for a cucumber bite, but as soon as the first monkey spotted the second monkey receiving a grape for the same task, it began to refuse its reward, instead pelting the researcher with the cucumber and vigorously rattling its cage.[4]

No one chooses to have an emotional response when one of these concerns is triggered; having a reaction to these concerns is simply part of our biological wiring. When one or more of them are stepped on in a conversation, our bodies will automatically unleash a rush of cortisol and adrenaline—hormones that produce immediate physiological effects. Cortisol and adrenaline slow down the blood flow to the prefrontal cortex of the brain where our higher reasoning capacities lie, drawing more blood into the limbic system of our brain where our flight and fight impulses reside. As a result, we become more visually attuned, but less auditory. Our capacity for remembering the sequence of events declines. We won't remember who said what and in which order, but we will remember how we felt treated in that moment. Understanding the neuroscience behind the emotional concerns has great import for us as preachers. Often when we prepare to speak, we will think, "If I lay out my argument in a reasonable way, I will win the

4. Sarah F. Brosnan and Frans B. M. de Waal, "Monkeys reject unequal pay," *Nature* 425, (18 September 2003): 297–299. De Waall's TED talk includes video of their experiment; see especially around minute thirteen: https://www.ted.com/talks/frans_de_waal_do_animals_have_morals.

congregation over by the excellent logic of what I'm saying." Or, "If I am just more clear, people will understand my point and be persuaded." Logic and clarity are important, but if we are inattentive to emotional concerns, emotional concerns will trump logic and clarity every time. Consider the following statements—typical of the kind of sentiments that might regularly be expressed in a preaching event:

- "The Church reminds us that when we step into the voting booth, the very first thing on our minds must be bolstering the culture of life."
- "The Gospel says you can't simply watch out for your own needs; you must also watch out for the needs of others. And, what you are currently doing is not enough."
- "We all know how tough it is to be married. We all know what it's like raising kids. So, take consolation in Jesus' words today, 'I want to give you rest.'"

Each of these statements may be basically true and well meaning, but by the way they are stated, they traipse upon hearers' autonomy, appreciation, and affiliation, respectively, turning up the volume of the internal voice. The listeners themselves might have a hard time identifying retrospectively when they leave the preaching moment; the dynamic is often so subtle. But, if one was to carefully track when listener attentiveness and sympathy dropped off, the field of negotiation would suggest a consistent correlation.

Knowing how powerful these emotional concerns are and the way that they can hinder hearing, is there anything we can do about it? The most obvious takeaway would be to avoid triggering them. That is not the same thing as saying, "Avoid bringing up difficult things with your congregation." Often as preachers we are called to preach a hard message that people may label offensive. But, it is the message that should challenge people, not how we say it. When we offend, it should be because of something intentional, not accidental.

Beyond avoiding negatively triggering emotional concerns, however, preachers might also consider how they might proactively engage these concerns as positive triggers. Neuro-economist Paul Zak is most well known for his research involving the Trust Game in which he took two groups of strangers and placed them in separate rooms.[5] The first group of strangers in room

---

5. Paul Zak, "Trust, Morality—and Oxytocin?" TED Talk available at https://www.ted.com/talks/paul_zak_trust_morality_and_oxytocin. For further information on Zak's research, see Mark Honigsbaum,

A received ten dollars—no strings attached. They were instructed that they could give as much of this money as they wanted to the second group in room B and that whatever they gave would triple for the people in room B. At that point, the people in room B would have the choice about whether to give anything back. Zak's initial trial resulted in the participants in room A giving an average of three to four dollars to the participants in room B. When asked why they had offered that amount, the participants in room A said things like, "Well, the money came to me free. It seemed like a nice thing to do. Maybe I would make something back. It was a low risk proposition."

The second time Zak ran the trial, he recreated the same conditions, but this time, before asking the people in room A how much they wanted to give, he had them inhale oxytocin. Oxytocin is another hormone, like cortisol and adrenaline. It is particularly prevalent in women who are giving birth and breastfeeding. Science believes it helps to create the strong mother-child bond. But, it can also be found at other times of intimate, meaningful encounter, both in men and in women. In the second round of testing, the average participant in room A gave eight to nine dollars to the participants in room B. When asked about why they had offered that amount, the participants in room A said things like, "Well, the money came to me free. It seemed like a nice thing to do. Maybe I would make something back. It was a low risk proposition." Note at the reasoning level, nothing had changed, yet they were two to three times more charitable.

Upon reading this, your own internal voice might be saying, "How do I get some oxytocin for my own congregation?!" The good news is that you can create it yourself at no cost. When the core emotional concerns identified earlier are honored—versus triggered—in an encounter, it unleashes a small amount of oxytocin in the brain. Whenever the preacher makes a move that helps the other feel appreciated or affiliated; whenever the preacher is clear about the desire to be fair; whenever the preacher elevates the status or autonomy of congregants, it opens the ears and hearts of congregants to work with—rather than against—the preacher. These moves can also be quite subtle:

- "The Gospel gives us a lot to chew on today and ultimately you are the one who will have to decide what this could look like in your own life."

---

"Oxytocin: could the 'trust hormone' rebond our troubled world?" *The Guardian* (August 20, 2011), available online at https://www.theguardian.com/science/2011/aug/21/oxytocin-zak-neuroscience-trust-hormone.

- "This is a reading that I struggle with as much as you . . . we are in this boat together."
- "Now to be fair, one could also say . . . "

While deceptively simple, they can nevertheless go a long way toward keeping a congregation leaning into the preacher's message.

## Seek Regular Coaching from Congregants

Thus far, I have highlighted things preachers can do to be attentive to the internal voice of congregants in order to increase their the capacity to hear in the actual preaching moment, but I want to close with a comment about what preachers can do to engage the internal voice of congregants outside the preaching moment through the practice of preaching feedback. While soliciting feedback might seem a natural way to get to know the internal voices of multiple congregants better, it is a practice that frequently meets resistance because it can be so frustrating. Preachers frequently complain, "Well, I ask and all I ever get is a handshake and 'Nice homily, Deacon.'" Or "I've tried but I don't have time to have long drawn out conversations with people nitpicking my preaching." Or "Oh, trust me, I've gotten lots of feedback. There are two people in my parish who write me an email every week with their thoughts on my preaching . . . right after they've written the bishop." Similar complaints exist in the business and government spheres: "I ask and the feedback I receive is anemic, unhelpful, too time consuming, etc." Trying to get quality, constructive feedback on one's work is apparently one of the toughest negotiations out there.

Labeling such feedback conversations as a negotiation can be confusing. There is no rule that says I need to agree with what the other person says or that we need to keep talking until we do agree. The primary negotiation in a feedback conversation is within ourselves. Internally, part of us really wants to learn and to grow and get better at what we do. But another part of us really wants to be accepted and appreciated just the way we are. Why does there always need to be a Preacher 2.0? Am I not okay as I am? As a result, our brains are wired to simultaneously desire hearing from others and also *not*. The biggest negotiation will be challenging *ourselves* to believe that getting feedback is an important part of our growth as preachers and to be proactive about getting the feedback we need, rather than passively waiting for it to come in our direction.

Once we've made that decision, again the negotiation sphere provides some insight on ways of gleaning higher quality feedback in a way that does not take a lot of time. In their 2014 book *Thanks for the Feedback*, Douglas Stone and Sheila Heen note that feedback is a generic term that can be interpreted by the hearer in a variety of ways.[6] When someone says, "I'm looking for feedback," it could mean, "I'm looking for some appreciation. I'd like someone to notice how much work I put into this." Or it could mean, "I'm looking for some coaching. I'd like to know how to get better at this." Or it could mean, "I need some evaluation. I want to know: Am I making the bar? Is this acceptable? How was this week's preaching in comparison to the others I've done?" Appreciation, coaching, and evaluation are *all* important. We need *all* of them in life. The challenge is that if we only ask, "Could you give me some feedback?" those being asked will not be clear about what it is that we are looking for at any given time and cross-communication can easily happen. For example, a congregant might respond, "Nice homily, Deacon" (appreciation) or "That was the best sermon I've heard this year" (evaluation) when what the preacher was looking for was a bit of coaching. The preacher is left thinking, "That's not what I was asking for. That's useless."

Hence, part of getting helpful feedback involves asking the right question. In their research, Stone and Heen highlight one question that elicits quality coaching without taking an expanse of time: "What is one thing you see me doing or not doing that gets in my way [as a preacher]?"[7] They recommend asking the question on a regular basis to different people, rather than the same person repeatedly. The question makes it easier for potential feedback givers, but it also reduces some of the awkwardness for the one receiving feedback. Congregants surely have many observations and impressions of a preacher, but often because of perceived status differential, they don't feel it is their place to say anything to the preacher. Unless the preacher asks, many will not share their feedback. But if the preacher initiates the conversation, they will. In asking this particular question, the preacher isn't asking for *everything* they'd recommend, but rather just *one thing*. This helps the feedback giver to focus attention on what they'd consider most important; it also means the receiver isn't left with a whole list of recommendations, which can feel overwhelming. The way the question is asked specifically invites coaching, rather than appreciation or evaluation, while at the same time it helps the person who is asked for their feedback to experience

6. Douglas Stone and Sheila Heen. *Thanks for the Feedback: The Science and Art of Receiving Feedback Well* (New York: Penguin, 2014), 29–45.

7. Ibid., 257–258.

appreciation and affiliation with the preacher—releasing a rush of oxytocin, heightening their readiness to hear future preaching.

If the preacher is in need of appreciation or evaluation—and all preachers are at varying points of time—the question can be tweaked. For appreciation: "What is one thing you see me doing [as a preacher] that you wouldn't want me to stop doing?" or "What is one thing you saw me do in this homily that you'd want me to do again?" For evaluation: "On a scale of 1 to 10, how well did that preaching work for you?"

## Conclusion

Are any of the recommendations made in this chapter magical? Will integrating them into one's preaching practice promise to perk up the ears of the congregation and put them on the edge of their pews forever? No, of course not, but they are tiny ways of loving our congregations, of letting them know that we care not only about whether the Word of God is spoken, but about whether the Word of God is received. That we care whether it makes sense to *them*; makes a difference in *their particular* lives.

It may be interesting to note that George Berkeley, the eighteenth-century philosopher who first posed the dilemma of trees falling and sounds being made, was also an Anglican bishop—the bishop of Cloyne, Ireland. And for him, the answer to the question he posed was clear: Even if there is no person, no squirrel in the forest, God is still there. God hears.[8] Some days that will have to be enough for us as well. Some days when a word has fallen flat, the only consolation I have is that at least God heard. At least God knows the work I put into it. At least God knows the good intent I had behind it. At least God knows I tried. In the end, I can't make anyone hear.

I find it equally intriguing, however, that the only surviving sermon that we have of Berkeley's—in contrast to his many philosophical works—speaks

8. Over a century later, Berkeley's stance was summarized in a limerick by Monsignor Ronald Knox (1888–1957), accessed at http://ronaldknoxsociety.blogspot.com/ (Friday, March 16, 2012)

*There was a young man who said "God*
*Must find it exceedingly odd*
*To think that the tree*
*Should continue to be*
*When there's no one about in the quad."*
*"Dear Sir: Your astonishment's odd;*
*I am always about in the quad.*
*And that's why the tree*
*Will continue to be*
*Since observed by, Yours faithfully, God."*

passionately of the importance of at least trying to be heard. It is a sermon preached before the Society for the Propagation of the Gospel in Foreign Parts, at the Church of St. Mary-le-Bow, on Friday, February 18, 1731. Berkeley states:

> By the Knowledge of God, is not meant a barren Speculation, either of Philosophers or Scholastic Divines, nor any notional Tenets fitted to produce Disputes and Dissentions among Men; but, on the contrary, a holy practical Knowledge, which is the Source . . . of Peace. . . .
>
> Whoever is a sincere Christian, *cannot be indifferent* about bringing over other Men to the Knowledge of God and Christ; but that every one of us, who hath any Claim to that Title, is *indispensably obliged* in Duty to God, and in Charity to his Neighbour, to desire and promote, . . . [that] they may become Partakers of Life and Immortality. For, this is Life eternal, to know thee the only true God, and Jesus Christ whom thou hast sent.[9]

In our own words and practice, may we be as devoted as Berkeley not only to speaking, but—for the sake of our neighbor—making a sound.

9. George Berkeley, "A Sermon Preached before the Incorporated Society for the Propagation of the Gospel in Foreign Parts at Their Anniversary Meeting in the Parish-Church of St. Mary-le-Bow" (February 18, 1731), available at http://ota.ox.ac.uk/text/4172.txt (emphasis added).

■ CHAPTER 4

# Emmaus Revisited: The Convergence of the Word Proclaimed and the Eucharist Celebrated

Bishop Sylvester Ryan

## Introduction

I will be focusing here on the preaching task within ongoing communities: parishes, Newman Centers, University pastoral centers, and the like. I choose this focus because it is the one with which I am most familiar. It is also particularly challenging since we are proclaiming the Gospel to many of the same faces Sunday after Sunday. Within that unique interaction, we learn to know our listeners even as they come to know us.

## Luke 24:13–35: The Road to Emmaus

I want to suggest a pastoral interpretation of the Easter Sunday encounter with two of Christ's disciples as found in St. Luke's Gospel. I believe the Emmaus story speaks in a unique and insightful manner to our contemporary preaching practices, and can provide an instructive model for our preparation for liturgical preaching. In particular, it links the proclamation of the Word with the breaking of the bread in the strongest possible way: the Risen Christ revealed in the scriptural narrative simultaneously in both Word and Eucharist.

So we enter the story.

> Now that very day two of them were going to a village seven miles from Jerusalem called Emmaus. (v. 13)

On Easter afternoon, the two disciples walked away from the Jerusalem community. We might begin this conversation with the question, "Weren't they walking in the wrong direction?" As we are aware, symbolism plays a part, sometimes more and sometimes less, in the interpretation of the Scriptures. I take this opening verse as a symbol of the critical relationship of the disciples (and ourselves) to the faith community. The symbolism and truth of this relationship comes into sharp focus at the close of the story.

"Two of them." The "two of them" describes ordinary disciples, not members of the Twelve! The story does not mention Peter, James, John, Andrew, or any of the rest of the Twelve. This is a contrast to many of the appearances of Jesus in the Resurrection period. It is noticeable as an element in the story because it provides a step whereby we may easily identify ourselves within the story. We can become this one unnamed disciple. We can take our place in this story because of our own experiences of the Word and Eucharist and the recognizing of Christ in our midst.

> And they were conversing about all the things that had occurred. (v. 14)
>
> And it happened that while they were conversing, Jesus himself drew near and walked with them, (v. 15)
>
> but their eyes were prevented from recognizing him. (v. 16)
>
> He asked them, "What are you discussing as you walk along?" They stopped, looking downcast. (v. 17)

Jesus joined in the conversation with a question. He asked and he listened! Preaching is speaking, to be sure; but serious preaching hangs on a careful pattern of pastoral listening to the hearts of those to whom we preach, especially in parishes or similar situations of preaching.

> And one of them, named Cleopas, said to him in reply, "Are you the only visitor to Jerusalem who does not know of the things have taken place in these days?" (v. 18)
>
> And he replied to them, "What sort of things?" And they said to him, "The things that happened to Jesus the Nazarene, who was a prophet. He was a prophet mighty in deed and word before God and all the people, (v. 19)
>
> how our chief priests and rulers both handed him over to a sentence of death and crucified him. (v. 20)

Some years ago in a priests' annual retreat, the retreat master shared this reflection: "Every once in a while it may happen that someone approaches Sunday Mass while aching inwardly, 'OK, one last time. I'll try it one last time for even a bit of hope . . . anything to make a difference.'" In this Gospel, these two disciples have left their community burdened with a numbing sense of loss. In this case, Jesus made the difference! He transformed their grief into amazement and recognition.

> But we were hoping that he would be the one to redeem Israel; and besides all this, it is now the third day since this took place. (v. 21)
>
> Some women from our group, however, astounded us. They were at the tomb early in the morning (v. 22)
>
> and did not find his body; they came back and reported that they had indeed seen a vision of angels who announced he was alive. (v. 23)
>
> Then some of those with us went to the tomb and found things just as the women had described, but him they did not see." (v. 24)
>
> And he said to them, "Oh, how foolish you are! How slow of heart to believe all that the prophets spoke! (v. 25)
>
> Was it not necessary that the Messiah should suffer all these things and enter into his glory." (v. 26)
>
> Then beginning with Moses and all the prophets, he interpreted to them what referred to him in all the Scriptures. (v. 27)

Jesus leads them to an initial grasp of the Paschal Mystery: it is God's will that makes a pathway throughout all these events! The Word of God unfolds for them a revelation of the mystery of Christ's redemptive action!

> As they approached the village to which they were going, he gave the impression that he was going on further. (v. 28)
>
> But they urged him, "Stay with us, for it is nearly evening and the day is almost over." So he went to stay with them. (v. 29)

They were free to believe or disbelieve! However, they chose to invite him to the table. I can see a possible parallel here from the earliest portion of John's Gospel that relates John the Baptist speaking with his disciples and pointing out to them Jesus as "the Lamb of God." Two of his disciples then choose to follow Jesus. Jesus turns and asks, "What are you looking for?" They said to him, "Rabbi, (which translated means Teacher), where are you staying," and he said to them, "Come and see." And they "stayed with him that day" (John 1:35–39). In the Emmaus story here, however, once he has revealed himself, he disappears. Perhaps this emphasizes the contrast here between the encounter with Jesus in the flesh and then, afterwards, Jesus raised from the dead.

> And it happened that, while he was still with them at table, he took the bread, said the blessing, broke it, and gave it to them. (v. 30)
>
> With that their eyes were opened and they recognized him, and he vanished from their sight. (v. 31)

These words, *take, break, bless,* and *give,* appeared for the first time in the Gospel accounts of Jesus feeding the five thousand. Here we have the first elements of what will become a clear pattern of the liturgy of the Eucharist.

> Then they said to each other, "Were not our hearts burning [within us] while he spoke to us on the way and opened the scriptures to us?" (v. 32)

As preachers of the Word, we would hope our words might sometimes at least draw our listeners to a similar response. Our homily preparation leads us towards a personal experience of Christ in words we later share with our communities. We also strive to reach their hearts and their minds. However, it takes the Spirit's singular touch to bring our words to possess such force. We also certainly can relish moments of hearing another preacher's message that touches our hearts as deeply as happened with the two disciples. Hardly any other experience would serve as a more powerful motivation for our own preaching than such moments.

> So they set out at once and returned to Jerusalem where they found gathered together the eleven and those with them (v. 33)
>
> who were saying, "The Lord has truly been raised and has appeared to Simon!" (v. 34)

They returned to the community! This direct experience of the Risen Christ drew them back to the Jerusalem community. In their sadness and confusion, they had left the community. Now, having recognized Christ, they were compelled to return! Once reunited, the members shared with them their personal accounts of the extraordinary events of this first Resurrection Sunday.

> Then the two recounted what had taken place along the way and how he was made known to them in the breaking of the bread. (v. 35)

Jesus interpreted the texts of the Torah and the prophets in the light of the Messiah. "As they perceived the true, messianic meaning of the Scriptures they were also 'able to see (recognize) Jesus in the breaking of the bread,' a dramatic response to the Word and Eucharist!"[1]

> Father Timothy Radcliffe, in the introduction to *A Handbook for Catholic Preaching*, connects the Emmaus story and our own pastoral preaching: "The disciples walking to Emmaus meet the Lord. Afterward they say, 'Were not our hearts burning within us while he was talking to us on the road, while he was opening the Scriptures to us?' That same hour they got up and returned to Jerusalem and found the eleven and their companions together. This short verse strongly lays out the challenge and the grace the preacher and homilist face in preaching in the twenty-first century."[2]

## The Liturgy of the Eucharist: A Preaching Link and Source

> Then the two recounted what had taken place along the way and how he was made known to them in the breaking of the bread. (Luke 24:35)

"A principle of liturgy highlights this truth: the homily does not stand apart from the liturgical action, the homily IS a liturgical action."[3] The Emmaus story provides a link to the intent and purpose of the homily. The homily is never just a performance, act, or entertainment! It can be joyful, but always, this Lucan story of the Resurrection presents us with a saving event that equates with how our preaching role connects with Christ's Eucharistic presence.

The Lectionary serves as a primary source of preaching the Mystery of Christ for the Sundays and weekday liturgies. Yet the Liturgy of the Word always points toward the Eucharist. *Preaching the Mystery of Faith*, a document from our US Conference of Catholic Bishops, states, "This is why virtually every homily preached during the Liturgy should make some connection between the Scriptures just heard and the Eucharist about to be celebrated."[4]

---

1. Luke Timothy Johnson, *Sacra Pagina: The Gospel of Luke*, vol. 3 (Collegeville, MN: Liturgical Press, 1991), 397.

2. Timothy Radcliffe, introduction to *A Handbook for Catholic Preaching*, ed. Edward Foley, (Collegeville, MN: Liturgical Press, 2016), xiv.

3. Timothy P. O'Malley, *Liturgy and the New Evangelization* (Collegeville, MN: Liturgical Press, 2014), 57.

4. *Preaching the Mystery of Faith* (Washington, DC: USCCB, 2013), 20.

The Lectionary of course speaks to the Mystery of Christ as revealed through the liturgical year. Timothy O'Malley speaks to this centrality:

> Every deed of Christ's is a mystery, a sacrament of the living God, which simultaneously bestows to us an example of what constitutes a flourishing human life. The wonder of the liturgical feasts of the church is that we are slowly presented with the entirety of Christ's life as deeper entrée into the Mystery of God and human existence.[5]

Preaching within the larger context of the Eucharistic celebration definitely serves as the preacher's best friend. A liturgy celebrated well on every level creates a welcoming expectation and appreciation of the homily! The inspiration, insights, or directions offered by the homily are supported through the full engagement of the people in the liturgy. When homilies touch the deepest levels of the human heart and experience, they lead people into the core of the liturgy and the Eucharist itself.

This connection of the Liturgy of the Word and the Liturgy of the Eucharist takes place within a single liturgical action and its connecting parts. Consequently, we can find many impressive expressions of faith within the Eucharistic Prayers that can fit well into our preaching. For example, if you were preparing the homily for Holy Thursday there is a Prayer over the Offerings in the Mass that speaks to the fundamental teaching of the Liturgy:[6]

> Grant us, O Lord, we pray,
> that we may participate worthily in these mysteries,
> for whenever the memorial of this sacrifice is celebrated
> the work of our redemption is accomplished.

The *General Instruction of the Roman Missal*, paragraph 2, quotes these same words. Our homiletic themes in the celebration of the liturgy include, in one or another manner, the good news of our salvation as the "work of our redemption." Our homilies point out and interpret how the Word proclaims Christ's salvation as the heart of the Eucharistic mysteries.

When the preacher is also the celebrant, the Opening Prayer, the Collect, may well express a theme in a way that lends itself to a homily or a neat summary of one. For example, the collect of the First Sunday of Advent:

> Grant your faithful, we pray, Almighty God,
> the resolve to run forth to meet your Christ

---

5. O'Malley, *Liturgy and the New Evangelization*, 65.

6. This section is adapted in part from Sylvester Ryan and Deborah L. Wilhelm, *Preaching Matters: A Praxis for Preachers* (Chicago: Catholic Theological Union, 2015), chapter 5.

with righteous deeds at his coming
so that, gathered at his right hand,
they may be worthy to possess the Kingdom.

These lines capture metaphorically the eschatological bent of the season, and invite comment and elaboration from the preacher.

As many of us know, one step toward an effective homily happens when the preacher can express the theme of the homily in one sentence. The Opening Prayer or other prayers of the *Roman Missal* might provide at times just such a summary. Here is a Prayer after Communion that has promise as an excellent homily theme:

Renewed and nourished
by the Sacred Body and Precious Blood of your Son,
we ask of your mercy, O Lord,
that what we celebrate with constant devotion
may be our sure pledge of redemption.
Through Christ our Lord. (Twelfth Sunday in Ordinary Time, Year A)

For the preacher who is also the presider, the Collect always gathers the intentions, hopes, and anxieties of the community. The presider prays on behalf of the entire community. The challenge is always in the inflection and voice with which one prays on behalf of the assembly. It cannot be a mere saying of words, but one prayed with an emphasis to effect and reflect the unity of the gathered community.

The Eucharistic Prayers contain numerous expressions of faith that may serve the purposes of a homily, especially with the number and variety of Eucharistic Prayers available today, such as Eucharistic Prayer II:

Therefore, as we celebrate the memorial of his Death and Resurrection,
we offer you, Lord, the Bread of Life and the Chalice of salvation,
giving thanks that you have held us worthy
to be in your presence and minister to you. (105)

How do we acknowledge and minister to Christ? We acknowledge him in his presence in the Eucharist and minister to him in serving the members of the Body of Christ! Pope Francis ceaselessly urges us to pray and serve the community of faith and especially to look out for those most in need.

The four *Masses for Various Needs* carry a clear reminder of the connections of the homily and the Eucharistic Prayer in these words:

Blessed indeed is your Son
present in our midst

when we are gathered by his love,
and when, as once for the disciples,
so now for us,
he opens the Scriptures and breaks the bread.
(Eucharistic Prayer for Use in Masses for Various Needs I, 2)

These lines carry in themselves a beautiful invitation to discover the living Christ in the liturgy, and this invitation could be unfolded in the homily.

## Preaching: A Privilege and Responsibility

> Were not our hearts burning within us while he spoke to us along the way and opened the scriptures to us. (Luke 24:32)

Barbara Brown Taylor, an Episcopalian priest, highly regarded nationally for her excellent preaching and writing, commented in her book *When God Is Silent* that we preachers owe our listeners a special courtesy:

> Courteous language respects the autonomy of the hearer. It also respects his or her ability to make meaning without too much supervision, which means it is language with some silence.[7]

I had never heard that expression before in relation to preaching and it touched a nerve. Courtesy requires a respect for the people to whom we preach because they are equal participants in the preaching moment. Pope Francis provides a similar reflection in *The Joy of the Gospel*:

> The preacher must know the heart of his community, in order to realize where its desire for God is alive and ardent, as well as where that dialogue has been thwarted and is now barren.[8]

In many instances today, our listening communities consist of people with substantial educational backgrounds and broad experiences in living the faith intelligently and courageously. Any reflection on our pastoral experiences reveals the depth of faith and understanding that spreads all across the members of our congregations. In fact, the faithful in the pews, regardless of their educational or social backgrounds or differing faith patterns, prove powerful collaborators in opening up the Word. So we act on this courtesy toward our listeners when we reverence and respect how deeply the Word

7. Barbara Brown Taylor, *When God Is Silent* (Lanham, MD: Cowley Publications, 1998), 111.
8. Pope Francis, *Evangelii Gaudium: The Joy of the Gospel* (Washington, DC: USCCB, 2016), 137.

is already present and active in their lives. Their dialogue in the liturgy is between them and God; that is the dialogue we lead.

Twenty-five years ago on a golfing trip to Scotland and Ireland, I sat in the clubhouse of a Scottish course we had played and picked up a local newspaper. I casually browsed through the paper and eventually came across the obituaries. The length and the detail of the obituaries caught my eye: lengthy and beautifully written. A recently deceased Presbyterian minister was the subject of the last obituary notice, which included this remarkable line: "The Reverend Steward, this shy, small man, became almost incandescent in the pulpit when the glory of being a herald of God took hold of him!" I wrote that line down right then and there.

Our Lord set the stage for such intensity: "I have come to set the earth on fire, and how I wish it were already blazing. There is a baptism with which I must be baptized, and how great is my anguish until it is accomplished" (Luke 12:49). We can't pass over the Letter to the Hebrews: "The Word of God is living and effective, sharper than any two-edged sword, penetrating even between soul and spirit, joints and marrow, and able to discern reflections and thoughts of the heart" (Hebrews 4:12).

We do not approach the Scriptures only to find a homily. In our preparation, we go to the Scriptures because as present and future heralds of the Word, we hunger and thirst for the Word: the Word made flesh in the person of Jesus Christ and the Word inspired in us through the Holy Spirit. We wrestle with the Word because our souls are at stake and because we want to open our hearts so that the Word may penetrate into the inmost places of our souls. When we give the Scriptures of the homily enough time in study and prayer to be at home with them personally, we gain more confidence in the action of preaching. When that preached Word appears to fit the community in much the same impact as it did for us, we will relish a deeply fulfilling experience.

Countless events cram our human journeys. We struggle to make sense of them, both as pilgrims and preachers. Especially trying are those that trouble the heart and sometimes devastate the soul. In our preaching role, we strive to discover through prayer and the Word of God the precise holy ground on which we can maintain our spiritual balance and perseverance.

The Scriptures we use for prayer and our homilies are not about the past. We search for what was meant in the past in order to know God's will for the present. The late Bishop Ken Untener, addressing the matter of preaching at an annual retreat for priests, challenged us with this comment: "Does this homily have the ring of real life? Is it spoken from inside or outside the real world?" Good preaching draws upon the past, but dwells in the present. It seeks a word from the Lord for today.

Passion in preaching happens when we allow the Spirit to carry the burning "ember" to our lips and our hearts (Isaiah 4:6). Bishop Robert Morneau, in his succinct booklet *The Gift of Preaching*, in a first chapter entitled, "Prayer," urges us as follows:

> Prayer and preaching must never be divorced. . . . If prayer does not precede preaching, people will sense an absence of fervor that moves and inspires the heart. Indeed, the homily might be eloquent, filled with literary references, humorous and engaging, but something is missing: an intimacy between God and the preacher that radiates the quality of authenticity.[9]

So, to approach our preaching as genuinely prayerful people, we too can become incandescent in the pulpit. Definitely, when our words are fired with the Holy Spirit, it makes all the difference in preaching effective homilies—even some which make for burning hearts!

9. Robert F. Morneau, *The Gift of Preaching: Exploring the Ten Principles that Bring a Homily to Life* (New London, CT: Twenty-Third Publications, 2015), 7.

■ CHAPTER 5

# Preaching Hope in a Postmodern World

Joseph J. Juknialis

Preaching over time has taken on different forms and styles and purposes. In much the same way communities of faith as well as individual believers within those communities come with various expressions of faith, expectations, and personal needs. Today when we are seated after the Gospel, that need may very well be quite different for each of us. Yet it always seems that in each of us there is a hunger to know that our God cares for us and is present to us. Frederick Buechner describes well that hunger, as well as the diversity from which that hunger springs.

> In the front pews the old ladies turn up their hearing aids, and a young lady slips her six year old a Lifesaver and a Magic Marker. A college sophomore home for vacation, who is there because he was dragged there, slumps forward with his chin in his hand. The vice president of a bank who twice that week has seriously contemplated suicide places his hymnal in the rack. A pregnant girl feels the life stir inside her. A high school math teacher, who for twenty years has managed to keep his homosexuality a secret for the most part even from himself, creases his order of service down the center with his thumbnail and tucks it under his knee.
>
> The preacher pulls the little cord that turns on the lectern light and deals out his note cards like a riverboat gambler. The stakes have never been higher. Two minutes from now he may have lost his listeners completely to their own thoughts, but at this minute he has them in the palm of his hand. The silence in the shabby church is deafening because everybody is listening to it. Everybody is listening including even himself. Everybody knows the kind of things he has told them before and not told them, but who knows what this time, out of the silence, he will tell them?[1]

1. Frederick Buechner, *Telling the Truth: The Gospel as Tragedy, Comedy, and Fairy Tale* (New York: Harper & Row, 1977), 22–23.

That is the world in which we live today. How then can the preacher speak the Word to each of them in such a way that each will hear what he or she needs and longs to hear?

## Stage 1—In the Beginning

Before there was the printed word, wisdom was passed on by word of mouth and heard via the ear. Thus preaching consisted of stitching stories together, stories that embodied the community's wisdom in such a way as to engage the listener. Repetition within the story was highlighted, both as a way of creating interest as well as a method of remembering the stories well enough to pass them on from one generation to the next. For example, in the creation account of Genesis 1 the narrative of each day begins with "Then God said . . . " and concludes with "God saw how good it was. Evening came, and morning followed—the first/second/third/etc. day."

In Genesis 18, Abraham's bargaining with God over the future of Sodom has a refrain of petition and response that keeps the storyline in place—Abraham pleading for fifty innocent people, then five less, then forty and thirty and twenty and finally ten, and God conceding each time a willingness to spare the city.

Wisdom, then, flowed from the particular to the universal. What was true in the situation of the story was presumed to be true in all other life circumstances. It was understood that there was a common natural order to all things. One only needed to know the story in order to know the wisdom and the behavior that was expected. It was and is typical right brain thinking, a natural way by which we learn. As Barbara Hardy has pointed out, "we dream in narrative, daydream in narrative, remember, anticipate, hope, despair, believe, doubt, plan, revise, criticize, construct, gossip, learn, and love by narrative."[2]

As believers, we continue to live faith by means of story. We pass someone stranded on the highway, and we think of the good Samaritan. We find our relationship with someone in tension, and we remember the story of the prodigal son. A loved one dies or we find ourselves in a difficult situation, and we recall Psalm 23 or the story of the Good Shepherd. We continue to think and remember in terms of story.[3]

---

2. Barbara Hardy, "An Approach through Narrative," in *Towards a Poetics of Fiction: Essays from Novel, a Forum on Fiction, 1967–1976* (Bloomington, IN: Indiana University Press, 1977) 31.

3. Richard J. Jensen, *Thinking in Story* (Lima, OH: C.S.S. Publishing, 1993), 17–88.

## Stage 2—Modernity

With the advent of print communication, humanity experienced a shift from oral to written communication. What was written down was considered reliable and trusted. Written contracts were more reliable than someone's word. The spoken word could be denied, disputed, held suspect. Even today, television advertising is understood to be biased and suspect as a source of authenticity.

Modernity ushered in a shift from the particular to the universal as a starting point. Real truth began with the universal proposition, a wisdom which was then applied to individual or particular situations. There is a natural law which is common to everyone in every situation. The universal truth always stands.

It was understood that every principle of truth was universal and would be true in every locale. The Latin Rite of the Catholic Church as it was celebrated in Rome was considered the proper way of celebrating the sacraments in the Far East as well as Africa or the most northern regions of North America. Though the Eastern Rites of Catholicism could celebrate the Eucharist in native languages, when the Roman Rite was brought to new lands, adaptations were not allowed.

Modernity had moved truth from the timely to the timeless. What was once true was presumed to be true for all time. As a result when Friday abstinence was no longer obligatory, many of the faithful found themselves confused and suspicious of all religious practices. If one tenet of faith was no longer true, what of every other tenet?

In the age of modernity, preaching ceased to be communicated through story and instead became linear. Truth was communicated by propositions in main points rather than by narrative. Left brain thinking prevailed. Faith became analytical in nature. In many dioceses liturgical preaching consisted of official outlines published each year, either on the sacraments or the commandments or the creed.

## Stage 3—Postmodern

Over the course of the last fifty to sixty years, the world view with which Western culture has existed has undergone a drastic revision. There has been a reversal of modernity, and our culture now exists in what has come to be called the postmodern age. I have found the reflections of Walter Brueggemann extremely helpful in exploring the ways of preaching to a world that has changed so greatly.

We live in a postliterate age, a time when we no longer learn about the world from books. Brueggemann refers to the observations of Stephen Toulmin.[4]

- We have moved from a written culture to an oral culture, from newspapers to television to the internet. Consider the simple fact that 1985 was the last time there were more books taken out of libraries than videos that were rented, to say nothing of the fact that video rental has become passé.
- We have experienced a shift from truth being universal to being particular, from general to local. "Only my experience matters" has replaced any notion of universal truth.
- There is no grand story that can any longer claim assent. We are left only with quite local stories.
- All knowledge is pluralistic, with many voices claiming to hold the truth depending upon one's perspective.

Why did this happen? Brueggemann points out that Langdon Gilkey has proposed four reasons for this shift in world view.

1. Intellectual know-how has failed to deliver the good life.
2. The political promise of the Enlightenment has failed to bring peace and has led to powerful tyranny.
3. The claim of "progress" has not worked out at all convincingly.
4. Confrontation with world religions has shaken the claims and domination of Western religions.[5]

James Zullo has described the consequent worldview of this age as having these characteristics:

- There is no such thing as absolute truth.
- There is to life a lack of coherence, and thus many paradoxes.
- There is little faith in institutions. As a result people trust only themselves.
- Human existence is random, impermanent, and nightmarish. Thus people search for meaning and purpose.
- Community has great value.[6]

---

4. Walter Brueggemann, *Texts under Negotiation* (Minneapolis, MN: Fortress Press, 1993), 6.
5. Ibid., 6–7.
6. James Zullo, "God and the Gen-X Generation," *Seminary Journal* 8, no. 2 (Autumn, 2002): 42–54.

I do not posit this shift in world view as either good or bad. I am simply pointing out what has taken place and is generally attested to by many observers of culture. This is the world in which we live and the world to which we preach. To ignore this reality is to preach to those in the clouds.

As a result, doctrinal preaching will have little appeal to the vast majority of individuals who do not believe in any absolute truth. Appealing to natural law will have little sway among those who do not see any grand story to human life. Attempting to convince by proclaiming the wisdom and authority of the Church and its teachings will not persuade those who are already suspicious of any institutions, including the institution of the Church. How then does the preacher offer hope to those who live with this world view? Again I refer to the work of Walter Brueggemann.

## Preaching to Postmodern Believers

Brueggemann argues the following:

1. People do not change, or change much, because of doctrinal argument or sheer cognitive appeal.
2. People do not change, or change much, because of moral appeal.
3. People in fact change by the offer of new models, images, and pictures of how the pieces of life fit together—models, images, and pictures that characteristically have the particularity of narrative to carry them. What is yearned for among us is not new doctrine or new morality but new world, new self, new future.[7]

Brueggemann goes on to propose three different ways of imagining ourselves as a means of offering hope to those in the assembly. First, he notes that God has not yet brought us to be all that we can be. We are not finished selves. He proposes that the preacher "*Imagine a self,* no longer the self of consumer advertising, no longer a self-caught in endless efforts of self-security, but a self-rooted in the inscrutable miracle of God's love, a self no longer consigned to the rat race, but one oriented to full communion with God."

Second, he posits a world that is incomplete, and so then the preacher is to "*Imagine a world,* no longer a closed arena of limited resources and fixed patterns of domination, no longer caught in endless destructive power struggles, but able to recall that lyrical day of creation when the morning stars

7. Brueggemann, *Texts under Negotiation*, 24–25.

sang for joy, a world no longer bent on hostility, but under God's presence as a place where creatures 'no longer hurt or destroy.'"[8]

Finally, Brueggemann describes the Church as yet unfinished, and thus the task of the preacher is to *"Imagine a community of faith* . . . drastically renovated" by God's love and presence, both "healed and made safe."[9]

Lest this all be pie in the sky, Brueggemann then adds another dimension. What he proposes in terms of preaching is to articulate God's promise in the face of the world in which we live. In other words, what of God's promise is revealed in the Word we hear on this Sunday, and where have we seen that promise being enfleshed? By articulating God's promise, the preacher brings us back to God's Word and the vision God has for us and all of creation. By then naming where that vision has begun to take root in concrete reality, the preacher offers hope in the realization that God is continually present and acting among us. By telling the stories of God's activity today, the preacher makes God's presence quite local and personal. In effect the preacher is preaching a spirituality for today that enables those in the pews to recognize God's activity in their own world. That reality is not something far off as if it were a distant day dream, but rather it is already in process, already becoming. What the preacher does is to proclaim both the "kingdom already" and the "kingdom not yet."

The generations of this age are in search of meaning and purpose for their lives. Because the world seems to be constantly changing—and, as a result, because truth also seems to be constantly changing—many individuals feel themselves groping through a darkness, or at least through shadows that obscure the path they are called to walk.

## An Approach

How might one then apply the wisdom of Brueggemann to preparing a Sunday homily? Using his approach let us consider the following Gospel for the Seventeenth Sunday in Ordinary Time, Year A, Matthew 13:44–52:

> Jesus said to his disciples:
> "The kingdom of heaven is like a treasure buried in a field,
> which a person finds and hides again,
> and out of joy goes and sells all that he has and buys that field.
> Again, the kingdom of heaven is like a merchant
> searching for fine pearls.

8. Ibid.
9. Ibid., 49–52.

When he finds a pearl of great price,
he goes and sells all that he has and buys it.
Again, the kingdom of heaven is like a net thrown into the sea,
which collects fish of every kind.
When it is full they haul it ashore
and sit down to put what is good into buckets.
What is bad they throw away.
Thus it will be at the end of the age.
The angels will go out and separate the wicked from the righteous
and throw them into the fiery furnace,
where there will be wailing and grinding of teeth.
Do you understand all these things?"
They answered, "Yes."
And he replied,
"Then every scribe who has been instructed in the kingdom of heaven
is like the head of a household
who brings from his storeroom both the new and the old."

Brueggemann proposes that we name the promise of God that we find contained in the biblical text out of which we will be preaching. One way of coming to name that promise is to identify what the text describes as God's action in the world and in human life. Biblical scholarship has given us to understand that the kingdom of heaven is not a particular place. Rather it is the reign of God in human life, the reign of God's peace and justice and love and mercy and compassion. In other words, the reign of God or the kingdom of God is wherever we find such divine presence alive and taking place, wherever people are embracing a new vision of life, wherever the dream of Jesus is discovered to be taking root. Some prayerful reflection upon the text above might suggest then that

- God plants the kingdom in our path as it awaits our discovery, or
- God guides us to discover or even stumble upon the kingdom, or
- God's kingdom will find us (rather than we needing to find it), or
- God waits to be discovered, or
- God instills in us a longing for what is of great worth, or
- God's net gathers in all sorts of folk.

By identifying in the text as many possibilities of how God works in human life, we are more likely to uncover some aspect of faith that is new for us, is intriguing, and is something which excites us. If it intrigues and excites us, it is more likely to be so for those to whom we preach.

Having named some ways in which God is active in human life, we are able to then translate one or another of those ways in terms of God's promise to us. For example,

- God promises to plant his presence along life's path, waiting to be discovered, or
- God promises to instill in each person a longing for the best of what life is meant to be, or
- God promises a banquet at which folks of every ilk will find life.

Among the possible messages, it is always important to winnow the possibilities to only one promise, one message for the homily. If we preach more than one message, the homily will lose its focus and sow only confusion among the assembly. As the saying goes, if there is mist in the pulpit, there will be fog in the pews.

The final step in the process, then, is to name instances when we see the promise we have chosen to preach as already in the process of being fulfilled. For instance, consider the following:

- As much as we want those we love to come to faith, it can at times seem futile to try to encourage them since each of us seems to choose our own path on our own terms. There is an abundance of stories, however, of those who have come to faith unexpectedly on their own timeline. They have stumbled onto faith when they were least attentive to what was taking place in their lives. *God's promise of planting God's presence along life's path and waiting to be discovered is being fulfilled in them,* like a buried treasure stumbled upon in some field.
- There are many stories of individuals who have spent a good portion of life seeking meaning and happiness. Always what they find quickly fades, and so they move on to another source that in the end also fades. The journeys of midlife crises are but one example. Some are fortunate to sort out the mix sooner than others, but *their quests attest to the fact that God's promise to instill in each of us a search for the true treasure of what life is about is already unfolding,* like the merchant in search of fine pearls.

- Faith does seem to spring forth in the most unexpected and unlikely individuals. Violent criminals come to genuine faith. Addicts surrender to a power greater than themselves. Teenagers once indifferent to anything regarding faith discover faith through service of others. Unchurched parents are brought to faith through their children. *All of these individuals may not become a part of institutional religion or perhaps may do so with little regularity; nevertheless their faith lives seem to nourish and guide them to the banquet of God's love and presence,* like the net thrown into the sea that collects fish of every kind.

Once the preacher has named for himself or herself instances of how the promise of God is being fulfilled in various aspects of human life, then it is always advantageous to find very specific instances of how that is taking place. Generalizations are valuable, but specific examples of events and places are even more effective in communicating the message of hope since they point to actual times and places when God's reign has become visible and has been recognized.

## Conclusion

Hope is so much more than wishing. In fact it is quite other than wishing, other than longing for something that might be. Hope is believing in the future. It is being sustained by the knowledge that what has been promised will be because the One who promises is faithful, and we have seen those promises unfolding already in our midst.

Reportedly, one of Carl Jung's favorite stories was the folk tale of the water of life. Early in creation, the water of life decided it wanted to spring up and be a source of new life for everyone. When it did, people began to gather in order to share in its bounty. Before long, however, those who had discovered its gifts began to protect it. They set a fence around it and a guard to watch over it. Someone else put a lock on the gate. Still others began to ration it and to decide who could drink from it and who could not. As a result, the water, which was life, became division and anger for those who had found it. This disturbed the water of life greatly, and the water decided it would cease flowing and find another place to bubble forth, which is just what it did. At first, however, the people did not notice and simply kept coming for more of the flowing gift of life. Before long a few of those who had gathered there realized what had taken place and with great courage they set out to find where the new site of the water's flowing might be. In time they found it, but eventually what had happened at the first sight repeated itself, and the water once again ceased flowing and sought out yet another site. And this has been going on throughout all of history.

As with any good story, it can be understood from a number of perspectives, and in the context of preaching with hope, it is a story of how God is always breaking into life in ways and places we do not expect. It is the task of the preacher to name those ways and places in order that people of faith may grow in hope, in order that those who have eyes to see and ears to hear may do so with hope.

CHAPTER 6

# The Ladder of Homiletics: Seven Steps to Effective Preaching

Guerric DeBona, OSB

Veteran homiletics teachers are asked a perennial question: what qualities make for great preaching? In 2016, the Kyle Lake Center for Effective Preaching at Baylor University's George W. Truett Theological Seminary took a survey on the dimensions of effective preaching.[1] The usual suspects were mostly all rounded up and present: make the sermon biblical, relevant, authentic, theological, and effectively communicated in delivery and form.

I am very well aware of the usefulness of cataloging a taxonomy of skills that makes for effective preaching. Typically, preachers scan the list and see what their strengths are, while congregants might survey the results and find their own preacher deficient in this or that category. Those responses are fine, as far as they go. Yet there ought to be a way of prioritizing these characteristics or, as I will suggest here shortly, *necessary building blocks of homiletic habits* leading to consistently good preaching. Otherwise, we are left with something like a wish list of preaching abilities that might apply with some preachers or congregations more so than others. Finally, I am not convinced that preaching is really made more effective by research alone, nor do I think anyone would make such a claim. It is up to the teachers of homiletics to apply the research gleaned from the pews to see what can be done in the pulpit. So here it is. *What about a necessary sequence of good preaching skills arranged in such a way so that the outcome is formational?*

In other words, are there aspects of effective preaching which build one upon the other, something like St. Benedict's famous ladder of humility (chapter 7 in the *Rule of St. Benedict*), which begins with "the fear of the Lord" and takes the monk through a process of twelve steps and ultimately arrives at the last rung in the ladder, where the outcome is expansion of love for God which casts out fear? Configuring dimensions of effective preaching one after the other, like steps going up Jacob's ladder, asks homilists to get

1. See https://www.baylor.edu/truett/doc.php/310994.pdf

a sure footing in one of these preaching steps before moving on to another. Briefly, I will now sketch out what seven of these stages might look like from my perspective.[2]

## 1. Claiming a Personal Theology of Preaching

The foundational principle of all-effective preaching rests on developing an integrated theology of evangelization. Why preach? To whom am I preaching? For the sake of what? When St. John Paul II and other contemporary popes called for a new evangelization, they were asking the whole Church to ponder and examine its mission to spread the Gospel from top to bottom. Interestingly enough, though, when teaching seminarians studying for the Roman Catholic priesthood, it is not unusual to hear in the Foundations in Homiletics course that the initial call to ministry had little to do with a call to preach the Gospel. Priestly vocations tend to be centered more generally on sacramental and pastoral engagement. From this horizon, preaching falls way down on the list and then becomes simply one of the pastoral tasks performed in priestly ministry, among the many others that make up a very busy week. Fair enough. Yet the USCCB has underlined for decades the importance of a developing a broad theology of preaching in order to make the liturgical homily a centerpiece in the life of the parish.

Drawing from *Sacrosanctum concilium, Fulfilled in Your Hearing* (1982) reminds us that the homily remains integral to the liturgy itself. It states that "we come expecting to hear a Word from the Lord that will again help us to see the meaning of our lives in such a way that we will be able to say, with faith and conviction, 'it is right to give him thanks and praise.'"[3]

Along these same lines, Pope Francis' postsynodal apostolic exhortation *The Joy of the Gospel* (2013) gives the liturgical homily pride of place and "serious consideration among pastors" as an essential pastoral and biblical encounter with the People of God.[4] Further, I would underline what *Fulfilled in Your Hearing* calls the preacher in the context of the liturgical homily: "the mediator of meaning."[5] The preacher must personalize evangelization and own the life-changing force of the Word made visible. Therefore, it is clear that unless the preacher can stitch together aspects of liturgical,

---

2. For a more expansive view on this topic see Guerric DeBona, OSB, *Preaching Effectively, Revitalizing Your Church: The Seven-Step Ladder toward Successful Homilies* (Mahwah, NJ: Paulist Press, 2009).

3. USCCB, *Fulfilled in Your Hearing: The Homily in the Sunday Assembly* (Washington, DC: USCC, 1982), 19.

4. *Evangelii gaudium: The Joy of the Gospel* (Frederick, MD: The Word among US, 2013), 101.

5. *Fulfilled in Your Hearing*, 7.

biblical, and pastoral theology into a personalized, seamless garment of proclamation, the Sunday homily will remain a series of observations or reflections on this or that topic, perhaps with some reference to the Sunday readings. Moreover, if the preacher intends to name grace by proclaiming God's Word, how can such gifts be disclosed to the liturgical assembly unless the preacher is a personal witness to God's saving action in the Bible and the world?

In developing a theology of preaching, the homilist comes to recognize that delivering the Sunday homily is more than just an activity one executes during the week; it is an *integrating discipline*, inviting the preacher to draw together the fruits of theological reflection, pastoral care, and biblical and liturgical study into a public testimony of faith. Committing to a personal spirituality of preaching focuses a vocational call in the light of the new evangelization and the Church's mission to spread the Gospel.

## 2. Preaching from the Table of the Word and Sacrament

St. Jerome famously said that "ignorance of Scripture is ignorance of Christ." It is worth the time and effort on the part of everyone who preaches to develop a learning plan with the Bible, which would include prayerful meditation in *lectio divina*, as well as reference to ancient and contemporary commentaries. Familiarity with the Bible forms the preacher through the use of a variety of literary genres traversing an enormous historical range. The most recent statement on preaching by the USCCB, *Preaching the Mystery of Faith* (2013), says that "an effective homily takes its cue from the very nature of the Scriptures themselves, which use a rich variety of literary forms to communicate their message: narratives, metaphors, hymns, prayers, proverbial sayings, and poetry all have their place within the pages of the Bible."[6] In a prayerful reading of the Scriptures and the liturgical texts for the Sunday liturgy, the preacher avails himself of a historical web of a tradition that continues to speak. That word then becomes fruit for others. In my estimation, however, one of the more challenging aspects of ministry in the Christian tradition these days remains articulating a unified story of salvation history to an American culture, which has very little sense of collective memory even for recent history. The Bible and the liturgy recall God working with the Chosen People through establishing an eternal covenant which is renewed in Christ. Scripture acknowledges a God who loved creation into

6. USCCB, *Preaching the Mystery of Faith: The Sunday Homily* (Washington, DC: USCCB, 2013), 27.

being, and who will one day set it "free from slavery to corruption and share in the glorious freedom of the children of God" (Romans 8:21). But in a Western culture that promotes largely episodic lives—untethered to historical memory—preaching faces intense competition with Instagram, YouTube, Twitter, and other social media platforms which thrive only in the disposable present. We have only to recall the way political candidates deployed their Twitter accounts in the 2016 election to recognize that the way our culture absorbs information has radically changed even over the last few years. The preacher should know the Scriptures intimately so that those inspired pages enliven prayer and can reorient the congregation with an ear towards salvation history.

In addition to Scripture, there are enormous resources available to the preacher in the rich Catholic historical and liturgical tradition, which continues to remember the saving work of God in Christ. A familiarity with the liturgical texts in the *Roman Missal* is a remarkable thesaurus for the liturgical homily, drawing from the language of the collects, proper prayers, and prefaces. The Church at prayer is also the Church remembering, an anamnesis of what God has done in the Pascal Mystery. Preaching inside the Church's memory in the language of Word and Sacrament repositions the liturgical assembly from the chaos of a busy world into God's sacred narrative of salvation. That mission is the preacher's unique call. Too busy for this? Then return to step 1 and (re)consider your call to preach. If we are on board, the wise preacher will know that how to arrange this material is of critical importance.

## 3. Crafting a Unified Homily

There is one underdeveloped aspect of the Sunday homily that drives listeners to distraction and often right out the doors: too many ideas. That may seem odd, since it appears counterintuitive that in a world craving information the hearer would resist more ideas. But when Bishop Ken Untener researched his book *Preaching Better*, he discovered that that "too many thoughts" was the most frequently mentioned complaint which far and away surpasses all others.[7] I would add that this misstep on the ladder of preaching remains close to fatal. One aspect of communication to keep in mind when we speak to a group of people is that the listening and comprehension process is slower in "group think" than such an interchange would be in a one-on-one

7. Ken Untener, *Preaching Better: Practical Suggestions for Homilists* (Mahwah, NJ: Paulist Press, 1999), 42.

encounter. One of the classic rhetorical skills that preachers and speakers on all different subjects have known for centuries is being able to underline an important point in not just one but rather two or three sentences, all of them saying the same thing in a slightly different way; that is how oral language works to gather the group consciousness. Preachers write for collective human ears, which require a center of gravity. If the congregation is not unified around the text then the preacher has not used the language of the homily to gather in the assembly into a unified whole. Every preacher needs to remember that the homily is a performance in public/ecclesial space; it is not a private meditation. The preacher diffuses the text by wandering into this or that side bar or digression. Introductions fail when they do not introduce the body of the text.

The choice of words is an obvious key to creating a unified text. If the homily fails to use language that imaginatively gathers the listener into that faith-filled liturgical space (appropriate to the generation and ethnic background of the listener), then the homily is not really doing its job. The homily is not a personal meditation meant for a pious diary entry; it is public witness and proclamation meant to deepen the faith of the baptized. A good homily, then, will take the listeners through a process requiring a faith-filled response. That will mean as many different responses as there are congregants, but moving the text along with the collective consciousness of the assembly is crucial. Therefore, the craft of preaching is far from pulling themes out of a text, still less about some observations about life lessons and moral dos and don'ts. The common reading device of a personal, thematic mining of the Lectionary ignores the fate of listening in the congregation. *How do they hear the text*? That is a much more important question than what themes are going on here in this passage. Ask the text questions. Do they trouble you? Ask yourself: what do your parishioners need in the midst of their busy (and often tragic) lives? Are you keen to hear their sorrows and joys? Ask what the Scriptures will do for them at this liturgy. Are you aware of what roadblocks might be present? This strategy becomes especially important when preaching "difficult texts," say, for instance, the so-called Binding of Isaac passage in Genesis 22:1–19. Do you find the passage tough? If so, why? How do you suppose a single mother with two small children hears that troubling text? What do all these questions posed for the listener yield? What emerges from a more productive encounter of dialogue partners is this: a silent, prayerful "conversation" between the preacher, the assembly, and the Scriptures during the preparation stage, which ultimately develops into *a single focus sentence*. What if the focus sentence for this passage read something like this: the story of Abraham and Isaac is meant to disturb us because a Word from God can often be troubling. Good preachers deploy what Untener refers to as a single "pearl" (but of great price) to carry the homiletic event through to the end—which is the heart and ears of the listeners.[8]

## 4. Finding a Homiletic Method

The beginning of unification in a text is a focus sentence. That is the one sentence the preacher wants the listener to take away with him or her. After finding a focus sentence, there is still more work to do which can be made easier by discovering a homiletic method. Creating unity comes from finding a kind of armature on which to hang the homiletic text. Without such a clarification of the preaching event through the *arrangement of the material,* the preacher and the congregation will be scattered. Too many unarranged ideas without a focus yield confusion and frustration in the hearer and a lack of unity in the text. Imagine a novelist or a screenwriter who just plopped down in front of the computer and randomly started piling on bits of description or dialogue with no awareness of the overall shape of the unity of the text. Good writers know how beginnings will engage their readers, and they know how to keep them hooked. Can we imagine a mystery novel without carefully planted clues? Here is the opening line of Otto Preminger's film noir murder mystery *Laura* (1944), narrated off-screen by Waldo Lydecker: "I shall never forget the weekend Laura died. A silver sun burned through the sky like a huge magnifying glass. It was the hottest Sunday in my recollection. I felt as if I were the only human being left in New York." The intention and suspense is clear from the beginning, and we want more of the plot to unfold. In his *Poetics,* Aristotle observed that plotting in narrative depends crucially on the arrangement of the material.

After reviewing countless student homilies over the years, I get the feeling that if a preacher can master the arrangement of the text for the sake of the hearer, the homily becomes immediately listener friendly—by definition. This process might be something like a playwright's vision when he or she is writing a play. What is the audience doing after this line? How are they reacting when we shift to this scene? Does this act follow upon the previous one logically? As it has been developed over the last several years by pioneers such as Fred Craddock, David Buttrick, and Eugene Lowry, narrative homiletics follow Aristotelian methodology in which preachers re-present the action of the biblical text in a kind of plot for the hearer to unpack through

8. Untener, *Preaching Better,* 42–47.

stages. These methods, then, allow for the hearer to become silent dialogue partners, as they would when they engage any narrative, such as a novel, film, or play. Using an appropriate form, homilies are plotted inductively with narrative tension and then are gradually resolved by the hearer. Paul Scott Wilson's method, for instance, includes a four-part paradigm: trouble in the text; trouble in the world; God's action in the text; God's action in the world. The method allows for an introduction and conclusion, but the method engages the hearer immediately by naming, perhaps shockingly, something troubling in the text or the world and then gradually coming to some sense of resolution. Overall, homiletic methods devised by David Buttrick, Eugene Lowry, Paul Scott Wilson, and others help the preacher to create the unity identified in the previous (third) step, by an effective arrangement of the text. But engaging this process means acknowledging the crucial importance of the listener, whose cultural circumstances will shape the text and be the subject of the final steps in the ladder of homiletics. As we shall see, having a method is not enough, if the homily is jettisoned from its local and historical setting. That topic brings me to step 5.

## 5. Communicating in Contemporary Culture

The New Evangelization cannot be other than a Christian encounter with the world within our contemporary horizon. As they say, context determines content. *Gaudium et spes*, the *Pastoral Constitution on the Church in the Modern World*, takes culture radically seriously; it calls the Church to recognize the commonality that the disciples of the Lord share with all humanity, especially the poor, a message that Pope Francis continues to emphasize in the Church's ongoing mission. If the homily is unified in its method by a deployment of inductive narration, then the preacher recognizes the crucial role of the listener in an engagement of the text. Rather than simply a series of sentences supplying information, the homily becomes an event—a kind of sacrament of the word made visible—which forms the Christian assembly of the baptized in the context of the liturgy. If the preacher has correctly understood what is at stake in a theology of preaching and that the listener is a necessary part of the preaching event, then the homily will emerge quite organically as integral to the liturgy. It is interesting to note that as conscious as we have been as a Church to reform the liturgy for engaging the congregation in full and active participation, the homily seems to be the one place where such active dialogue falls short. Preaching then becomes a kind of series of observations, rather than a prayerful, prophetic centerpiece on the Word of God requiring a response. On the other hand, when viewed as a *formational text* in the context of the liturgy, the homily gathers and shapes the listener in Jesus' name with a pastoral imperative to reach the contemporary ear. In this regard, the preacher keeps substantial collateral developments in contemporary language and culture at the ready. Some general familiarity with the contemporary rhetoric of advertising and mass media is a necessity for preachers who encounter an assembly schooled by an oversaturated, overstimulated society. For a number of years, we have required students in the Foundations in Homiletics course at St. Meinrad Seminary and School of Theology to read Chip and Dan Heath's *Made to Stick: Why Some Ideas Survive and Others Die*. The authors say that what tends to find a home in people's imagination are six principles: simple, unexpected, concrete, credible, emotional, and stories.[9] Some church folks shy away from secular media and advertising. That is a mistake for one who strives to be a "mediator of meaning." We must remember the other half of the famous equation Jesus has given his disciples on the road to evangelization: we are not only to be as simple as doves, but wise as serpents. How can the Gospel's countercultural demands be recognized if those who evangelize are media-ignorant of contemporary culture in its rapidly changing forms? Attending to the signs of the times does not necessarily mean inviting the congregation to tweet during the homily, but understanding media does suggest that those gathered for an hour of worship on Sundays have been substantially engaged in rhetorical forms which may have robbed their attention span and repositioned them in a variety of ways, well outside ecclesial space. Do preachers recognize that multigenerational preaching will involve a familiarity with the images and language patterns of a variety of age groups? Pardon me: there is a reason that laxatives are discussed in television ads by older adults after the evening news, while toy and cereal commercials are meant for Saturday morning. We are all made and remade by language depending on who and where we are. Metaphors shape us. Preaching is an invitation to reshape the hearer by deploying a methodology appropriate to a particular cultural stance. But now we must also remember the larger Church, which brings us to the next rung on the ladder.

## 6. Understanding the Globalized Homily

If we are to take seriously the Lord's Resurrection and the sending of the Spirit at Pentecost, then the call to mission can never exist in a vacuum. The

9. See, Chip Heath and Dan Heath, *Made to Stick: Why Some Ideas Survive and Others Die* (New York: Random House, 2007).

Samaritan woman (John 4:4–42) and later Mary Magdalene (John 20:11–18) took on new identities in the face of new circumstances. As we see him depicted in the Acts of the Apostles, Peter was transformed from the quivering disciple who denied the Lord around the campfire to the courageous preacher in the midst of a diverse—and sometimes hostile—assembly. As the face of the Church changes, so also does its preaching. If we are committed to preaching for the listener and understanding the hopes and joys, the heartbreaks and sufferings of the People of God, then an empathic, globalized understanding of the homily is in order. In my estimation, the key to unlocking a globalized homily resides in the ear of the assembly. Effective homiletics will depend on preachers who exegete not only a text but their people. To lack an understanding of the people before us makes the text a personal monologue and not a homily. Here, I would suggest the crucial link between pastoring and the homily. What has been going on in the parish and the lives of the parishioners will orient the homily. Could it be otherwise that, if a young child and member of the parish school is killed suddenly in a bike accident, it would not affect the way the preacher and the listener respond to the following Sunday's Gospel, which happens to be the Fifth Sunday of Lent (Year A), the raising of Lazarus? Additionally, anticipating the needs of an immigrant population (especially the Hispanic community), whose worldview may not be shared by North Americans, will require a conversion for many preachers and parishioners. That means letting go of safety nets and allowing the People of God to transform the preacher. Contemporary preachers are like missionaries who live and breathe the diversity of the flock entrusted to their care, all of which may challenge traditional economic and political safety nets. Increasingly, that Catholic Christian community faces political and cultural opposition when it comes to evangelizing because of real or supposed threats to national security. Racism is alive and well in the USA. Over the last several decades, the US bishops have reimagined a North America where there are "Strangers No Longer," because the Hispanic community is a gift and "blessing."[10] Receiving such a graced population carries with it the risk of transformation by and for the People of God, who come as the Body of Christ without borders.

---

10. For an informative take on this subject, see *On "Strangers No Longer": Perspectives on the Historic US-Mexican Catholic Bishops' Pastoral Letter on Migration*, ed. Todd Scribner and J. Kevin Appleby (Mahwah, NJ: Paulist Press, 2013).

## 7. Confronting the Obstacles to Effective Preaching

The biggest step to improving preaching is this: feedback. We know from a variety of research studies, notably Lori Carrell's study (2000) from a University of Wisconsin at Oshkosh grant, that what will make good preaching better is feedback from the listener. That exchange is more than something like "nice homily" or "thanks for the thoughtful words." I have identified a series of questions which might be printed on cards and distributed to the congregation. These comments are not simply affirmations, but tools for homiletic reassessment:

> In one sentence, can you say what you heard?
>
> Did the preacher use the biblical readings from the
>
> Lectionary well?
>
> The homily motivated me to ______________________.
>
> The homily did not really motivate me.
>
> I felt it ______________________.
>
> The delivery of the homilist was: excellent; good;
>
> needs to improve in this way: ______________________.

Consider that the first question is really asking if the listener heard the focus sentence. Additionally, the question about the Bible is really an integration question because it asks if the texts were used well and not just referenced or explicated in isolation. Indeed, there is the all-important motivational or personal application question, which might be phrased more bluntly as, "so what?"

When it comes to delivery, preachers whose native language is not English face a special challenge. Those who struggle with English might be served by replacing bad sound systems or printing up the homily ahead of time for distribution to the congregation. We might remember the special difficulties the elderly endure when it comes to hearing effective proclamation.

Lastly, using small groups for feedback also provides an effective way to transform preaching. A new area of exploration is emerging in homiletic circles: group supervision. Those who have come from good homiletic training know the invaluable experience of classroom feedback from peers and instructors, as well as one-on-one video monitoring supervision. But the teaching does not have to stop in the classroom. Local pastors and catechists might gather to share their homilies, before or after preaching them. Recently, thanks to Fr. Mike Connors, CSC, a Lilly grant was awarded to the

Marten Program in Homiletics under their Strengthening Preaching Initiative. The resulting project is the Fr. William Toohey, CSC, Notre Dame Preaching Academy that supervises several cohorts of preachers in order to develop some models of homiletic continuing education. We get feedback by checking in with the listening assembly, peers, or a supervisor, so the homily is bound to improve with some amount of mirroring. In addition, Lorri Carrell noted a second way to improve preaching: developing a solid spiritual life. That leads us back to our foundational step 1 in effective preaching. If the spiritual life is either rusty or on shaky ground, the preacher will be on a very difficult scaffold indeed.

There is no question in my mind that preachers can benefit from sequencing the skills we know make for effective preaching. We can discuss the variables, such as what makes for good preaching or even the order they might occur. But step by step, *poco a poco* makes for sure progress when it comes to preaching effectively.

■ CHAPTER 7

# Making a Scene in the Pulpit!

Alyce M. McKenzie

I begin with a sermon that illustrates the principles we will highlight below.

## The Yellow Backpack: Mark 10:42–56

Today Jesus is coming through Jericho. He is about to encounter a blind beggar named Bartimaeus. Bartimaeus is not one of the original disciples. But he shows us what it looks like to be one. Right before this encounter James and John argue over who is going to get to ride shotgun with Jesus in the world to come (Mark 10:35–37). Right after that, Jesus enters Jerusalem to shouts of "Hosanna!" in Hebrew, "*Hoshiya na*!" which means, "Save us, please!" Then the Palm Sunday parade will fade, and the disciples will scatter like cockroaches. Mark places Bartimaeus' story here, just as Jesus heads toward Jerusalem and the cross. His purpose is to say to us, "This is what it looks like to be a disciple!"

A few years back our oldest daughter Melissa was getting married. I somehow thought I could perform the ceremony at First United Methodist Church of Allen, Texas, host a houseful of out-of-town company, and help with wedding details all without breaking a sweat. I thought I was doing pretty well in the days leading up to the wedding. That is, until I overheard our middle daughter Rebecca say to her younger brother Matt, "Just stay out of her way. She is in full freak out mode."

Two days before the wedding, I was up early, list in hand, in my car, and on a mission. Fill up with gas. Drive through car wash. Pick up non-wedding party family suits and dresses at dry cleaners. Go to grocery store. Pick up deli trays for lunch at home before wedding. Go by drugstore. Pick up sewing kits for bridesmaids' gift baskets in case of last minute wardrobe malfunctions. Lastly, drive through the ATM. I pulled up at the ATM, put my card in, punched in my pin number, pulled out my fast cash, and peeled out, heading home on Exchange Avenue toward our neighborhood. I hate being tailgated, especially when I am already going at least ten miles over the speed limit.

This minivan pulled right up behind me and then beside me and motioned for me to pull over. I thought to myself, "It's ten in the morning. You have two children in the car. You're drunk!" And then the driver held up a small rectangular plastic card.

I wish life were like that. I wish that every time I lost something, I got it back. Every time I lost something Jesus would ask me, "What do you want me to do for you, Alyce?" And I'd say "I want it back," and he would drive up in his minivan and hand it over into my car window.

Life doesn't work that way. A lot of things we lose in life we never get back.

I still remember the rejection letter I got when I was applying for a teaching job. It would have been nice if it had started out with "Dear Dr. McKenzie, we appreciate your interest in our position and value your background and gifts." But no, it simply said, "Dear Dr. McKenzie, while our search continues, it no longer includes you."

A pastor walks into the waiting room outside the obstetric unit. There is her church member, a young man who had hoped to be a father in a few months, rocking back and forth in his chair, asking "What did we do wrong that we lost the baby? What did we do wrong?"

A woman almost eighty enrolls her husband in a dementia unit at a facility near the apartment they've shared together since he retired. He is getting good care. But last night after she visited with him and came home, it hit for the first time: "I'm alone now."

Think of Gabby Gifford, representative from Arizona shot in the head January 8, 2011, in a grocery store parking lot near Tucson, in an attack in which thirteen others were injured and six were killed. She lost her career, and her ability to walk, speak, read, and write. While she has made progress and has a great spirit, she has lost some things that are not coming back.

Bartimaeus was born able to see but through an accident or an illness he lost his sight.

And that's not all he lost. When he lost his sight he lost his community; he lost his livelihood; he lost his future. Why these losses? Because of the false belief that pervaded his day and seeps into our own: that blindness, illness, and poverty were punishments from God for some sin the person had committed. As he began to believe that bad theology, as his confidence leached away year by lonely year, he began to lose faith in himself.

But there is one thing Bartimaeus had not lost: his faith. Sometimes we think if we don't feel joyful and peaceful all the time, we don't have faith. Allow me to introduce us to the faith of Bartimaeus. His is not a faith based just on feelings. This is not how the story goes. When he heard it was Jesus of Nazareth coming to town, Bartimaeus felt his heart flood with warm emotions. This is how the story goes. When Bartimaeus heard that Jesus of Nazareth was coming to town, he gathered up the one thing he hadn't lost, his single shred of stubborn faith, and he goes and spreads out his beggar's cloak at the corner of desperate and driven and begins to call out Jesus' name. Every time the crowd tells him to shut up he shouts out even louder: "Jesus, Son of David, have mercy on me!"

A single shred of stubborn faith. That kind of faith reminds me of the psalmists. They vent their anger and pain in the same breath that they stubbornly expect God to save them. Psalm 42 could have been written by Bartimaeus in the long years of his darkness and isolation.

> As the deer longs for streams of water,
> so my soul longs for you, O God.
> My soul thirsts for God, the living God.
> When can I enter and see the face of God?
> My tears have been my bread day and night,
> as they ask me every day, "Where is your God?" (vv. 2–4)

> I will say to God, my rock:
> "Why do you forget me?
> Why must I go about mourning
> with the enemy oppressing me?"
> It shatters my bones, when my adversaries reproach me,
> when they say to me every day: "Where is your God?"
> Why are you downcast, my soul,
> why do you groan within me?
> Wait for God, for I shall again praise him,
> my savior and my God. (vv. 10–12)

It is in this tradition of faithful lament that Bartimaeus calls out to the Son of the God addressed in the psalm as he strides through town: "Jesus, Son of David, have mercy upon me!"

Now maybe you're not the shouting type. Maybe you're more private about your losses and your faith. Maybe you are the type who suffers in silence and doesn't want to draw yourself to Jesus' attention.

Dr. Theodore Parker Ferris, preacher, author, and preaching professor served Trinity Episcopal Church in Boston, an old downtown church founded in1733, from 1942 to 1972. One morning Dr. Ferris' administrative assistant came in and said, "Dr. Ferris, there is a man here who wants to see you." When the man was seated in Dr. Ferris' office, he leaned forward and said, "I'd like to thank you for saving my life." "But I've never seen you before!"

Dr. Ferris answered. "Last Sunday night I was on my way to the Charles River with my pockets full of rocks. I saw the lights on and heard the music. I came in and sat in the gallery behind a pillar. What you said saved my life. I came to thank you." "From that day on," Dr. Ferris later said, "I always preach to the man behind the pillar."

There is no hiding from Jesus behind the pillar. And Jesus is passing through your town this morning, about to embark on the road to Jerusalem, asking, "Who's coming with me?" And like it or not, when he stands still, it's because he has noticed you and he has noticed me. And he is calling us along with Bartimaeus to come and stand before him. And he is asking all of us the same question: "What do you want me to do for you?" That is a tough one. What do you think is the best answer?

I asked myself, how should I answer Jesus' question, "What do you want me to do for you?" The evening of Tuesday, March 10, I fell asleep mulling that over. And while asleep I had a dream. The kind of dream that makes me wonder if God thinks I'm a better listener when I'm asleep than when I'm awake. I was coming home from Europe after a long trip. I was filled with this yearning to go home, to be home. I had checked my fifty-pound suitcase. I was at the gate. I was planning to take just two pieces of luggage on board—my roller board and my yellow backpack. I had a heavy wool coat which I had gone ahead and put on so I wouldn't have to carry it. I sat on the edge of my seat and double-checked that I had everything. With a sharp intake of breath I realized that I did not see my yellow backpack. I broke into a sweat under my coat. I searched under the seat. I went to the counter and asked a young man whose nametag said "Matt," "Has anyone turned in a yellow backpack?" "No, ma'am." "But it has my passport, my driver's license, wallet, and phone in it. I can't get home without my yellow backpack." "Calm down, ma'am," said Matt. "We'll look around." He searched behind the desk. No yellow backpack. He searched in the closet where employees keep their belongings. There were yellow hats, yellow scarves and yellow shoes, but no yellow backpack. He announced to the indifferent people in the waiting area that if they had seen a yellow backpack to please bring it to the desk. He called over to the lost and found and had them checking. No, no yellow backpack. Then they began calling out all the categories of people who had better seats on the plane than I did. Advantage Platinum. Advantage Gold. One World Emerald, Sapphire, Ruby. Priority Access. They were about to call group 1. I was at the brink of panic when suddenly Matt put his arm around me and patted me on the back. Several times. And then he said, "Ma'am, either you are a hunchback, or there is something under your coat." He helped me struggle out of my coat and we both discovered that I was wearing my yellow backpack. He smiled like they are trained to do, ruining the effect a bit by rolling his eyes. And then I woke up.

"What do you want me to do for you?" Jesus asks. The best answer for me is: Lord, help me to remember that I have on me everything I need for the next leg of my journey. I don't need to get back everything I've lost in order to move forward with you. I don't need you to promise me that no losses lie ahead to move forward with you. Help me to remember that I have everything I need to continue my journey home because I make that journey with you.

Help me to take a page out of Bartimaeus' book. He doesn't say, "Give me back the job, give me back the friends, give me back the years, give me back the tears." No, he says to Jesus, "I would like to see again . . . Not so I can go back. But so I can go forward and bless others as a follower of yours." And immediately after he regained his sight, he followed Jesus on the way. In this brief exchange, Bartimaeus becomes the only person Jesus heals in the Gospels who immediately follows him.

"What do you want me to do for you?" Jesus asks each of us. Lord, we do not ask you to restore all that we have lost. We ask that you remind us of what you have already done for us. What I already have by your Presence, by your Love.

When I lost the opportunity to teach at the school that rejected me, God comforted me with the knowledge that God has accepted me. And God encouraged me to apply again somewhere else. And through the years God has helped me encourage other young scholars at low points in their job searches.

When the young parents lost their baby, they still had the arms of God who was embracing their child and also embracing them—encouraging them to embrace other couples in their losses and struggles with infertility and miscarriage.

When the woman whose husband had dementia and no longer recognized her walked into her empty apartment, she found that she was not alone. God who knew her name was there. And turned her mind to dwell upon the other lonely people in her building and how she might reach out to them.

When Gabby Gifford lost her career, her motor skills, her ability to speak and read and write, God was with her through her husband and many friends, encouraging her to press on. When a terrible loss struck Sandy Hook Elementary School in Newtown, Connecticut, on December 4, 2012, I believe it was God who motivated her and her husband, Mark Kelly, to visit the parents and grandparents of the children who were killed and offer them presence and comfort from the depth of their own loss.

When the man hides behind the pillar, feeling all hope is lost because of his guilt over his past, Jesus speaks a life changing, lifesaving word of forgiveness to him: "Your life has meaning and purpose. It is not over yet."

My favorite anthem in the choir in which I sing has words by St. Thomas à Kempis, a German priest who lived in the 1400s. His beautiful poem has been set to music in the gorgeous classic choir anthem by K. Lee Scott. It is called "Write Your Blessed Name." It is my answer to Jesus' question, "What do you want me to do for you?"

> Write your blessed name, O Lord, upon my heart
> There to remain so indelibly engraved
> That no adversity, no prosperity
> Ever move me from thy love."
> Oh, Jesus, my only Savior.[1]

## Part 1: Make a Scene!

In everyday life, we most often advise people, "Don't make a scene!" A father may say this to a toddler on the brink of a tantrum at Target. A lawyer may say this to her client on the way into the courtroom. Don't make a scene means: Don't draw bystanders into our drama. My advice as a preacher and teacher of preaching today is just the opposite. Make a scene! For God's sake, make a scene! Because now more than ever, we need to pull out all the stops to draw increasingly indifferent and disaffected bystanders into the drama of the story of salvation. I suggest we activate the power of a strategy the Bible uses so masterfully: the scene!

My first encounter with scenes for preaching was when I was in graduate school at Princeton Seminary in the early 1990s. I was late for a class in Old Testament interpretation for preaching and got stuck with writing a thirty-page paper on what most preachers regard as the least preachable genre in the Bible: Proverbs!

Remembering the witticism by Will Willimon that "reading the book of Proverbs is like taking a long road trip with your mom," I began to read through Proverbs that evening. There I encountered a number of scenes.

1. Copyright Hope Publishing Company, 2014.

- It is not good to eat too much honey, or to seek honor on top of honor (25:27).
- Like a city breached, without walls, is one who lacks self-control (26:28).
- The crucible is for silver, and the furnace is for gold, so a person is tested by being praised (27:21).
- The fear of others lays a snare, but one who trusts in the Lord is secure (29:25).
- Sometimes there is a way that seems right, but in the end it leads to death (14:12).

The sages responsible for coining and collating the Book of Proverbs did not follow the advice "Don't make a scene!" Scenes were their stock in trade.

Proverbs are compressed one-liners of wisdom drawn from the sages' observations of repeated cause-effect patterns in the realms of nature and human relationships. Their rhetorical intention is for the reader/hearer to gather a constellation of experiences to the proverb with which the reader/hearer deems it to be an "apt fit."[2] After writing that first paper, I found myself alert to other scenes from Old Testament wisdom literature beyond Proverbs: those painted by the authors of the books of Job and Ecclesiastes: the outraged Job on the ash heap (Job 2), the humbled Job before the whirlwind (Job 38–41) and the melancholy Qoheleth observing life's injustices (Ecclesiastes 4:1–3).

## Jesus Makes a Scene in His Proverbs

And then it was on to another sage, who also taught in proverbs. Jesus often used sayings that caused listeners to picture a specific, exaggerated scene, and made a command in relation to it that challenged daily norms of behavior.

- "If your hand or foot or eye causes you to stumble . . . " (Mt 18:8; Mk 9:43–48).
- "It is easier for a camel to go through the eye of a needle than . . . " (Mt 19:24 = Mk 10:25 = Luke 18:25).
- "Follow me and let the dead bury their own dead" (Mt 8:22 = Luke 9:60).

---

2. Alyce M. McKenzie, *Preaching Proverbs: Wisdom for the Pulpit* (Louisville, KY: Westminster John Knox Press, 1996), xvii.

- "If anyone strikes you on the right cheek, turn the other also; and if anyone wants to sue you and take your coat, give your cloak as well; and if anyone forces you to go one mile, go also the second mile" (Mt 5:39–41).

In his classic work *The Sword of His Mouth,* New Testament scholar Robert Tannehill calls these scenes "focal instances."[3]

Jesus also taught in parables, a longer narrative cousin of the proverb—both from the genre known in Hebrew as *meshalim* (plural of *mashal*). Both proverbs and parables are born from somebody closely observing scenes from everyday life, discerning patterns in them, and offering advice based on those observations which we call wisdom. A parable is, according to C.H. Dodd's definition from 1935, "a metaphor or simile drawn from nature or common life arresting the hearer by its vividness or strangeness leaving the mind in sufficient doubt as to its precise application as to tease the mind into active thought."[4]

Jesus' parables feature powerful religious and political figures in an unflattering light (arrogant Pharisees, unjust judges) and lowly and despised individuals in a flattering light (Samaritans, tax collectors).

## Jesus Makes a Scene in His Parables

- Pharisee and tax collector: Luke 18:10–14
- Sower: Mark 4:3–8; Matthew 13:3b-8; Luke 8:5–8a
- Workers in vineyard: Matthew 10:1–15
- Good Samaritan: Luke 10:30–35
- Prodigal son: Luke 15:11–32

The greatest experts in making scenes in the Bible, as we have seen, are the wisdom teachers, of whom the authors of the Books of Proverbs, Job, and Ecclesiastes and Jesus are prime examples. Their fundamental skill was what I call the "knack for noticing." It is the alertness to one's inner life, one's life in community and one's religious traditions and writings. I call this an attentiveness to inscape, landscape, and textscape. Essentially this means being

---

3. Robert Tannehill, *The Sword of his Mouth: Forceful and Imaginative Language in Synoptic Sayings* (Philadelphia: Fortress Press, 1975), 72–88.

4. Alyce M. McKenzie, *The Parables for Today* (Louisville: Westminster John Knox Press, 2007), 22.

attentive to the elements of scene in all these areas: setting, plot, character, and theme.[5]

# Part 2: Scene Crafting

## Principles of Scene Crafting: Concrete Significant Detail

A general rule that applies to scene crafting in general is what fiction writers call "concrete significant detail." *Concrete* means that there is an image, something that can be seen, heard, smelled, tasted, or touched. *Detail* means that there is a degree of focus and specificity. *Significant* means that the specific image is related to the theme of the scene.[6] The use of the color yellow is an example from my sermon. Dream analysts tell us to pay particular attention to brightly colored objects in our dreams. We need to *focus the listener's attention on something in particular* for a *reason* that pertains to our theme and purpose by means of an *appeal to one of the senses.* This is how we convey information through vivid detail. We direct our listeners' intellects and emotions toward the meaning of the details. While description is important, over-description is deadly. Why? Because it diffuses rather than directs the reader's intellect and emotions.

## Principles of Scene Crafting: Show, Don't Just Tell; Show Me Character

Josip Novakovitch's advice to writers is, "In description, directly show what can be seen and allow readers to infer the rest. You must show emotion. Don't just say outright how your characters feel. Give the reader evidence. How do we know that Joan is bored, that Peter is ashamed, that Thomas is skeptical? Show how they look and behave, what their hands are doing, and the reader will infer the emotion."[7] So in my opening sermon the man behind the pillar said, "I was on my way to the Charles River with my pockets full of rocks." I don't need to explain to the reader that his purpose was not to go swimming. Screenwriter Karl Iglesias suggests that aspiring screenwriters watch silent films to learn how to show instead of tell.[8]

---

5. Alyce M. McKenzie, *Novel Preaching: Tips from Top Writers on Crafting Creative Sermons* (Louisville: Westminster John Knox Press, 2010), 14–15.

6. Sondra B. Willobee, *The Write Stuff: Crafting Sermons that Capture and Convince* (Louisville: Westminster John Knox Press, 2009), 93.

7. Josip Novakovitch, *Fiction Writer's Workshop* (Cincinnati: Story Press, 1995), 179.

8. Karl Iglesias, *Writing for Emotional Impact* (Livermore, CA: WingSpan Press, 2005), 139.

## Show Me Setting

The vivid description that is the key to showing characters' emotions and personalities is also the key to portraying scenes and settings. Whether you are portraying a biblical setting or a contemporary one, use details that engage all five senses. These could be details of weather, geography, food, smells, textures, place, windows, light, or furniture. They can be used to convey both concepts and emotional dynamics.

Sensory details can do justice to the blood, sweat, and tears of the biblical world. The smell of martyrs' blood mingled with the dirt of the coliseum floor. The sounds of flames licking at the buildings as Rome burned. A wild glint in an emperor's eyes. The taste of bread and wine as they share their holy meal. Their hands tremble as they reach out to receive it. This is the Gospel of Mark. Probably written at the outset of a persecution, possibly by Nero. It's written in a crucible: this accounts for its high blood pressure, urgent feel, for its stress on sacrifice, and for its terse language. There isn't much time; there is lots of danger. Persecutions are imminent. Are you in or are you out?

Sensory details can make a contemporary scene come alive on the screens of listeners' imaginations.

> He sat across from me, his face chalky except for the maroon gash over one eye. About to tell me a story I'd heard before and would hear again. Drinks at the bar. Driving his buddy home. Single car accident. Friend in ICU fighting to live. His cut hadn't even needed stitches. He picked up the Bible we kept on the coffee table, his hands brushing off the dust. Somebody had given it to us for our wedding. It was white naugahide, with the face of Jesus on it in Velveteen. Auburn hair. Limpid blue eyes. He began tracing the face of Jesus, around the chin, the outline of nose, eyes, brow, hair and back again, tracing the face of Jesus.[9]

## Show Me Truth (Theme)

Does your sermon consist of a series of statements about God and the life of faith, each followed by conceptual explanation? "We reach a place in life where we realize that we are living a superficial existence." "In our relationship with Christ, God gives us the gift of discovering our deepest identity." "We need to live in such a way that the values of our faith take priority over the values of the world." "The Incarnation is God's action to meet us in our grief." "Despite the instances of violence and hatred in the world over the past

9. See chapter 6 of Alyce McKenzie's *Novel Preaching* for more examples of the use of sensory details in sermons.

several months, God is at work in the world bringing redemption and reconciliation." All these statements are edifying and, I believe, true. But we need to give the listener examples, not just expect them to take our word for it.

## Part 3: Scene Sequencing: Think Plot with Scenes, Not Points with Illustrations

We preachers tend to think of the segments of our sermons as points in an outline. Instead, try thinking of your sermon as unfolding in a series of scenes. In some scenes, you might do some teaching in the framework of a setting, dialogue, or image.

The word *scene* comes from theater, where it describes the action that takes place in a single physical setting in continuous time. Novelist and screenwriter Raymond Obstfeld advises his students to think of each scene in their work as an inner tube designed to keep the larger work afloat. The more memorable scenes there are, the more we see the entire structure floating in front of us and, therefore, the more we appreciate the whole work. The fewer memorable scenes there are, the quicker that work sinks to the depths of mediocrity."[10]

Sometimes the problem with the coherence of a sermon is that its scenes are out of sequence. Make sure your scenes are both coherent and compelling in the order in which you have placed them. Sometimes preachers, after offering the good news, revisit the problems and sorrows of the world. This is a prime example of bad sermon sequencing. In my sermon I tried to move from the reality that there are things in life which we lose and never get back to the spiritual reality that with God's presence we have all we need for the journey. In circling back at the end to the scenes of loss at the beginning (job opportunity, child, husband's company, Gabby Gifford's experience), I brought those losses into the present reality of God's providing new energy, faith, and positive influence despite what has been lost. Obstfeld advises writers to be clear in their own minds about the purpose of each scene in their novel. The same goes for preachers and sermons. When you finish reading a scene, says Obstfeld, ask yourself:

- Is this scene necessary?
- Is it memorable apart from the overall movie?
- Does it propel us into the next scene?

10. Raymond Obstfeld, *Novelist's Essential Guide to Crafting Scenes* (Cincinnati: Writer's Digest Books, 2000), 2.

Effective sermon sequences move from problem to solution, or human condition to divine response. Some recent options include the following.

- The Lowry Loop (Oops, Ugh, Aha, Whee, Yeah!):[11] The problem in the world or text is identified. We are made to feel the itch. The divine key or good news that overturns the bad is revealed and the preacher makes concrete the difference it makes in our lives.
- Detective Novel (Craddock):[12] The sermon follows the journey the preacher takes through the exegetical process to final insight. The form is "Not this, or that, but this!"
- Four Pages (Wilson):[13] Trouble in the text, trouble in the world; good news in the text, good news in the world.
- Celebration (Mitchell;[14] Thomas[15]): A false belief about ourselves or God is identified by the preacher. For example, we are not worthy of God's love. Our best days are behind us. We are saved by grace and so do not have to do anything. The truth of the Gospel through the text(s) of the day is proclaimed that overturns the false belief. The preacher offers reason for the congregation to celebrate liberation from falsehood and life in the Truth.

## The Benefits of Good Scene Sequencing: It Avoids Common Pitfalls in Sermon Construction

- Dull Hook: The sermon begins with a tedious recitation of biblical history or an anecdote that lacks luster and relatability.
- Sudden Drop Off: The opening story is interesting, but its connection to the Scripture is tenuous and it is presented in a more interesting manner than the Scripture.

---

11. See Eugene Lowry, *The Homiletical Plot: The Sermon as Narrative Art Form* (originally published 1980; expanded edition, Louisville: Westminster John Knox, 2000).

12. See Fred B. Craddock, *Preaching* (Nashville: Abingdon Press, 1985).

13. See Paul Scott Wilson, *The Four Pages of the Sermon: A Guide to Biblical Preaching* (Nashville: Abingdon Press, 1999).

14. See Henry H. Mitchell, *Celebration and Experience in Preaching*, rev. ed. (Nashville: Abingdon Press, 2008).

15. See Frank A. Thomas, *They Like to Never Quit Praisin' God: The Role of Celebration in Preaching*, rev. ed. (Long Island City, NY: Pilgrim Press, 2013).

- Bloated Midsection: The middle of the sermon is filled with information with no illustration and the initial interest wanes.
- Tangled through Line: The preacher doesn't have a clear theme and sense of purpose throughout. The focus seems to change.
- String of Pearls with No String: The sermon consists of a series of stories with no connecting thread.
- Awkward Goodbye: The sermon circles the airport and fails to land. Listeners become increasingly annoyed.

So in conclusion, my advice to preachers is "Make a scene! For God's sake, make a scene in the pulpit!" The Bible is the best example of effective scene making. The sages, wise teachers of Israel, including Jesus, knew how to activate their knack for noticing scenic elements of setting, plot, and character in their inner lives, their communities, and religious traditions. The best preachers in homiletical history have been those who didn't just offer a series of abstractions, but activated the power of scenes. Key principles of scene crafting are the use of concrete significant detail and the principle of "show, don't just tell!" Effective sermonic scene sequences move from the human condition to the difference made by the character and the actions of God in the world. Effective sequencing is an antidote to common pitfalls in both sermon construction and sermon delivery. Making a scene in the pulpit means drawing all the bystanders we can into the drama of salvation!

CHAPTER 8

# Story/Point/Passage: Ten Rules of Thumb for Homilists

John Shea

The preparation, planning, and performance of a homily is a complex process. It has many elements; and those elements can come together in a variety of ways. However, I do not want to wade into this complexity or try to identify and connect its elements. I only want to suggest one possible element—a language tool that may enhance the homily and contribute to the homilist's purposes. Also, I want to suggest ten rules of thumb for using this tool.

This language tool is a story/point/passage package. The homilist should learn how to tell a story, distill its point, and connect it to a scriptural passage. The homilist doesn't have to keep that order. The sequence could also develop as scriptural passage, story, point, or any other combination—as long as all three are present and connected to one another. This tool has the advantage of having an interest-capturing story, the succinctness of a chiseled point, and a connection and illumination of a scriptural text. This sequence is usually used at the beginning of a homily. But, with a little creativity, it can also be imported into the middle or the end.

## Spiritual Teaching Stories

One group of stories that can be used in this way is spiritual teaching stories. These stories are found in all religious traditions, and they usually resonate with the perspectives and teachings of biblical texts. They can be found in abundance by searching the internet for "spiritual teaching stories." The following is an example of a spiritual teaching story.

**STORY:** I do not know where this teaching story comes from, but it is a story that has something to say.

A man went into a marketplace. He looked around at all the shops and vendors. He saw a sign, "God's Fruit Stand." Although he was alone, he said out loud in a frustrated voice, "It's about time."

He went into the shop and said to the woman behind the counter, "I want a perfect apple, a perfect banana, and a perfect pear." The woman replied, "We only sell seeds."

**POINT:** There is no perfection. There are only seeds and soils.

**PASSAGE:** "A sower went out to sow some seed and as he sowed some of the seeds fell" (Luke 8:5) . . . on us. What we want to reflect on is: What seeds have come our way and what type of soil are we becoming to welcome them?

## First Rule of Thumb

Do not tell a story that has not been first told to you. In other words, the story should have an impact on the homilist before the homilist tells it with the hope that it will have an impact on those who are listening. This background personal experience gives the homilist an inside track on the potential of the story.

## Second Rule of Thumb

The story has to be practiced—pauses, tone of voice, punch lines, etc. It is an oral happening, and it is most effective when it is performed with the best practices of that skill. Although homilists may rate themselves as good or poor storytellers, all homilists can improve. They are not professional storytellers, but they can become good enough storytellers to use the medium effectively in a liturgical setting.

## Third Rule of Thumb

Respect the liturgical context. Delivering an oral story within a homily harness means the story has to be decently short as well as decently fitting. Entertainment is acceptable as long as it is not the only value. Always remember the sacredness of the setting and the homiletic contract with the congregation.

## Telling Experiences in Story Form

Besides spiritual teaching stories, there are experiences told in story form. In my opinion, these stories can be very relevant to homilists. Homilists have their own experiences, people are continually telling them about their experiences, and they are reading about people's experiences in books, newspapers, and articles. Some of these experiences can supply the raw material for homilies. The task is how to craft them into stories and tell them so they serve the homily's purpose.

Therefore, telling experiences in story form can be distinguished into three areas:

- telling your own experience in story form
- telling an experience that someone told you in story form
- telling an experience in story form that you have read

Each of these areas has its own distinctiveness. If homilists are telling their own experience, they should always be a learner or observer in the story, not the hero or the major actor. If homilists are telling an experience in story form that has been told to them, they should tell it as a respected listener. If they are telling an experience they have read about, they should tell it as thoughtful reader. Here is an example of telling your own experience in story form:

---

**YOUR OWN EXPERIENCE:** In 1960, when I was eighteen, I took a summer job as a camp counselor at an inner city Catholic parish. I taught baseball, basketball, and religion. Baseball and basketball I could handle. I was definitely over my head with religion, but I had a book!

However, the classrooms of the school were being painted. So the religion class was held in a gangway, a narrow strip between the stone walls of the church and the brick walls of the school. Fifteen eleven- to thirteen-year-old boys sat on rickety, wooden folding chairs. I stood in front of them with my book. They paid no attention to me and were talking and hitting one another.

Suddenly, they fell silent. They were looking at something behind me. I turned around and there was Fr. Brown, the pastor.

He walked in front of me, picked up one of the rickety, wooden folding chairs and began banging it against the bricks of the school. It fell into pieces. Then he picked up one of the pieces and banged it against the stones of the Church. It splintered more.

The kids watched, paralyzed.

When Fr. Brown had broken the last of the pieces, he looked at the kids and said, "That's what they are going to do to you unless you have something inside you."

**PASSAGE:** "Everyone who listens to these words of mine and acts on them will be like a wise man who built his house on rock. The rain fell, the floods came, and the winds blew and buffeted the house. But it did not collapse; it had been set solidly on rock. And everyone who listens to these words of mine but does not act on them will be like a fool who built his house on sand. The rain fell, the floods came, and the winds blew and buffeted the house. And it collapsed and was completely ruined" (Matthew 7:24–27).

**POINT:** Fr. Brown and the Gospel thinks there is something inside us that can withstand storm. Are they right? And if they are, what is it that has that power?

---

## Fourth Rule of Thumb

A story particularizes and a point universalizes. The story above is about an eighteen-year-old camp counselor who watches a priest demonstrate a lesson in withstanding destruction. The listeners were not there and the story is not about them. But hopefully the story has kept them awake and interested. When the point is spoken, the listener becomes the target. What is it about them that can withstand storm? This is sometimes called the window/mirror effect. During the storytelling, listeners look in on the actions of others through the window of the story. When the point is spoken, the window turns into a mirror and listeners see themselves and are confronted with the point. What starts out as someone else's story becomes theirs.

## Fifth Rule of Thumb

Storytelling weaves together setting, description, characters, and direct/indirect dialogue. All of these are needed, but memorable dialogue holds a special place. A memorable piece of dialogue often articulates the point and stays with the listeners.

## Sixth Rule of Thumb

The point has to be chiseled. Homilists must work on sharpening the point and finding succinct and powerful language to communicate it. "What do we have within us that can withstand storm?" is an attempt to say what the homily will develop in a way that captures attention and is relevant to the listeners. Preparation is not only getting the story down: it is also wordsmithing a direct and impactful point.

Here is an example of telling an experience that someone told you in story form:

---

**ANOTHER'S EXPERIENCE:** A teacher told me about an experience that caused him to do a great deal of soul-searching.

He was teaching a course on "Death and American Culture" at a community college. The course was one day a week between 6:30 and 9:00 PM with a break at 7:45. The usual students for a course like this were those whose schedule it fit. Their interest in death and American culture was far down the line compared to their interest in not being inconvenienced. The teacher was aware of this, and so students had to sign in. Attendance was always an issue.

The teacher told me he noticed that a young woman was arriving on time, but after the break she was not present. He had seen this behavior before and was prepared to confront it at the midcourse meeting he had with each student. He told me he had been around this block before. This was not his first rodeo.

When the student entered his office, she had a doll in one hand and a folder filled with papers in the other hand. Before he could confront her on her attendance, she said, "I suppose you're wondering about the doll. I am a twin, and this doll was between me and my sister in the back seat of our car when we were in an accident. That was twenty years ago. My sister died, and I have been in therapy ever since. I saw your course advertised and I thought, 'Why not?' I've tried everything else. But it is a little too much for me to sit through the whole thing. So I leave at the break, go to the library, and read the stuff on the bibliography you passed out. Here are my notes."

She handed him the folder.

"Jack," he said to me, "I felt this big."

He held his thumb and his forefinger very closely together.

**PASSAGE:** "Be compassionate as your heavenly Father is compassionate" is a daunting imperative from Jesus (Luke 6:36). But he does not tell us how.

**POINT:** But the teacher's story makes a suggestion. Withhold judgment until you enter the world of the other. This is not an easy action, but let's talk about how to do it.

---

## Seventh Rule of Thumb

Pay attention to the experiences people tell you. The homilist is always on a homily hunt. Since most homilists are ministers, they are constantly interacting with people in serious situations and people are often telling them things that are powerful connections of faith and experience. Although there are confidentiality restrictions, many of these experiences can be used in homilies. People hand homilists their homilies—if homilists know how to listen.

## Eighth Rule of Thumb

Keep a notebook. Not everything you hear will be immediately useable. But if it strikes you, chances are it will be useable in the future. For example, last night my wife and I had dinner with a man who had recently undergone a serious illness. At one point, he said, "It was really quite something to look into the eyes of people who love you and see the terror of their helplessness." That is a powerful observation, and I felt my eyes must have often communicated that "terror of helplessness." If I were still a homilist and I kept a notebook, that observation would find its way into it. It smacks of future use.

Let me give you an example of telling an experience you read about in story form:

---

**READING AN EXPERIENCE:** Rachel Naomi Remen is a doctor on the West Coast who writes wonderful books that reflect the humanity of the medical world—like *Kitchen Table Wisdom* and *My Grandfather's Blessings*. In one of her books, she tells about a time she was asked to come into a clinic that was having staff problems—poor communication, interpersonal friction, etc. In preparation, she asked all the staff members to bring an object/icon of their work in the clinic.

All the staff sat in a circle around a table. She asked them to put their objects/icons on the table. Then she asked a man to come forth, pick up his icon and tell the group what it meant.

The man went to the table and picked up a small bridge, an erector set piece. He said, "I connect people who are hurting with people who will help them heal." Then he sat down.

Rachel asked what he did at the clinic.

"I answer the phones," he said.

**POINT:** We often focus on our tasks like answering the phones and not their deeper purposes like connecting the hurting with those who can help.

**PASSAGE:** "For, brothers and sisters, you have been called unto liberty; use . . . liberty by love to serve one another" (Galatians 5:13). Maybe we are serving one another more than we know, but we have to look at our lives in a different way.

### Ninth Rule of Thumb

All stories have to be introduced to satisfy the listeners' curiosity. But not all stories have to be introduced in the same way. Spiritual teaching stories can be introduced by mentioning the spiritual tradition they are part of or by confessing, as I did above, you do not know where the story came from. Stories of your own experience and another's experience can be introduced with pertinent information that sets up the story—not too much and not too little. Stories about experience taken from written material can be introduced by citing the written work and something about the author.

Introductions are important, but they are "slide-ins" to the more important story. The homilist's voice should reflect that.

### Tenth Rule of Thumb

Written stories of personal experiences provide good material, but any story taken from written material almost always has to be edited for oral delivery. Although it is good to read novels and short stories, the better material for homilies comes from authors who are writing about their own or others' experience. Their writing says in effect: here is what it is like to be sick, to be a mother, to lose your job, to suffer a divorce, to be grateful, to reconcile with a person you have held a grudge against, to be an immigrant, to meet someone who changes your life, to finally understand what is wrong, etc. However, these written experiences will most likely be too long and complex for the oral harness of homilies. They will have to be strategically edited to fit into the overall agenda of the homily.

## Conclusion

I will not rehearse at any length the benefits and limits of storytelling in homilies. But since the topic of this reflection is stories, points, and passages, I will tell one story about how storytelling, despite the best intention of the homilist, can miscommunicate.

I preached on weekends for eight years at an upper-middle-class parish. When I was moving to another parish, they had a "coffee and . . . " for me after the last Mass. A handsome, stylish couple, perhaps in their late thirties, came up to say good-bye. The man opened with this comment. "Well, we came to like you."

It is a line that is difficult to ignore. I couldn't let it go by.

"I take it there was a time when you didn't like me."

"You always spoke down to us."

That was serious and I had to pursue it.

"That was certainly not my intention. Tell me about it."

The woman chimed in. "You always told stories. Stories are for children. The people in this parish are highly educated and are looking for a higher level of discourse."

"Thanks for the feedback," I managed to muster.

Ah, the joy of using stories in preaching!

■ CHAPTER 9

# Plotting a Path for People to Follow

Richard L. Eslinger

As preachers, we are concerned with shaping liturgical homilies that listeners at the Eucharistic Feast may hear in their hearts and minds and become more fully transformed into the faithful people of God. Another way of putting this goal is to proclaim with the Apostle Paul that "faith comes from what is heard, and what is heard comes through the word of Christ" (Romans 10:17). Such a witness places a serious burden on our preaching beginning with the qualification that our words need to be heard by the assembly. Before we get to our discussion of how the homily is shaped, I'd like to mention a pitfall. Pope Benedict XVI cautioned in *Verbum Domini* that generic and abstract homilies that obscure the directness of God's Word should be avoided, as well as useless digressions that risk drawing greater attention to the preacher than to the heart of the Gospel message.[1]

The apostolic exhortation *Verbum Domini* deals constructively and at length with the ways and means of developing liturgical homilies that do faithfully proclaim the Word of God and the joy of the Gospel. Attention there is directed to the liturgical context of the proclamation of the Word of God and its essential grounding in the Scriptures of the Old and New Testaments. The proclamation also details specific teaching regarding the church's preaching and the suffering, the poor, and the entirety of creation.[2] On the other hand, Benedict XVI also speaks to various pitfalls in preaching a liturgical homily that hinders the hearing of the Word of God. Generic and abstract homilies lack an essential incarnational identity; they are rather docetic, in that the Word does not become enfleshed.

Preaching that results in useless digression by focusing more attention on the preacher than on the Gospel represents a failure of such preachers to

1. Pope Benedict XVI, *Verbum Domini: Postsynodal Apostolic Exhortation on the Word of God in the Life and Mission of the Church* (September 30, 2010), 59.

2. See Benedict XVI, *Verbum Domini*, 106, "The Proclamation of the Word of God and the Suffering"; 107, "The Proclamation of the Word of God and the Poor"; 108, "The Proclamation of the Word of God and the Protection of Creation."

grasp the crucial role of the Scriptures in Christian proclamation. Moreover, such self-centered preaching constitutes a failure to comprehend how thoroughly the homily is to speak to and be in dialogue with the world of the baptized. Instead, as Robert P. Waznak states the situation, such preachers "blithely indulge in narcissistic preaching Sunday after Sunday since they claim it is what the people want."[3] To be sure, some preachers have modeled their homiletical style on that of a succession of television celebrities whose personas are crafted to appeal to a slice of contemporary viewers. However, the preacher who sees his or her vocation as proclaiming the Word of God in Scripture in such ways that it speaks to the lived experience of the assembly and leads these listeners toward a full and joyous participation in the Eucharist will avoid such narcissism. If the people seem to want such preacher-centered offerings, perhaps the core issue is that they have not been offered the richer fare of Scripture, tradition, and a prophetic engagement with the culture in the homilies they have experienced.

## The Homily Shaped by Narrative Scriptures

Given any number of pitfalls on the way to a hearing of the homily, our task now is to return to the scriptural foundation of our preaching. How does the text itself serve to shape the liturgical homily such that it is heard, and that faith will be strengthened by that hearing? The seminal statement on Catholic preaching in the United States, *Fulfilled in Your Hearing,* teaches that the liturgical homily "is not so much *on* the Scriptures as *from* and *through* them."[4] Preaching that is chiefly *on* a Scripture implies some distance between the interpreter and the text as well as a notion of control over what is distilled out of the text. A much more immediate relationship to the biblical Word is proposed as we preach "*from* and *through*." The first criterion in Catholic homiletics is that the liturgical homily is grounded in Scripture. "Good homiletic preaching begins and ends with an engagement with the word of God."[5] Two further criteria are essential companions to this insistence on preaching "*from* and *through*" the Scriptures. On the one hand, the homily must speak to the "deepest levels of the human heart and address

3. Robert P. Waznak, *An Introduction to the Homily* (Collegeville, MN: The Liturgical Press, 1998), ix. Also see further analysis of such preacher-centered homilies in chapter 2, "The Homilist as Herald, Teacher, Interpreter, and Witness."

4. Bishop's Committee on Priestly Life and Ministry, National Conference of Catholic Bishops, *Fulfilled in Your Hearing: The Homily in the Sunday Assembly* (Washington, DC: USCCB, 1982), 20.

5. United States Conference of Catholic Bishops, *Preaching the Mystery of Faith: The Sunday Homily* (Washington, DC: USCCB, 2013), 44.

the real questions of human existence."[6] On the other hand, a further criterion for effective preaching is that it will lead the faithful to "full, conscious, and active participation"[7] in the Eucharistic celebration that follows. Given that liturgical homilies embody all three of these core criteria, it is salutary to explore more deeply what preaching *"from* and *through"* the Scriptures implies as regards homiletic method (as we speak, as well, to the human condition of the listeners and invite them to the fullness of their Eucharistic celebration). An initial proposal is that such "from and through" preaching will take seriously the genre and surface level movement and structure of the text. This approach, then, offers a means to fulfill the mandates of *Preaching the Mystery of Faith* by way of allowing the Scripture to shape the homily.

Biblical narratives offer the most evident and accessible expression of the three traits of the liturgical homily—that they are preached "from and through" Scripture, that they speak to the heart and mind of the assembly and relate to their lived experience, and that the hearers are led to a full and faithful participation in the Eucharistic Feast. Here, in the narratives of the Old and New Testaments, a sequence of scenes or moves are encountered inviting the preacher and the assembly to follow along a path (a plot) that wants to be "fulfilled in our hearing."[8] It is in the parables of Jesus that this narrative plotting with its scenes may be most evident, and we therefore begin our project of shaping the homily by selecting the parable of the Good Shepherd (the Gospel for the Twenty-Fourth Sunday in Ordinary Time, Year C). We may identify three scenes that comprise the plot of the parable. Importantly, the scenes are expressed as moves in contemporary speech and not in past tense language:

- Sheep get lost. It is not at all unusual. At times we seem in the business of losing sheep.
- But our Good Shepherd leaves the ninety-nine and goes for the one, searching without pause or rest.
- Finding the lost one, the Shepherd calls friends and neighbors to rejoice. A feast is ordered and the celebration begins. The lost is now found.

6. Ibid., 15.

7. Second Vatican Council, *Constitution on the Sacred Liturgy* (*Sancrosanctum concilium*), December 4, 1963, II.14.

8. See Guerric DeBona, *Fulfilled in Our Hearing: History and Method of Christian Preaching* (New York: Paulist Press, 2005).

Notice, here, that the three moves are derived from the shape of the parable. What is not intended is a search for three points as we interpret a scriptural text. Points are propositional statements presumably based on a text, while these moves are derived "*in* and *through*" the movement and intention of the pericope. (We will remain with three moves in our homiletical explorations since each move takes about three to three-and-one-half minutes to form and the brevity of the liturgical homily usually constrains the preacher to three moves.)

Having identified the component scenes of the parable, the preacher's task now is to explore the ways in which each scene may by analogy relate to the lived experience of the assembly. Moreover, an alert homilist will be on the lookout for opportunities to prepare the faithful for their journey towards the Holy Eucharist. With regard to the former task, that of spotting the analogies to the lived experience of the congregation, several examples come readily to mind.

## "Sheep Get Lost."

If the context is that of a parish in or near a rust belt city in the Midwest, the familiarity with jobs being lost and even entire industries dying out or moving elsewhere is a constant reminder of what has been lost. Other contexts may evoke images of almost an entire generation of young adult "nones" being lost to Christian faith and practice. In other contexts, the epidemic of opioid addition is resulting in horrendous losses to those suffering the addiction and their families and communities. More immediately, in particular parish contexts, the preacher may make bold to recall a time when some other persons used to be present at Mass, but now are no longer present. As David Buttrick notes, we may assemble a modest series of examples within the same move, such as here with "sheep get lost," provided that they are shaped "in a similar, stylized manner."[9] In such example chains, a refrain may be added as a tag line to each example, such as the obvious "sheep get lost." (If such a recurring refrain is employed following each example, the last example's refrain should disrupt the somewhat hypnotic repetition of the prior tag lines. Therefore, the final refrain could be "More lost sheep!" or words to that effect.)

9. David Buttrick, *Homiletic: Moves and Structures* (Philadelphia: Fortress Press, 1987), 132.

## "The Good Shepherd Seeks Out the Lost."

The second move's meaning focuses on the Shepherd who does not abandon the search for this one that is lost. Ignoring the daunting odds of ninety-nine to one, the Shepherd goes for the lost sheep. Selecting an illustration as the means to establish contemporary analogy with the move becomes a happy option since we have deployed an example system in the first move. (It is best to vary the type of analogy used as the moves progress in a homiletical plot. Therefore, it is inadvisable to use all example systems or, alternatively, to provide a story illustration in every move.) In any case, the illustration will need to avoid a purely personal, saccharine pathos. Also, the illustration will not be extended into a huge story that threatens the assembly's focus on the narrative of the parable. One brief illustration, then, may be shaped as follows:

A nurse decided that it was time for a new vocation. Now she needed to shift her care giving towards abused women and those attempting to escape from human trafficking situations. She founded a safe house, raised funds for its operation, and took on the responsibilities as its director. She relates that her "sheep" often tend to get lost again, returning to their old places of abuse. But she never tires of seeking the ones that are lost and leading them into new life. Her safe house is named The Shepherd's Fold.

The example intentionally selects a woman who is shepherd-like in her agency and care, one who does not tire of seeking the lost. (This story also draws largely from the contemporary ministry of this woman of faith.) The brief story also avoids the either-or distortions of individualism or social-institutionalism. Both models for interpreting evil and grace in Christ are operative in the churches. The model of individualism locates sin and evil within the individual heart of the listeners, urging each to repent and turn to God. The social-institutional model of interpretation, on the other hand, insists that "the most decisive bearers of human reality are not individuals but groups, classes, races, nations, corporations, bureaucracies."[10] Neither the individualism model nor the social-institutional come close to embodying the fullness of the biblical witness to both sin and evil on one hand or the decisive work of God in Jesus Christ that overcomes evil and makes all things new on the other.

10. Edward Farley, *Practicing Gospel: Unconventional Thoughts on the Church's Ministry* (Louisville: Westminster John Knox Press, 2003), 59.

## "The Lost Is Found; a Feast Abounds."

Here, the opportunity is presented to develop an analogy between the shepherd's call to friends and neighbors to "rejoice with me" (Luke 15:6b) and the forthcoming opportunity to join in a joyous celebration of the Eucharistic celebration. Our imaging such a vibrant analogy, though, will be guided by several principles stemming from the liturgical words and actions of the Eucharist as well as the Church's teachings on the sacrament. The principle that is at the core of this work of analogy is that "the Lord's Paschal Mystery becomes the basis of all preaching."[11] A related principle at work in the shaping of analogy within this third "scene" of the parable is that we will weigh the imagery well toward the communal and covenantal pole rather than focusing on individual Eucharistic piety. (Remember, the shepherd's family and neighbors were all invited to the feast.) Then, too, our analogy will provide a journey the listeners are able to follow from the feast within the parable to the celebration of the Eucharist. Here, we are alert to the "double feast"[12] of the Sunday Mass. Our proclamation of the Word in the homily is organically connected to the proclamation of the Word at the Eucharist.

Given these principles, a number of lived "feast" experiences may need to be set aside. Once more, the theological as well as imaginative task of the preacher is called into play. For example, having grown up in Baltimore, Maryland, one joyous, communal meal of family and friends for me was that of the "crab feast." However, the analogy fails dismally! Yes, there is some parallel in the parable's reference to the rejoicing (obviously involving a feast) announced by the shepherd and to the "crab feast" held by family and friends near the Chesapeake Bay. On the other hand, as David Buttrick insists, the analogy or illustration must be appropriate to the content of the move.[13] Beyond the fact that the analogy does involve a feast in both cases, the "crab feast" proposal is entirely devoid of any Eucharistic content whatsoever or even an allusion to the Paschal Mystery. The most appropriate analogy, then, is one drawn from the lived experience of the assembly, perhaps a notable recent Mass at which the Gospel was read and proclaimed and the Eucharist was celebrated with joyous passion. Since the Ordinary Time Lukan Gospel

11. USCCB, *Preaching the Mystery of Faith*, 9.

12. See Michael Monshau, ed., *Preaching at the Double Feast: Homiletics for Eucharistic Worship* (Collegeville, MN: Liturgical Press, 2006).

13. Buttrick, *Homiletic*, 134. David Butrrick develops his move theory in *Homiletic*, 23–79. Also see Michael Monshau, "A Catholic Conversation about Preaching," 28–35, and Mary Alice Mulligan, "Teaching Disciples to Preach in the Service of Word and Table," 61–91, in Michael Monshau, *Preaching at the Double Feast*. Also see my work *The Web of Preaching: New Options in Homiletic Method* (Nashville: Abingdon Press, 2002), 151–200.

reading of the parable of the Good Shepherd occurs in late August or early September, the example of a powerful and joyous Pentecost Sunday Mass may well be considered. Other liturgical occasions prior to the Twenty-Fourth Sunday in Ordinary Time could include the Feast of the Transfiguration or one of the recent feasts within the sanctoral calendar. Our task as preachers, though, is clear—illustrations and examples will need to draw deeply on analogy and will be appropriate to the content of the move.

The example of the Good Shepherd pericope was chosen with reference to its modest sequence of scenes that would translate easily into the homily's plotted moves. However, we repeatedly encounter much longer narrative readings as we preach through the liturgical year. These lengthy stories present a challenge with regard to the necessary brevity of the liturgical homily. Pope Francis notes that "if the homily goes on too long, it will affect two characteristic elements of the liturgical celebration: its balance and its rhythm."[14] When opening up longer readings, there are two homiletical strategies available that may treat an extensive narrative text with integrity while maintaining the brevity appropriate to the homily at Mass. The two strategies include introductory *reach* and plotted *conflation*. The former is simple to define. Given a long narrative pericope, the preacher may compress several initial scenes into the introduction and reach well into the narrative for the homily's first move. So, for example, when preaching on the parable of the prodigal son (Luke 15:11–32) instead of the parable of the Good Shepherd on the Twenty-Fourth Sunday in Ordinary Time, Year C, the material up through the second son's fall in the far country could be traced in the homily's introduction. The three moves that become the plot of the homily, then, could include:

1. A focus on the prodigal son's coming to his senses and deciding to return home.
2. The son's attempt to exert some control over his fate and the response of his father ("Father, I have sinned against heaven and against you, . . . treat me as you would treat one of your hired workers.").
3. The father's actions that wipe away any attempts at control by his son. The father runs to him, embraces him, restores him within the home, and commands a feast in celebration.

---

14. See Pope Francis, *Evangelii gaudium: Apostolic Exhortation on the Proclamation of the Gospel in Today's World* (November 24, 2013), II, 138. Also see Gregory Heille, *The Preaching of Pope Francis: Missionary Discipleship and the Ministry of the Word* (Collegeville, MN: Liturgical Press, 2015).

Notice that the whole of the part A of the parable is embraced within the homily. If the part B issues with the older son are the subject of the homily (vv. 25–32), an even more extensive reach will be called for in the introduction.

The strategy of conflation comes into play when the preacher encounters a longer narrative text of Scripture. The Gospel reading for the Year A catechetical Third Sunday in Lent is John 9:1–41 or an abridged version. There are several stages of increasing faith revealed as the man born blind is opposed by the religious authorities. First, when asked as to Jesus whereabouts by his neighbors, the man replies, "I don't know" (v. 12). After growing opposition from the Pharisees, who describe Jesus as a sinner, the man blurts out, "He is a prophet" (v. 17). Then, as the attacks by the religious authorities increase, involving even an interrogation of the man's parents, he finally proclaims that Jesus is from God (vv. 24–34). He is then expelled from the synagogue. A final move deals with Jesus coming to the outcast, engaging in a dialogue, and revealing his identity as the Son of Man. Joining with all the other implied outcasts, the man born blind believes and worships the Lord. The homily on this Fourth Sunday in Lent can take the following form:

Introduction—a reach across the opening material of the reading through the man's first comment that he does not know where Jesus is.

Move 1—The growing opposition to the man by the Pharisees results in a sequence of confessions of faith, each building on the other (all after the man initially did not even know where Jesus was!). This first move contains the material leading to the man's second declaration in response to the anger-filled charge that Jesus is a sinner: "He is a prophet." The reflection on this new stage of faith may be related to the disciples' question to Jesus at the opening of the narrative when they asked, "Who sinned . . . ?" Jesus does not engage with the disciples regarding the flaws in their theology of suffering and affliction; he simply spits in the dirt, makes clay, and anoints the man's eyes. The man comes back from the pool called "Sent" with his blindness behind him. By word and action, Jesus is a prophet.

Move 2—The opposition by the Pharisees continues to grow, beginning with the poignant scene of their questioning the man's parents. Then, they return to attack the man born blind, shouting "Give God the praise!" (an action he will soon be about). But this time, the man does not passively accept the continued derision. He confesses to them, "I was blind and now I see." Since they continue to ask him about Jesus, he then asks, with all their inquiries, whether they perhaps want to become Jesus' disciples as well. He adds that Jesus is "from God," and is immediately expelled from the synagogue!

Move 3—Jesus seeks out the man now outcast from his old place of worship. He asks the man if he believes in the Son of Man. His reply is a request: "Who is he, sir, that I may believe in him?" (v. 36). Based in the sign Jesus performed to the man born blind, the Lord announces, "You have seen him, the one speaking with you is he" (v. 37).[15] Now the man born blind ironically conforms to the admonition of the Pharisees and gives glory to God. He worships this Son of Man, taking his place among all the others who have been cast out and who are now found and claimed. Healed and gathered together, they worship their Lord.

Now that the three moves are identified and the narrative reach of the introduction is established, the task turns to that of imaging each move, whether by one story illustration, one or more examples, or the deployment of a compelling image. Again, the principles related to analogy become prominent in homiletical preparation. In every move, an analogy will be clearly drawn between the conceptual material and the imagery. Then, as we have noted, David Buttrick calls for a parallel between the content of the material of the move and the shape of the illustration or example. So, for example, as the second move deals with the repeated attacks by the man born blind's opponents, a series of examples may be assembled that point to contemporary situations of similar accusation and even persecution. Since the move concludes with the man's confession that Jesus is "from God," we may well focus these examples on persons or communities of faith suffering abuse or persecution. Then, we have noted that two other principles are at work as we seek analogies within each move—the homily will be grounded in the Paschal Mystery and it will lead the faithful on towards the celebration of the sacraments. Since the location within the liturgical year is the catechetical Year A season of Lent, it may well serve best to allow the baptismal meanings of the Pool of Siloam ("Sent") to have prominence, especially if the parish is blessed with catechumens who are journeying toward the sacraments of Christian initiation at the Easter Vigil.

## Plotting Non-narrative Homilies

Other kinds of biblical literature also may be plotted so as to directly shape the order and movement of the homily. However, we find other texts of Scripture that do not offer such an immediately traceable plotting. In these instances, David Buttrick's mode of reflectivity offers another approach to

15. For an extensive analysis of the meaning of a "sign" in the fourth Gospel, see Raymond E. Brown, *The Gospel According to John* (New York: Doubleday, 1985), 525–32.

the shaping of the homily's plot. Remaining nearby the biblical text, we design the homily to relate to "the *pattern* of meaning in consciousness."[16] What is meant here is that attending to the Scripture involves our own reflection on it on behalf of the assembly *in present tense speech*. We will build a field of meaning evoked by the passage of Scripture that again is plotted according to a series of moves. We shift from the mode of immediacy to that of reflectivity frequently in our daily experience. A performance of bluegrass music by a family of musicians from Southwest Virginia is totally engrossing and we become completely immersed in the song. Later, we reflect on the odd tension in the music when the Gospel is being sung and played, yet in a rather solemn, minor key style. It is like a meal having a sweet-sour dissonance that can be so rewarding. Here, we first engage deeply in the immediacy of the performance while later we reflect deeply in a different way about what we have experienced.

We encounter a perfect opportunity for employing the reflective mode as we anticipate the epistle reading for the Third Sunday of Lent, Year B, 1 Corinthians 1:22–25.[17] A series of moves may be plotted that offer the assembly a homily shaped by St. Paul's epistolary convictions. The sequence of moves in this reflective homily may be shaped as follows:

1. The world looks at the cross and sees folly.
2. But the cross of Christ sees the folly and arrogance of the world.
3. Now, St. Paul proclaims, the cross is the wisdom of God to redeem the world!

Each of these reflective statements will now be fleshed out into a full move—opening and closing language that is not complex, but simple; some present tense analysis inviting the listeners more fully into the conceptual; and a vivid analogy that is appropriate to the text and the liturgical, parish, and worldly context. To be sure, the analogy the preacher draws for a parish, say, in Seattle's Washington University District will be from a different cultural and ideological context than that of a parish in Alliance, Nebraska. Yet, by virtue of the ways in which the media connect the parishioners in both settings with the world, some possible analogies may well be shared between the two parishes. Therefore, when preachers at the University

---

16. Buttrick, *Homiletic*, 367.

17. See Joni S. Sancken, *Stumbling over the Cross: Preaching the Cross and Resurrection Today* (Eugene, OR: Cascade Books, 2016) and Brad R. Braxton, *Preaching Paul* (Nashville: Abingdon Press, 2004).

District parish in Seattle and at the two churches in the Alliance parish engage in an imaginative investigation of the first move of this homily, quite similar examples drawn from media could serve well in both contexts. Parishioners in both contexts are aware of the sports and film celebrities who decorate themselves with huge gold crosses, or have them inked boldly somewhere visible to others. Yet for some their talk about themselves and others reveal character issues in opposition to the Gospel and the cross. In any case, possible analogies that take the form of illustrations or examples will need to be carefully assessed as to their appropriateness to the move at stake and to the assembly's context.

## Conclusion

What we propose is a way to shape our homilies in order to provide forms that evoke and strengthen faith. The Scriptures may shape the homily through the mode of immediacy in which the plot of the homily is aligned with the "scenes" in the biblical text (typically a narrative). On the other hand, many texts in Scripture do not offer up such a clearly traced plot for the hearers to follow. In such cases, which include many nonnarrative genres of Scripture, the mode of reflectivity is proposed as a means of remaining faithful to the text's movement and meaning while shaping a homiletical plot that forms in the assembly's consciousness. Moreover, just as our own experience can shift easily between a mode of immediacy and reflectivity (recall our bluegrass concert and our later musing on the experience), some of our homilies may be "modal hybrids." The homily may open with a move derived in immediacy from the biblical passage and then turn in a subsequent move to some reflection with the listeners as to our response to what has been heard. We will not want to inflict a Wimbledon tennis match kind of back and forth between modes throughout the homily, but a reflective move carefully placed within a plot otherwise shaped in immediacy can bring the assembly even more deeply into the proclamation of the Word. There is a more biblically grounded back and forth at work in our practice of preaching.

The homily in its most effective form enables the hearer to understand the meaning of the Scriptures in a new way and, in turn, helps the message of the Scriptures, proclaimed in the context of the liturgy, to illumine the experiences of the hearers.[18]

18. USCCB, *Preaching the Mystery of Faith*, 29.

We shape our homilies such that the Word of God in Scripture may be fulfilled in the hearing of the faithful as they are invited and led to the Paschal Meal.

CHAPTER 10

# "Murder Your Darlings": How to Edit for Effective Preaching

Deborah Wilhelm

## First: The Eight Little Pigs

We were at the county fair with our children, doing all the kid stuff—riding the Ferris wheel, eating cotton candy, petting the baby rabbits—when suddenly a loudspeaker sliced through the carnival sounds and the August afternoon heat: "Thirty minutes until the pig races, everyone, only thirty minutes until the pig races!" Pig races did not sound particularly attractive to my husband and me, but they sounded very delightful indeed to our youngsters, Jeremy and Angela (who reminded us, inconveniently, that we had promised to spend the day doing "all the kid stuff"), so we wandered over to a dirt track with a dozen other families, leaned on the fence, and waited for the big event.

Pig races, it turns out, require quite a buildup. After a spirited welcome, the emcee explained the race rules at length and introduced each of the eight racing pigs by name: "This is Harriet! Harriet is two years old! She was born in Iowa!" while Harriet, elegant in her racing silks, looked at us with a wise and imperturbable gaze. Apparently, pigs don't naturally sprint around dirt tracks, so race officials placed a big box of Oreos at the finish line as an incentive, and after another twenty minutes of prerace fanfare, Harriet and her competitors were herded into the starting box. A bell rang; the box opened, and the pigs dashed for the cookies. The whole thing was over in ten seconds, fifteen counting the cookie-gobbling time, and my husband and I traded exasperated told-you-so looks over the tops of our kids' heads. Talk about bitter disappointment, about buildup for nothing. The only pleasure we could salvage was to spend the rest of the afternoon making fun of how stupid pig races were, how we'd been bamboozled, how gullible we were to fall for such an obvious gimmick. We groused our way through the rest of the day and all the drive home that evening.

Later that night, tucking four-year-old Angela into bed, I asked her which part of the fair had been her favorite. Was it riding the Ferris wheel? No. Eating cotton candy? No. Petting the baby rabbits? Angela shook her head, silent, and looked down. Finally, I cupped her face in my hands and looked into those big four-year-old eyes: "Sweetie, what was it?" At last her tiny voice said, "The pig races." Then she began to cry.

That was more than twenty-five years ago, and I still feel like the world's worst mom. Using only words, our entire family had rolled right over our smallest member. Our verbiage filled the afternoon, filled the fairgrounds, filled the car, and never considered the precious small person with us, the one who lacked the sophistication and power to break into the conversation, the one who depended on us for affirmation and who had been made to feel unworthy. Our words had taken precedence over an actual human being, a cherished child made in the image and likeness of God. We had not intended to hurt her—we simply didn't consider her. No wonder she'd felt shamed; no wonder she'd resisted the urge to share her own response, her own joyful experience. No wonder she'd cried.

## A Call to Consider

Similarly, we preachers may find ourselves so captivated by our own experience or interpretive stance that we forget to enlarge our circle of consideration. Yet, the contributors to this book challenge preachers to shift their gaze outward. Karla Bellinger, for example, described the ways that preachers must reverence the word and the hearers; Fr. Mike Connors cautioned preachers to preach for encounter and transformation; Fr. Ron Rolheiser spoke about "words that enflesh the Word"; Suzanne Nawrocki argues that since only 7 percent of preaching communication comes from the words spoken, preachers must attend to the integrity of their nonverbal speech; and Bishop Sylvester Ryan reminds preachers not to underestimate their hearers. Each of these experts demands that the preacher attend to the listener who, like my four-year-old daughter, is typically not invited—or even allowed—to speak any words during a preaching encounter and whose human ideas, joys, and sorrows may never be sought or revealed.

One way to nurture this outward gaze on behalf of the listener is so obvious that many preachers look right past it: the neglected skill of editing. As someone who preaches regularly, who teaches preachers, who writes about and presents on preaching, I have observed that many preachers do not practice this basic task. And as someone who spent fifteen years teaching technical writing to engineering students at a large university, I strongly believe that editing skills are not only valuable but also highly accessible. Most preachers attending my workshops acknowledge that they should edit but do not. Why don't they? Part of the problem may be that the word *edit* itself seems attached to images of that high school English teacher who assigned papers with a minimum length requirement ("Please write an essay of at least 2,500 words comparing symbolism in the short stories of Kate Chopin and Edgar Allan Poe") and then returned those efforts weeks later, bleeding with red-pen notes in the margins and admonitions to learn the difference between the comma and the semicolon—or else. Hints of such academic-memory leftovers are visible in a list of common editing-avoidance reasons from a recent group of preachers in one of my workshops. Some of these answers to the "Why not?" question may sound familiar:

- I don't have the time.
- I haven't acquired the habit.
- I'm not a writer, thank you very much, I'm a preacher.
- I'm still creating my preaching right up until I give it.
- I've never heard any complaints.
- I like what I have.
- I know that it's bad, and I don't want to be confronted with the evidence.
- I can hide my lack of preparedness with my sincere delivery and a good opening joke.
- I worked hard on that sentence and I'm not changing it!
- I tuned out that part of sophomore English class.
- I don't really know how.

The items on this list, although understandable, share an interesting characteristic: They're all focused on "me," on "my" history, on how busy "I" am, and on what "I" want. Under scrutiny, however, this "me/my/I" catalog looks unappealing, even selfish. All of the energy that preachers devote to prayer, *lectio divina,* study, organization, writing, and practice is intended to move them out of the "me/my/I" orientation—to reorient themselves toward God, toward God's Word and God's world. Editing, too, comes from and manifests this basic shift from inward- to outward-gazing preparation and sharing.

## What Editing Really Is

For preaching purposes, *to edit is to attend to the written and spoken word at the level of language itself in service to God's Word,* particularly in terms of focus, connections, and cutting. Bishop Sylvester Ryan and I have written elsewhere about focus. By focus, we mean that preachers should understand that their preaching should have only one idea, that the idea should matter, and that preachers can learn how to recognize the one idea that matters. We have also written about connections, that is, how the bits of language that link sentences, paragraphs, and sections are vital to the listeners' understanding by enabling listeners to make the right kinds of connections.[1] The emphasis in this chapter, instead, is on the final item on that list: cutting—that is, ruthlessly deleting redundant, pompous, abstract, or distracting words. This struggle for conciseness is not new,[2] but Sir Arthur Quiller-Couch may have offered the most succinct solution a hundred years ago in his instruction to writers: "Murder your darlings."[3] These days, I have argued in writing seminars and preaching workshops alike that the key word in his advice is *your.* When, in the role of preacher, I concentrate on what I want to say, on my story, told in my witty or sophisticated or evocative language, grown out of my study and the amount of time that I spent looking up that etymologically or theologically or philosophically interesting word, on my understanding of what you, my listeners,[4] need to hear, using language that I have inflated so that I sound smart or look like I have the Scriptures figured out, then I'm thinking about myself and what I'm saying, *instead of about God and what God is saying.* The subsequent words are darlings—my darlings—when, as I've written before,[5] the only darlings that belong in the preaching are God's.

---

1. See Sylvester Ryan and Deborah Wilhelm, *Preaching Matters: A Praxis for Preachers* (Chicago: Paul Bechtold Library, 2015). Again, note that most preachers already know that they should be doing these things—they just don't. Therefore, we offer help for practicing these skills.

2. See, for example, Augustine's fourth-century *De Doctrina Christiana,* or Humbert's thirteenth-century *On the Formation of Preachers.*

3. Arthur Thomas Quiller-Couch, "XII: On Style," in *On the Art of Writing: Lectures Delivered in the University of Cambridge, 1913–1914* (New York: Putnam, 1916), 281.

4. Notice here that even the listeners have become *my* listeners!

5. See, for example, Deborah Wilhelm, "'Murder Your Darlings': Still Good Advice," *New Theology Review* 30 (September 2017): 59–62.

Cutting, especially in terms of figuring out what language should go and what should stay, sounds difficult. It isn't—it just takes practice, particularly if the preaching's content has already been narrowed to the single idea that matters. Even in the most ideal circumstances, however, the first draft of any preaching is likely to include many extras that arose during the prayer and preparation process but that aren't really contributing to that single core idea. The key to removing these extras is to be able to identify and delete them without feeling emotionally attached to them ("But I worked so hard on that one . . . "). The practice here is simple:

1. Take a detached look at the draft.
2. Cut everything that isn't contributing to the single idea that matters.

Like the word *cut*, the word *draft* may seem intimidating, implying as it does a written text that will have more than one version. Yet words that are obstacles for the listeners are most easily discovered and deleted when the text has been written far enough ahead to have a chance to cool off.[6] Alas, those who preach from a written text may often find under time pressure that they end up just using that first draft, extras and all, simply because it's "done." The first-draft-only-draft may seem fine at the time that it is written, but anyone who has ever pulled a previously preached script out of a drawer or up on the computer screen knows that rereading often reveals problems that went unnoticed in the original version. While a preacher is preparing, the ideas and sentences are still fresh and easily accessed in his or her thoughts, so the mind easily fills in the missing pieces and glosses over the distracting ones. Months (or weeks or even days) later, however, the memory fades and the response is much more likely to be something along the lines of, "What was I thinking when I wrote that?"

Preachers who use notes or an outline may not see the need to edit multiple drafts or even write a fully developed single draft. Others may think that editing wastes their time because they do not use a text at all.[7] I have never met a preacher who did not feel overwhelmed in terms of the demands on his or her time. Nevertheless, writing out the preaching is a good discipline, not least because it enables the kind of interrogation and polish that come

---

6. The cooling-off period varies by preacher, but at least one overnight is key. For those who preach every day, a lengthy cooling-off period probably is not realistic, but in my own preaching life, even during times that I have preached daily, I work to have a solid draft the day before, which I can edit the next day.

7. Just for the record, I am a notes-free preacher myself. However, nine times out of ten, I have prepared a text, neither to read nor to memorize, but to encourage my own deep understanding of the message and to allow appropriate editing.

from proper editing. Examining a complete text reveals immediately and clearly that four important ideas, none of them related, are competing for space; or that the main idea has been presented only in abstraction, without the benefit of specific detail for support, interest, or relevance; or that the details are dumped together without connecting language; or that the preacher is saying for twenty minutes what could be said better in ten. Moreover, a text can be repaired, polished, or otherwise modified and will reveal improvements just as immediately and clearly. Yet while seeing a text in its raw disorganization or unskillfulness is painful, that detached vision is what creates the space for effective revision (literally, "re-seeing"). Writing out the preaching thus honors the preparation process and the people who will hear the polished version, by whatever delivery method.

## Content-Level Cutting

Now, to cut: The energy devoted to tasks like prayer, *lectio divina*, study, and planning will manifest itself best when the energy devoted to the words themselves (that is, editing) receives a similar investment. The process may not be intuitive, but I offer here two main cutting skills to practice, plus some suggestions for getting started. The first of these involves looking at the big picture of the preaching and cutting out extraneous content. Consider the following partial list of delete-worthy content:

1. *Throat-clearing language.* "Throat-clearing" means platitudes, truisms, or empty constructions that may have helped start the writing process but that do not actually contribute meaningful material to the message itself. Examples include statements like "There are many important issues facing us in the world today" or "Today's society is composed of different groups of people, each group with its own unique sets of goals and ideas." Listeners already know these things, and to open with this kind of language is a clear signal to them that listening will be neither required nor rewarded.

2. *Material that rehashes the Scripture reading.* I hesitate to include this item because some preachers may argue that it falls under the category of truism just mentioned! Nevertheless, in my preaching classes and workshops and in my own experience as a listener, needlessly repeating the Scripture is a chronic problem. Moreover, not once have I heard a preacher tell the scriptural story better than, well, better than Scripture does.

3. *Jokes.* Perhaps a perfect joke is out there that perfectly leads into the Word of God in the lives of this assembly. If so, tell it (perfectly). But avoid any joke designed to win over the hearers and predispose them to like the preacher or the preaching, a category which includes nearly every joke that I have ever heard from a preacher.

4. *Words that tell a preaching-preparation story.* Cringe-worthy examples include, "I have to confess that I did not have a lot of time to prepare today's homily," and "I looked through the *New Interpreter's Bible* and the *Anchor Bible* because I was so enthused about nuance of this Greek grammatical construction," and "So I woke up from this strange dream about a rotten orange . . . " Enough said.

5. *Ideas that are not the main idea.* Listeners are listening, not reading, so honor them by offering only one idea and focusing on developing that idea. Additional ideas do not simply compete—they actively interfere by displacing the mental space available to the one key point. No preacher can say everything that there is to be said about any particular bit of God's Word, but every preacher can look deeply and carefully into one idea, considering it a gift of the Holy Spirit, and share that deep look with others. And the other ideas? They will still be around for next time.

6. *Ideas that do not matter.* How to tell whether or not an idea matters? Preachers can ask themselves the question that writers ask themselves: *So what?* This question reveals and resolves myriad problems. If the listeners have been following the preacher's explanation, for example, of how Matthew's Gospel presents Jesus as the new Moses, they also need to know what this comparison means and why it's important —that is, why it matters or should matter to them. *So what?* How does this idea open a more powerful experience of God, a deeper communion with God, a fuller advancement of God's reign?

7. *Abstract language.* Words like "love" and "pride" come immediately to mind. These concepts invite, even demand, illustration. For example, picture "faith." Picture "devotion." Now picture a sixty-years-married couple reaffirming their marriage vows at Saturday's Vigil Mass. Which image is easiest to call forth? In fact, much language can be made less abstract, even when it is not referring to a large-scale idea (imagine "participating in all the activities that a county fair has to offer" versus "riding the Ferris wheel, eating cotton candy, petting

the baby rabbits"). Concrete language is more powerful and easier to remember, which helps the main idea that matters to shine through.

8. *Clichés.* Consider a few practice clichés by filling in the blank: Pretty as a _____. Stiff as a_____. Eating like a_____. Hotter than _____. A phrase is cliché if the blanks are easy to fill in, and in preaching, these words are wasting space that will be much better spent on effective specific development.
9. *Long quotations.* Truth to tell, most quotations, long or short, function better on the written page than they do spoken aloud. The listeners have the Scriptures and the preacher, and in most cases, that should be the maximum number of degrees of separation. As is true with clichés, the limited time available can almost always be better spent.
10. *Material that reasonable people will not understand or be able to remember.* The listeners do not have the preacher's theological training. They did not spend hours in *lectio* and study. They probably do not have their Bibles in their laps. They are not taking notes (sorry). They may be cranky because they've observed that there's going to be a Baptism, a second collection, a speaker after Mass, or a missionary asking for support in the vestibule. Their children are crushing Cheese Nips in the songbooks. They're wondering whether the car alarm braying outside is theirs. And yet they are longing to hear God's Word and to be transformed by its power. The preaching, then, must be both accessible and memorable.
11. *Material that fails to grant reasonable people their reasonableness.* Sometimes preachers underestimate the listeners, assuming that theycan't or don't want to understand difficult concepts. Other times, preachers may oversimplify complex ideas so much that listeners no longer find those ideas relevant or worth additional reflection. And at still other times, preachers may avoid complex or contentious issues because to speak of them properly requires too much energy and time, both of which are in such short supply. Preachers need to assume that hearers both need and want to be challenged, avoiding language that sounds condescending, simplistic, or childish.
12. *False endings.* The preaching is certainly allowed to contain words that signal an ending, but only at the end.

13. *Any material that deprives the listeners of something good to talk about in the car on the way home.* I am a preacher, but I am also a listener. My husband, a Roman Catholic deacon, also preaches sometimes and listens from the pews at others. We long to hear good preaching and to forget that we are preachers so that we can truly be preached to. After Mass, we always talk about the homily, and our opening question is usually, "What did you hear?" Our conversations move outward from there as we think and talk about how the preaching that we heard might—or might not—come to life in our own experience. Where does God's Word proclaimed and interpreted resonate for us at work, in our family, out in the community, to the universe? We are not unique—most of the families we know have, or long for, similar conversations. Effective preaching is meant to go out from the liturgy in just this way.

These tips probably contain few surprises—and yet they emphasize the power of editing. The first draft of any preaching (mine included) may be full of extras like the items on the list above, plus other excess verbiage, and I hesitate to call such material "useless" because it helps inspire the thinking and writing processes that lead to effective preaching. The material turns into trouble when it is still present after the initial draft, either because I can't bring myself to murder my darlings—or because the first draft is the only draft. The novelist Stephen King offers some expert advice for fiction writers that is relevant for preachers as well when he quotes one of his early editors, who said, "When you write a story, you're telling yourself the story. When you rewrite, your main job is taking out all the things that are *not* the story."[8] We preachers can benefit from a similar approach to our own words.

Deleting an interesting idea or much-labored over sentence (paragraph, section) may sting a bit at first. For those who cannot bear to send their words into electronic oblivion, I suggest creating a computer file called "Awesome Stuff That I Deleted from My Preaching" and paste all cut material there. While I have never used any of my own deleted gems, I am comforted knowing that they are available if needed.

## Cutting the Word Count

The second, equally key, component of successful cutting is simply decreasing the overall word count. Because generating written words is so much easier today than it has been at any time in human history, and because most

8. Stephen King, *On Writing: A Memoir of the Craft* (New York: Pocket, 2001), 57.

preachers learned to write by being required to come up with at least a certain number of words, most preachers' writing experience lends itself to a type of wordiness that does not add meaning. Thus, listeners are subjected to extra words that not only do not contribute to understanding, but (as noted above) actively obscure it. Some of these extras come in the form of multiword substitutes for single words, like these:

*in the event that* . . . versus . . . *if*
*at the current time* . . . versus . . . *now*
*in spite of the fact that* . . . versus . . . *although*
*it is often the case that* . . . versus . . . *often*
*there is a possibility that* . . . versus . . . *possibly*

Sometimes, simple action words grow extra length, like these:

*was desirous of* . . . versus . . . *desired*
*is envious of* . . . versus . . . *envied*
*moved to object* . . . versus . . . *objected*
*performed a waving action* . . . versus . . . *waved*
*undertake an analysis of* . . . versus . . . *analyze*

And other times, redundant language fattens the phrases, like these:

*fast in speed* . . . versus . . . *fast*
*small in size* . . . versus . . . *small*
*red in color* . . . versus . . . *red*
*gathered together* . . . versus . . . *gathered*
*rise up* . . . versus . . . *rise*
*the reason is because* . . . versus . . . *because*

And at still other times, words delaying the start of a sentence add unnecessary length, like these:

*There were a number of people waiting* . . . versus . . .
*A number of people were waiting*
(or even better, *Seven people were waiting*)
*It is my belief that* . . . versus . . . *I believe*

Consider the results of word-count cutting at the sentence level, as in the examples below:

A large multitude of people had assembled themselves in order to hear the words of the prophet Jeremiah. (18 words)

*A multitude assembled to hear Jeremiah prophesy. (7 words)*

One of the members of the crowd proceeded to ask Jesus a question. (13 words)

*One crowd member asked Jesus a question. (7 words)*

It was decided by the disciples to undertake a journey to the city of Jerusalem, which they did. (18 words)

*The disciples journeyed to Jerusalem. (5 words)*

Even Mark, which is the shortest among the four Gospels, has a significant number of parables that have an agriculturally related theme. (22 words)

*Even the shortest Gospel, Mark, has six agriculturally themed parables. (10 words)*

It has been determined by biblical scholars that a number of interpretations of the word *rebiristos* are possible and that of these multiple interpretations, two are considered the most likely. (30 words)

*Biblical scholars offer two main interpretations of the word* rebiristos. *(10 words)*[9]

Notice that none of these editing examples is focused on learning the difference between a comma and a semicolon. Instead, we are considering the listeners, concentrating on the unglamorous work of subtraction, making sure that the words we've chosen are the best words.[10] Some of the over-loaded words and phrases above might seem like bit players. After all, what's the big deal about cutting a hundred words out of a ten-minute homily? But stack all that cut material together, and throw in a few other offenders, and the result is a pile of darlings just waiting to be murdered—er, edited.

So What?

Perhaps most importantly, the habit of editing helps develop the habits of mind that lead to effective speaking. In my own preaching life, to edit is to consider the beloved four-year-old child at the pig races instead of my own oh-so-sophisticated self. We do not cut for the sake of making the preaching as brief as possible, nor for meeting an arbitrary time standard, but rather for the sake of cutting away the excess so that our words point clearly and directly to the holy and living God. To edit is to acknowledge that our preaching words are effective only to the extent that they accomplish this

9. Would you like to know what scholars are saying about *rebiristos*? If only it were a real word.

10. Stephen King offers help with this equation: "Second draft = First draft – 10%." See King, *On Writing*, 222.

task. To edit is to step back from the "me/my/I" approach to speech, to esteem the listeners and invite them to recognize and experience the transformative power of the God who speaks all creation into life. To edit is to undertake the humbling work of paring back, of removing the clutter to see the work of God, the breath of the Spirit, and the face of Christ wherever they are, which is everywhere.

The most effective words for preachers are those that are carefully chosen to spark the hearers' hearts. Jesus tells his listeners, "I have come to set the earth on fire, and how I wish it were already blazing" (Luke 12:49, NABRE). As I speak, write, teach, and preach, I picture him now, right here among us, out there in the world, and across the cosmos, and waiting to come and light that fire in us. I picture him still wanting to set the world aflame with the word, still longing to see *his* word moving across the earth, alight and alive, with real hands and feet—and with real effect. That is our work, and Christ is waiting for us to take it up seriously. At the end of Luke's Gospel, the disciples who had encountered Christ on the road to Emmaus pose a powerful question: "Were not our hearts burning within us while he spoke to us on the way and opened the scriptures to us?" (24:32). Their words speak a worthy preaching goal: That we preachers would hear the call of the Holy Spirit and that our hearts would burn with God's Word, and that when we invite listeners into a similar encounter with the risen Christ, their hearts would burn, too.

CHAPTER 11

# Focus and Function: Kindling the Fire

Edward J. Griswold

Each year I say to our new homiletics students: "I got this job, teaching homiletics, not because I am the best preacher in town, but because I did some homework." I would like to share some of that homework with you. I want to (re)visit the why and how of developing stronger focus and function skills for more effective preaching. To approach this topic, I turn to the work of Thomas Long. He is truly the father of the focus and function phenomenon.

In his wonderful book *The Witness of Preaching,* Long defines and promotes the critical importance of developing focus and function statements in the early stages of homily preparation. Personally I am so convinced of their importance that they are among my greatest concerns in teaching and evaluating student homilies. It is what we spend much of our time on in our preaching practicum sessions. I am sure I drive students crazy insisting that they be able to articulate and critique each other's preaching in light of focus and function statements.

Here are two brief stories that reinforce my obsession with the discipline of focus and function.

The first story took place when I was teaching for about three years. Even then, I was working hard to get students to understand and to appreciate the value of crisp, clear focus and function statements in preparing their homilies. That summer I went down to MACC, the Mexican American Catholic College in San Antonio, to study Spanish. Almost immediately after we began the course, we were celebrating Eucharist in Spanish but preaching in English. Thank God!

After Eucharist each day we would gather for lunch. One day as I sat down at one of the refectory tables, a seminarian from Assumption Seminary said, "Thank you, Father, for your homily. Your focus and function were so clear." Well, I almost fell off my chair. It was the first time outside a homiletics classroom that I had heard anyone speak of my two good friends, focus and function. I experienced his words as a gift from God, a small reinforcement to keep up my classroom efforts. It is always a source of encouragement when you realize that students actually do remember some of what they hear in the classroom. I remember thinking, "I hope someday the seminarians and permanent deacons back at St. Mary's in Baltimore will be able to make the same kind of homiletic assessment."

A second experience that confirmed my obsession with focus and function statements took place rather recently. At the end of a semester, our registrar called me. She was reviewing the student class evaluations and could not quite figure out what one student had said in evaluating my Preaching II course. She explained, "I can get the first word. It is 'focus' but the second word is not clearly written." I said laughingly, "I am sure it is the word 'function.'" She said, "Oh yes, that's it." She then continued, "The student had written, 'I can even hear the words *focus* and *function* in my sleep.'" Ah, a small sign of success! When teaching preaching in the seminary even the smallest positive sign means a great deal. But of course, knowing the concepts and using them well are two very different things.

You may come to feel like many of my students: overexposed to the words *focus* and *function*. Don't say I didn't warn you. I am excited about the opportunity to share this important part of my homework with you. I know that many of you are already familiar with Tom Long's focus and function discipline. For others it may be new or just remotely familiar. But I have found for myself that it never hurts to revisit basic principles and practices in order to renew my skills and my awareness of their value. So I invite you not only to think about focus and function, but I also want to suggest ways for us to sharpen our focus and function skills.

Long speaks of focus and function statements as providing a bridge between biblical text and homiletic text. He points out that biblical texts do many things but most importantly they shape the identity of members of the Christian community. They are not merely a collection of sterile thoughts and ideas.[1] I would add that the biblical claim upon the congregation ought not to be lost in homilies that are intended to communicate mere thoughts and ideas, no matter how insightful or interesting those ideas might be. Our homilies, like our Scriptures, are meant to do more than that.

A homily should attempt to accomplish the same task as the biblical text. It should not only say something but also do something. Long points out:

1. Thomas G. Long, *The Witness of Preaching*, 2nd ed. (Louisville: Westminster John Knox, 2005), 105–106.

> And it is here in the interplay between saying and doing, that we find the key to building the bridge between text and sermon. The bridge must be able to bear the weight of both word and event. The preacher should bring to the sermon both what the text says and what the text does; or, to put it another way, what the text does by its saying.[2]

This "saying" and "doing" are often referred to as the "claim" of a biblical text. Basically the claim is the outcome or synthesis of the saying and doing of the text under consideration. This should also be what the preacher wants to accomplish in the homily. I emphasize this with students because the biblical claim ought to be the basis upon which they make the important decision as to what form the homily will take. The homiletic form is sometimes referred to as the structure, or the plot or perhaps even the movement of the homily. Whatever name we give it, I can tell you that for beginning homiletic students form is a very foreign concept. Yet I have found that after studying the contributions of some well-known homileticians such as Fred Craddock, David Buttrick, Paul Scott Wilson, and Eugene Lowery, students begin to get a handle on homiletic form. However, even with that background, all too often they tend to skip right over homiletic form unless they are required to deal with it in the classroom.

Many experienced preachers seem to pay little attention to what the form of a homily should be as well. Even effective preachers who use other important homiletic tools can get into a homiletic rut, using the same form in homily after homily. They seldom ask the question as to which form would best communicate the focus and function of this homily to this community. I always encourage preachers to give more attention to the variety of forms that are available. Otherwise their homiletic effort can seem like the same old thing week after week. Boring is not a label that any of us would seek. Yet it is one of the common pitfalls of preaching that our Holy Father warns against in a number of his many statements on preaching. Homiletic form is so closely related to focus and function that I could not speak of them without giving some attention to the often neglected issue of homiletic form.

Now we can get back to our friends, focus and function. Preachers in preparing their homilies at times neglect these as well. Some see the process as too time consuming. I suppose they feel they don't have enough time in their busy schedules. Recall what Pope Francis said in *Evangelii gaudium* to priests about being too busy to give adequate time to homily preparation. He said very bluntly they should take time from other important things

2. Long, *The Witness of Preaching*, 106.

in their ministry because effective homilies are that important in the life of the Church.[3]

What preachers need to keep in mind is that their listeners are involved in a purely oral-aural experience—i.e., mouth to ear. In most cases the listeners have no text to read along with or to refer back to. As a result preachers have the responsibility of providing as much clarity as possible in the development and movement of the homily. It must be a clarity that makes it possible for the listeners to take in and experience the preaching without benefit of a text. When following the development of a homily takes too much effort, hearers often give up listening before the homily is concluded. This is especially a problem in this age of brief sound bites and text messaging. Clarity of focus and function can be very effective in making the oral-aural experience of preaching more user-friendly.

Long offers these observations on how well crafted focus and function statements can make homilies more engaging:

> The place to begin in creating a sermon is with the focus and function—what the sermon aims to say and to do. If we keep our eye firmly on these, the sermon form will have unity, since the whole sermon will be shaped to accomplish these aims. Everything the sermon needs to accomplish the focus and function should be included in the structure, and anything that does not help us to achieve these aims is extraneous and should be weeded out.[4]

Focus and function statements are useful guides for preachers in writing and editing their homilies. They ought not to be overlooked.

> Now let's look more precisely at what Long has to say about each of these statements. In *The Witness of Preaching,* Long gives a brief but clear definition for each of the concepts. He explains: *A focus statement* is a concise description of the central, controlling, and unifying theme of the sermon. In short, this is what the whole sermon will be "about."[5]

In the development of the homiletic focus, a leading question is: "What does this biblical text mean for us as disciples today?" The answer to that question must lead to a single idea. Only then will it provide a unifying and controlling theme for the homily. Now this is not as easy as it may sound for the student who is new to this discipline. On the one hand, students often

3. Francis, *Evangelii gaudium,* 145.
4. Long, *The Witness of Preaching,* 137.
5. Ibid., 108.

want to say too much about the focus. They frequently need to be reminded that we are looking for just one theological or spiritual idea that has been uncovered in the exegesis of the biblical text. Having too much to say in a focus statement can often lead to homilies that leave the listener confused because the homily is too hard to follow. More than one parishioner has said on a Sunday morning, "I wonder what the preacher was trying to say today." On the other hand students may seek too much brevity which results in focus statements like this, "God loves us!" This, of course, captures very little of the biblical text and is so generic that it contributes almost nothing to clarifying and unifying a central focus for the homily. It provides no guidance at all.

Read now Long's definition of the function statement:

> *A function statement* is a description of what the preacher hopes the sermon will create or cause to happen for the hearers. Sermons make demands upon the hearers, which is another way of saying that they provoke change in the hearers (even if the change is a deepening of something already present). The function statement names the hoped-for change.[6]

Therefore, a well-crafted function statement will prevent a preacher from developing a homily that is merely an exposition of exegesis or a collection of theological and spiritual ideas. Instead, it should enable the preacher to create a homily that will cause something to happen in the hearer's life. Think of the scene in chapter 4 of Luke's Gospel. We find Jesus in the temple. After proclaiming a passage from the Book of Isaiah, Jesus states, "Today this scripture has been fulfilled in your hearing" (Luke 4:21). Jesus' statement, "fulfilled in your hearing," indicates that the Scriptures were doing something in the minds and hearts of the listeners as they experienced his proclamation. Long maintains that such a doing, such a happening, should be the goal of every homily as well.

Now let us take a brief look at some of the qualities that Long suggests are essential in developing clear and helpful focus and function statements.

*1. The focus and function statements should grow directly from the exegesis of the biblical text.*[7] Preachers bring their personal experience to an exegesis. This includes their theological and spiritual background as well as their perceptions of the congregation. As a result, preachers must be vigilant to see that the homiletic claim flows clearly from the biblical text, not from their personal agendas. Such agenda statements are of no service to effective

6. Ibid., 108f.
7. Ibid., 108.

preaching since they do not flow from the scriptural texts. A helpful reminder here: the focus statement expresses an *idea,* a noun, if you will. The function statement on the other hand, expresses something that the sermon *will do,* a verb. Both of them should be clearly rooted in the biblical text.

Long gives the following examples of effective focus and function statements rooted firmly in the scriptural text, Romans 8:28–39—the famous "all things work together for good" passage. He suggests the following focus and function statements:

> *Focus:* Because we have seen in Christ Jesus that God is for us, we can be confident that God loves and cares for us even when our experience seems to deny it.
>
> *Function:* To reassure and give hope to troubled hearers in the midst of their distress.[8]

Clearly, we can see how deeply rooted in the biblical text these statements are. There are of course other valid ways to express the focus and function for this text. A preacher in a different congregation, in different circumstances, would most likely express the claim of the text in a very different way. What should be the same, however, is that the homilies should grow out of a focus statement that expresses a central idea directly from the biblical text and a function statement that expresses just what the biblical text was meant to do.

*2. The focus and function statements should be related to each other.*[9] It hardly needs to be said, but it is important to keep in mind, that the focus and function statements should be interrelated. The function should grow out of the focus, otherwise it will do very little to build unity and clarity in the homily. Long gives an example of faulty focus and function statements. The statements are based on Luke 6:12–16. Recall that in that passage, Jesus chooses the twelve apostles after praying during the previous night. Here are a preacher's focus and function statements that are not clearly related to each other:

> *Focus:* Today, just as it was in the beginning, the leadership of the Church and the shape of the Church's mission grow out of the prayers of Christ.
>
> *Function:* To encourage a spirit of greater openness in the Church to many diverse people that Christ calls into leadership.[10]

8. Ibid., 110.

9. Ibid., 112.

10. Ibid., 112.

Both statements are certainly commendable thoughts, but clearly, they are not integrally related to each other. The problem is that the function is not a "doing" statement of what the focus is stating. It appears that the preacher has brought his personal agenda to the function statement.

*3. The focus and function statements should be clear, unified and relatively simple.*[11] Although this principle sounds easy to observe, it is anything but that. It is where we spend much of our class time in reviewing focus and function statements. Many preachers, after praying with a text or doing a *lectio* and after doing the necessary exegesis, often have so much to say about a text that they find it hard to remain concise and on point. Their minds and hearts are so filled with worthwhile theological and spiritual insights from the text. Unfortunately, when faced with this overabundance of inspiration, preachers are often inclined to string together too many ideas by invoking a number of ands or buts or the all-too-popular semicolon in the focus and function statements.

This is where the discipline of focus and function statements make another valuable contribution. Preachers need to be sure that both statements put forth a single, unified claim. If not, the homily will most likely be scattered and unfocused, making it very difficult for the hearer to be engaged. As a result, it will be ineffective in engaging the consciousness of the listeners.

Long gives two examples of unhelpful focus and function statements and then he offers a well-crafted set. The first unhelpful statement is too general, while the other is too complex. These statements derive from John 5:1–18, the story of the lame man at the pool of Bethesda. First a focus and a function that are too general:

> *Focus:* Jesus was a controversial healer.
>
> *Function:* To help the hearers understand the importance of this for their lives.[12]

Clearly, these statements would give very little guidance or direction for the development of the homily. Because they are so general, they barely reflect a meaningful claim of the passage.

Secondly, a focus and a function that are too complex:

> *Focus:* Jesus unsettles our comfortable illnesses (blindness to injustice, paralysis of love, deafness to the cry of the needy) with the disturbing question, "Do you really want to be healed?" When people are healed, in the power of Christ, of such illnesses, opposition comes, not from evil

11. Ibid., 113.

12. Ibid., 114.

people but ironically from good people who mistake their religious traditions for the will of God.

*Function:* To enable hearers to become aware of Christ's continuing challenge to the sometimes comfortable complacency of our illnesses, and to enable hearers to perceive how our allegiance to religious traditions can sometimes stand in the way of the saving and healing work of God in our midst.[13]

There are clearly two different claims expressed in these statements. What makes this situation problematic is that it will lead to a confusing homily with disparate parts or, just as bad, the homily will be experienced as two separate, smaller homilies that leave the hearers confused.

Thirdly, Long gives us two statements for this text that are on the mark:

*Focus:* Jesus unsettles our comfortable and complacent illnesses with the disturbing question, "Do you want to be made well?"

*Function:* To challenge the hearers to leave their comfortable "mats" and to live out the health Jesus offers.[14]

We can see that this last set of statements exhibits the important principles that Long proposes. They are brief, clear, related to each other and rooted in the biblical text. They would be helpful guides for a preacher developing a homily for the oral-aural experience of the congregation. Of course, as I often repeat to my students, the preacher must keep in mind that every paragraph, sentence, phrase, word, and punctuation mark of the homily should lead to the homiletic destination as identified in the focus and function statements.

If we need any further support for employing the discipline of focus and function statements, let's look at the homiletic pitfalls that such statements can help us avoid:

*1. The temptation to say everything we know about an idea, an issue or a biblical text.* In his excellent textbook *Preaching Effectively: Revitalizing Your Church,* Benedictine Father Guerric DeBona speaks of this temptation as "a string of pearls." He describes this as "having too much to say, not knowing how to cut or edit our seemingly important ideas, and not understanding the focus and function."[15] The problem here is that in the midst of many pearls, the "pearl of great price" could easily get lost in the clutter. By

13. Ibid., 114–115.

14. Ibid., 115.

15. DeBona, *Preaching Effectively, Revitalizing Your Church: The Seven-Step Ladder toward Successful Homilies* (Mahwah, NJ: Paulist Press, 2009), 81.

the way, Bishop Ken Untener used this "pearl of great price" image famously in his very practical text *Preaching Better.* By using the pearl image, Bishop Untener was saying that the claim of the homily ought to be something worth listening to.[16] The busy people, who set aside a Sunday morning to hear the Word of God, deserve to be fed with something that is truly worthwhile for their everyday lives.

*2. The temptation to inflict upon the congregation ideas and issues that are the preacher's favorite themes.* Often these are the ideas that flow from the preacher's own agenda whether it is ecclesial, political, or something totally unrelated. Some have suggested that preachers need to "murder their darlings" when they get up to preach (see chapter 10).

*3. The inability "to land the plane."* This is a complaint that you hear quite often, "I thought the preacher was bringing the homily to a conclusion three or four times before it ended." In such homilies, preachers seem to be concluding but then they take off on another issue or idea. Sadly this can happen more than once or twice in the same homily. This lack of a single clear homiletic destination can be both confusing and frustrating for the listeners.

## Conclusion

We have been considering one of the important homiletic contributions of Thomas Long: the discipline of focus and function statements. I have tried to share with you the reasons why I feel so strongly about this discipline. It really works, in my experience! It is especially helpful for the less gifted preacher. If a very ordinary homily is built upon well-crafted focus and function statements, the listeners have a much better chance of leaving the church with an awareness of a claim that the Word of God is making on their lives that day. With well-crafted focus and function statements, even less talented preachers can create unified, clear homilies that work well for the oral-aural experience of their listeners.

Finally, I have found that the development of solid focus and function statements can assist preachers in having greater control of the text, the material that they are preaching. The clarity and brevity of the statements express a homily's destination in so concise a way that preachers are better able to own the claim of the homily. Only then can they deliver that homily with the passion of their convictions. The People of God are hungering for that kind of passionate witness in our preaching.

16. Untener, *Preaching Better* (Mahwah, NJ: Paulist Press, 1999), 43.

As you can see, I could not be more convinced of the value of well-formulated focus and function statements that are used effectively in homily preparation. They are worth the time and effort. The People of God certainly deserve at least that much from us who are called to proclaim God's Word in their midst.

Let me conclude with Long's own words:

> It is important to realize that a good set of focus and function statements indicates where a sermon is headed; they are a description of a sermon's overall destination. When they are formulated well, the preacher has a clear idea where the sermon is going and can begin to make coherent plans for how the sermon will get there.[17]

What could be more helpful to us preachers or more valuable to God's people as together "we set the earth on fire," one homily at a time?

17. Long, *The Witness of Preaching*, 116.

■ CHAPTER 12

# Entertain or Else! The Preacher as Performer in Attending to Augustine's "Delight"

David J. Shea

St. Augustine is considered one of the foremost teachers in the art of Christian preaching.[1] His seminal document *De doctrina christiana (On Christian Doctrine)* is judged to be one of the most significant sources for the development of preaching in the Western Church. In its time, it was considered to be a foundational preaching manual. While the first three volumes of *De doctrina christiana* focus on Scripture and how it must be the source of the preacher's insights on the "wisdom of God's word,"[2] the fourth volume addresses the subject of "preaching with eloquence."[3] Even after all these years, Augustine's work is still relevant and still deserves our serious attention. This is particularly true in the area of rhetoric, the art of finding and using the available means of persuasion in verbal communication. Augustine convinced us, and is still convincing us, that we must employ rhetoric in our preaching. Augustine believed that a homily should teach, delight, and persuade, suggesting that the combination of these three qualities creates an effective homily. Further, Augustine says that we can find some degree of teaching, delighting, and persuading in every homily. While some homilies may have a strong teaching orientation, there must still be elements that delight and persuade in order for the homily to be effective. If we examine, in particular, the function of teaching in a homily, we can refer to Augustine's description of the "hammer of error."[4] By this he meant that as preachers we have to be about truth; we must be the advocates and defenders of truth

1. Michael Dominic O'Connor, "Preaching to the Whole Person: Classical Wisdom for the New Evangelization," *Homiletic & Pastoral Review* (October 25, 2012) https://www.hprweb.com/2012/10/preaching-to-the-whole-person-classical-wisdom-for-the-new-evangelization/.

2. James A. Wallace, "Preaching with Style: But Whose?" *Preach* (July/August 2006): 27.

3. Ibid.

4. O'Connor, "Preaching to the Whole Person."

and enemies of error, striking at it and smashing it wherever we find it. Preaching the truth is essential in Catholic homilies. In his first homily as Archbishop of Boston, at the Chrism Mass on April 6, 2004, then Archbishop Seán O'Malley said that our place of martyrdom is the pulpit when we preach, underscoring the importance of truth in our homilies, "to a dominant cultural influence that is incongruent with our faith and with our destiny."[5] There are many ways to preach the truth, some of which have to do with content and others which have to do with style of delivery, which we will address here.

In contrast, the function of delighting in preaching refers to something that is pleasant, even tantalizing, and a joy to hear. Augustine underscored the reality that delight must be employed in order to hold the attention of the audience. With regard to the function of persuading, Augustine indicates that the listener needs to be swayed, that we must move those in the congregation to act. Our hope in every homily is to change the way people think and even change the way they behave. Augustine indicated that by means of persuasion—the preacher is to guide and move the congregation toward doing what they already know they should be doing.

To help his message win a reception, Augustine employed numerous rhetorical devices in order to present the truth eloquently and capture the imagination of his audience. He commonly used figures of vivacity, adding liveliness and animation to his speech, in order to delight his audiences. Augustine also used *interrogatio*, a technique of giving a speech in a questioning form of expression, not for the sake of information, but for the effect it will produce in the hearer. Augustine intentionally *entertained* his audiences with the use of a great variety of rhetorical devices.

The greatest challenge for preachers today is determining if a message is received and how it is received. The vast majority of us preach in a vacuum without any feedback from our congregations. In primary research that I conducted on the subject of the "Unmet Needs in Catholic Preaching,"[6] I learned that both adults and teens—teens more so than adults, but both—said they want their Sunday preaching to be *entertaining*. What do they mean by this? My research began with focus groups, the purpose of which was to derive a comprehensive list of homily attributes. The participants in the focus groups came up with a list of sixty-three different homily attributes that can

---

5. Sean O'Malley, "April 6, 2004—Archbishop Sean O'Malley's Homily at the Chrism Mass," *The Boston Pilot*, last modified 2015, accessed July 14, 2017, http://www.thebostonpilot.com/article.asp?ID=1795.

6. David J. Shea, "Unmet Needs in Catholic Preaching: A Project of the Archdiocese of Cincinnati," *Seminary Journal* 16, no. 2 (September 2010): 33–42.

be grouped into four categories: homily content, the impact of the homily on the listener, preaching styles, and preacher characteristics. The first quantitative study followed with an online survey of eight hundred Catholics in the Archdiocese of Cincinnati. A similar study was then conducted among teenagers in Catholic high schools and parish youth ministry organizations. The results of the quantitative studies revealed that key attributes of an effective homily are that it be inspirational, motivational, and relevant. In order for a homily to be *inspirational*, people thought it must be thought-provoking and make a difference in their daily lives. The *motivational* aspects of a homily are a great deal more elusive and difficult for people to describe. The most common response was that a homily should bring people closer to Christ. Bringing people closer to Christ, or bringing them to an encounter with Christ, is the goal of every homily we preach. The other two *motivational* parameters were providing something concrete to think about and delivering a clear message. When listeners attempt to describe a motivational homily, they struggle to find the words to do so. Interestingly, they use such words as concreteness and clarity underscoring how difficult it was for people to explain what they meant by a motivational homily. Finally, according to respondents, *relevance* is an essential attribute of a successful homily.

Over and above every other attribute, teens prefer homilies that *entertain* and engage them. To no one's surprise, teens reported disliking homilies that are boring, uninteresting, too long, and that do not speak to their issues, concerns, and interest. The word "abhor" was used to describe their disposition towards boredom. Teens are less concerned about truth, doctrine, and knowledge in homilies, and more concerned about "stuff" that relates to and is relevant to their lives. They want to remain engaged in the preaching event and this necessitates that the preacher use a dynamic approach in his delivery. Teens specifically mentioned the use of props, as well as moving away from the ambo and coming down into the midst of the congregation. They want a homilist who is energetic and passionate about what he is preaching. They also mentioned the need for concise language and tight delivery. Overall, teens indicate very strongly that religious issues should take a backseat to secular references in homilies. Teens went on to say that they want a homily that is spiced with humor and stories that will help the preacher to make a lasting point that they will remember.

There is an important related study conducted by a colleague on the subject of "Effective Preaching to the College Congregation."[7] Rev. Thomas Gaughan, CSC, studied preaching preferences of students at four Catholic colleges. In an approach very similar to mine, a list of homily attributes was the outcome of focus groups that were hosted at the University of Notre Dame. Those attributes were then ranked by a survey of 1,200 students across four Catholic colleges. The study derived the top six homily characteristics including: relevant to life, challenging and *inspirational*, emotionally compelling, and funny. For college students, the interesting characteristic which appears to separate them from both adults and teens is that of a homily being emotionally compelling. The survey instrument that was used in the study included one open-ended question as the final question. Students could say anything they wanted about preaching. Many used it to clarify their responses on homily characteristics while others used the question to make personal appeals to preachers about how they wanted homilies to be preached—"Have to be emotional," "Use refined public-speaking skills," "Deliver from the heart," and "Pull us in!" In short, college students want a homily that is stirring, one in which there is an emotional appeal, and they want preachers to convey that they truly care about what they are preaching.

As we continue to explore the issue of delighting people in our preaching, I'd like to draw from an article from the September 12, 2014, *Wall Street Journal*. In J. Perry Smith's article "The Elements of Sermonizing Style," the author cites what he considered to be one of the best homilies he ever heard, preached by Rev. Dunstan Stout, a Roman Catholic missionary to the African community in Mexico City in the 1960s. In the author's assessment, "Father Stout could deliver a four to six minute homily that was hard hitting, even accusatory, and everyone in the church believed he was speaking directly to them. . . . It was gospel-centered and relevant to the listeners."[8] He went on to mention another sermon preached by a Rev. Michael Curry, an Episcopalian priest, at the Washington Cathedral. "He preached that sermon with the passion of an old fashion tent revivalist and it included solid theology with lots of references to the Scriptures that were made real for his listeners."[9] The tent revivalist style of preaching calls to mind a preacher who is loud, emotionally charged, and someone who preached with a cadence in a rhythmic delivery. It was highly participatory and demanded a response

7. Thomas Gaughan, "Effective Preaching to the College Congregation" (presentation at Notre Dame Preaching Conference, Notre Dame, IN, June 27, 2012), https://www.youtube.com/watch?v=I3i3pP9kRFk.

8. J. Perry Smith, "The Elements of Sermonizing Style," *The Wall Street Journal*, September 12, 2014.

9. Ibid.

from the congregation: "Are you saved?" or "Do you profess Jesus Christ as your personal savior?" I remember years ago attending a program of the late Rev. Billy Graham at Paul Brown Stadium in Cincinnati with a group of parishioners. Even though Graham was advanced in years and lacked some of the energy and passion that he once had, it was still exciting and inspirational to hear him preach the Gospel and then invite people to come down for an altar call.

In his article, Perry Smith offered the opinion that the highest profile preachers today are those who lead nondenominational megachurches. He mentions Joel Osteen as one such preacher. Perry is not especially complimentary of Osteen's preaching style, indicating that "he captures listeners with his toothy grin, beautiful hair, and seeming sincerity."[10] He asserts that Osteen, "is scripted, stiff, trained in the media, and delivers repetitive incantations that, 'Jesus loves you, and because it is so, all will be well.'"[11] Whether we believe that Osteen is a good preacher or not, we cannot deny the reality that thousands listen to Osteen in person each week and millions watch him on television and feel assured or encouraged by his gentle style of delivery.

In Perry's assessment, "Scripture has to come alive; that the heart has to be set on fire; that the sermon has to have meaning in people's lives and help them to learn to love God and grow in faith."[12] One particular preacher who knows how to deliver sermons in this manner is Pope Francis. "He lives the gospel he preaches, he understands relevance, he is authentic and passionate, and 'He clearly believes what he says and does what he believes.'"[13]

As a homiletics professor, I have gained valuable perspective from my students during their learning processes and maturation as homilists. The self-evaluation of one seminary student was particularly insightful as it pertains to the *entertaining* dimension of preaching. Throughout the semester, I require that all of my second theology seminarians look at videos of their homilies and do a written self-evaluation. They are asked to address the following questions: What worked in this homily? What didn't work? What has to change? In his remarks, this seminarian acknowledges the importance of energy in his delivery, but at the same time stresses that forcing himself to add that energy seems repugnant to him. He adds that he has always felt uncomfortable about acting and views the artificial forcing of energy into his delivery as a kind of acting. Despite this hesitation, he indicates that he

10. Ibid.

11. Ibid.

12. Ibid.

13. Ibid.

wants to be more excited, increase his enthusiasm, and employ variations of volume and inflection in his next homily. He then ends his self-assessment with the question, "But *entertaining* or acting; is that what I really want to do in my preaching?" This seminarian was not yet convinced that this is what he should or could do.

An examination of acting and its relationship to preaching might be helpful. The seminarian raised the issue of acting in a pejorative sense, suggesting that it is out of place in the pulpit. However, there are many areas where acting and preaching are the same. The use of voice and all verbal and nonverbal parameters are inherently significant. Gestures, facial expressions, and overall physicality are critical to how an individual actor or preacher conveys meaning and is understood. There are a number of qualities that make acting unique; an actor takes on the identity of the character, in effect becoming that character. They study the role very carefully, look at the history of the individual, his or her behavior, mimic their mannerisms, and immerse themselves into the life of that character. Actors authentically communicate another's experience of the world. In preaching, the character of the preacher serves as a medium of the message. In other words it's not just about what the preacher says in his homily; it's also about (or much more about) communicating who the preacher is when he is away from the pulpit and out of the sanctuary. An authentic *performance* of this character is an essential component of how well a homily will be received. While there are important fundamental differences between the actor and the preacher, both must be expert *performers* and communicators.

So, why does there appear to be such a hesitancy and a reticence on the part of the preacher to *perform* his homily and thereby delight and entertain his congregation? In the context of preaching, is there a negative connotation associated with the use of the terms *delight*, *perform*, and *entertain*? The first time I use the word *perform* in the seminary classroom, I encountered a great deal of resistance. "We're talking about the Word of God, after all, and *performing* has nothing to do with proclaiming." Perhaps there are better words to use other than *perform*. What about Augustine's word, "delight?" Delight can connote an authenticity, and we do tend to delight in what is dear to our hearts. What about the word *encounter*? In my first homiletics course some twenty-four years ago, the professor stressed the fact that the purpose of every homily is to lead people to an *encounter* with Christ. That being the case, *encounter* might be a more accurate and less negative word than delight or *entertain*. Even if we learn how to frame this concept for preachers and seminarians, how can we better train them for this type of communication?

In its simplest form, preaching is communication, and while the homily is built upon knowledge and information, it's much more than that. As we all know, communication is anything but simple. There are countless variables influencing how we communicate as speakers and what we hear and understand as listeners. When we add the content of our communication to the mix (verbal cues, changes in inflection, and nonverbal variables), then add expectations and perceptions of the speaker and listener, communication becomes an incredibly complex process. It's no wonder, theoretically speaking, the homily can be heard in as many different ways as there are people in the congregation. If you're anything like me, there have been many times when people tell me what they heard in my homily, and as I listen to them I'm thinking to myself, "Where did that come from?" Ultimately, the only thing that matters is what people heard.

For a moment I want to return to the study I did on the unfulfilled needs in the Sunday homily. In that study, parishioners indicated that the Sunday homily was most seriously lacking in these areas: the preacher draws you into the homily, the homily touches you deeply, and the homily is clear and preached on your level. Moreover, people indicated that they want to feel challenged to act and moved to action. These underscore the importance of how a homily is preached and delivered. The improvement of public speaking skills, which has everything to do with style, is a critical issue in preaching.

An essential aspect of effective communication in preaching is the proper use of nonverbal skills. Nonverbal communication can be incredibly dominant. I like this quotation from Jack Rang: "The truth is that what we see is often far more vivid, more response producing, than what we hear."[14] I continually remind my students that long before we open our mouths, people are already making judgments about us by our appearance, by the condition of our vestments, by how we walk, and by the kind of attitude that we project by our facial expressions. Some people decide that they don't like us even when they've never had a chance to hear us speak. If the congregation is going to judge us (positively or negatively) before we even speak, then when we speak, it better be good! Without qualification, nonverbal communication is important and it makes voice skills all the more important. It is the visible language of the body that enables the preacher to embody the homily, give it life, and preach it with passion with his use of gestures,

14. Jack Rang, *How To Read the Bible Aloud* (New York: Paulist Press, 1994), 15.

facial expressions, empathy, and other elements of bodily action. Faces do important work when we preach—our faces communicate as we smile and frown, when we furrow our foreheads, and express emotions with our eyes. All of these come together to inject life and vitality into a homily. A very high percentage of a congregation's understanding of the spoken word is based upon the visual aspects of communications. Rocco Dal Vera, professor of voice and drama at the Cincinnati Conservatory of Music, suggests that as much as 93 percent of understanding is based upon context. Context, or how we preach a homily, is highly determinative of what people hear and understand.

In his book *Why Preach? Encountering Christ in God's Word,* Peter Cameron says, "in trying to recapture the amazing happening for someone who did not see it, we use an appropriate style and only as many words as are needed to re-create the event in such a way that the other can experience it."[15] The average preacher can devote several hours each week to preparing and finalizing his homily, but only invests a small fraction of that time to practicing the delivery of the homily. There is a real tension between content and context, with the latter falling a great distance behind the former. Many preachers struggle with the issue of style because they believe that the best we can do is to put out the Word of God and then get out of the way; it is God's Word and he will do what needs to be done. We can only interfere or impede that Word. In his book *The Word Made Plain: The Power and Promise of Preaching,* James Henry Harris makes the point, that "black preachers and parishioners understand the nature of homiletics and recognize that style without substance is typically more acceptable than substance without style."[16] That is not to suggest that the content of our homilies isn't important, but the best written homilies can be very poorly preached and the results very poorly received by the congregation. The point to be made here is that the dialogue between the preacher and the hearer must be communicated with appropriate style. Father Jim Wallace in his article "Preaching with Style—But Whose?" indicates that a preacher's style is an instrument that assists achieving full, conscious, and active participation in the liturgy.[17]

So what exactly is style? The Oxford English dictionary defines it as, "elegance, refinement, or excellence of manner, expression, form, or

---

15. Peter John Cameron, OP, *Why Preach? Encountering Christ in God's Word* (San Francisco: Ignatius Press, 2009), 55.

16. James Henry Harris, *The Word Made Plain: The Power and Promise of Preaching* (Minneapolis: Fortress Press, 2004), 78.

17. James A. Wallace, "Preaching with Style—But Whose?" *Preaching,* July/August 2006, 26.

performance."[18] There's that word *performance* again. Jim Wallace provides a little more extensive definition when he describes style as "the manner of a person's expression in the choice of words, in the manner of presenting content and the rhythm of speech that conveys the thoughts and feelings a speaker wishes to invite listeners to consider and even share."[19] The preacher's style takes time to develop, and versatility is essential as different contexts and homilies will require different styles of delivery. How one preaches at Sunday Mass is different from how one preaches at the funeral of a teenager who committed suicide. These preaching events will be delivered in fundamentally different ways, and they will be heard and experienced in fundamentally different ways. Similarly, the style we use to preach at a wedding or Baptism of four infants will be significantly different than how we preach at weekday Mass. Wallace suggests that the preacher should develop skills in three distinct styles of expression: simple style for teaching, a moderate style for giving delight, and a grand style for moving listeners to a particular end.[20] The simple style is characterized by clarity and it leads listeners to understanding and instruction. When we employ the simple style we speak to the mind. When the moderate style is used the goal is to please listeners. It is marked by expressions that will interest and engage listeners. It gives delight and pleasure and it speaks to the imagination. The grand style is aimed at persuasion and moves listeners to a particular goal. It is aimed at the heart. Fr. Wallace says, "The most effective style is one that flows from the truth of the preacher's being and from the heart of one who ministers by fulfilling preaching's ultimate purpose,"[21] to give people a message that brings healing and helps people to deal with the great assortment of baggage they bring with them to Mass, to lead them to celebrate the Eucharist with hope, "and go forth to be God's presence in the world under the leadership of Christ and in the power of the Holy Spirit."[22]

Given the essential demands of the job, you might think that the ministry of preaching would attract only the vocally gifted, the most eloquent, and the most charismatic. While that might be true in certain cases, with certain people, we also know that preaching attracts a great diversity of personalities and temperaments, from the over-the-top extrovert who brings a natural energy and drama to the homily, to the soft-spoken introvert, who

18. Ibid.

19. Ibid.

20. Ibid., 27.

21. Ibid., 29.

22. Ibid.

brings hesitancy, an uneasy demeanor, and shyness into the pulpit. Shyness has two main tracks: performance anxiety and reticence. Performance anxiety is common and we know that even professional actors and performers experience varying levels of nervousness. I like to tell my students that a certain measure of anxiety and nervousness is a good thing—that extra adrenaline increases our sharpness, it helps us to do a better job, and it is a reminder that what we are doing is very important. If there is an absence, altogether, of anxiety, then that in itself could be a problem. Reticence is different and more complicated. There is an understandable hesitancy when we impose a more dramatic interpretation on the Word. To be more expressive can be experienced as performing. I remember a homily I preached in the fall of 2015, on a weekend when my preaching was being evaluated at all Masses. It was a homily in which I had employed lots of projection, dramatically raising my voice to emphasize a point. One of the individual evaluations I received from a woman was very critical, indicating that I yelled at her, and she was upset with me. Sometimes we can be overly expressive and accomplish something altogether different from what we intended. We also have to realize that an expressive approach can sometimes be perceived as being egocentric and can shift the focus of our homilies away from the Word and to ourselves.

So how do we adjust, more naturally, our demeanor in our speech? We speak one way to someone sitting next to us and another way when giving a toast at a wedding. We certainly sound differently as spectators at a sporting event and when we're having an intimate one-on-one conversation. These are all things that we do without even thinking; we do them naturally. The trick is to do them in a homily and have them sound natural. For example, in intimate speech, we lower volume and reduce energy; we may speak in whispers, speak more emotionally, or work hard at being empathetic. These are the very things that we need to do so that people receive a personal, pastoral, empathetic, and natural homily. There is the concept of scaling, which is nothing more than being in a relationship with every single person in the church. If it is a large space, then the person in the back is our most important partner and that individual must be able to hear and understand us and experience us in a personal and natural way. Of course, volume is important, but microphones only amplify what we give them. If we are having a private conversation with the microphone, then we will be *heard* in the back of the room but we won't be *felt* in the first row. Above all things, the question of intention is essential. We must realize that preaching is completely about the other person, the people listening and what they hear, understand, and experience. Our intent as preachers is to connect with every single person, to register the message, and to change their lives—that is essential. We can all benefit by working much harder at preaching style; by pushing our voices, by ratcheting up our energy and our passion and by using all of our voices and all of our bodies to preach the best possible homily we can.

So we return to our opening question, "What do people mean when they say they want to be *entertained* in the Sunday homily?" They want to enjoy the homily, pay attention without struggling, find relevance to their lives, hear a message spoken directly to them, feel an emotional reaction to it, remember it, and most importantly, they want to encounter Christ in it. Is that too much to ask? Accomplishing this begins with the best use of our imaginations with vision, story, symbol, and images as we write our homilies, and we should follow Augustine's lead by using every kind of rhetorical device available to us. It necessitates the best use of our voices and the involvement of our bodies. It stresses the criticality of the preacher's character. We must live what we preach. We must communicate how human we are and that we struggle with some of the same temptations that they do. We must realize how strong the connection is between who we are and what we stand for in the pulpit on Sunday and in our interactions with people during the rest of the week. Delighting our congregations requires an embrace of the importance of the preacher's style and how truly significant it is in inspiring our own excitement, enthusiasm, and passion. While there is heavy emphasis on the moderate style for giving delight, all styles can and must be used because "Preaching is for the whole person."[23] Similarly, it necessitates an understanding as to how the three preaching styles work together: a calm style for teaching with an appeal to the intellect, the moderate style for delighting with its appeal to the memory and imagination, and the grand style for persuading with its appeal to the will. All of these can work together, sometimes in the same homily.

Happy preaching, and go *delight* and *entertain* your congregations!

---

23. C. Colt Anderson, *Christian Eloquence: Contemporary Doctrinal Preaching* (Chicago: Hillenbrand Books, 2005), 33.

■ CHAPTER 13

# Igniting the Flame of Intentional Listeners

Sharon Schuhmann and Rev. Jeff Nicolas

The listening assembly is essential to the preaching encounter. The first chapter of both *Fulfilled in Your Hearing: The Homily in the Sunday Assembly*[1] (hereafter, FIYH), published in 1982, and *Preaching in the Sunday Assembly: A Pastoral Commentary on Fulfilled in Your Hearing,*[2] published in 2010, are dedicated to the assembly. In both works, the authors correctly give great emphasis to the assembly because what they hear in the homily and how they hear it is of great importance in determining the success of the homily. Of course, part of these publications' emphasis involves identifying the assembly and how the preacher fulfills the role as mediator of meaning:

> What the preacher can do best of all at this time and in this place is to enable this community to celebrate by offering them a word in which they can recognize their own concerns and God's concern for them.[3]

Chapter 4 of FIYH also suggests that a small focus group made up of members of the congregation could be involved in the homiletic preparation process. It would be "an effective way for preachers to be sure that they are addressing some of the real concerns of that congregation."[4] This is true, yet more can be done with the assembly to deepen the preaching encounter.

In this chapter, we will focus on how we were able to inform and form the assembly into intentional listeners. We developed a course to help our parishioners understand the world of preaching by using a systematic approach. Sherry Weddell's book *Forming Intentional Disciples: The Path to*

1. National Conference of Catholic Bishops, *Fulfilled in Your Hearing: The Homily in the Sunday Assembly* (Washington, DC: United States Catholic Conference, 1982).

2. James Wallace, ed., *Preaching in the Sunday Assembly: A Pastoral Commentary on Fulfilled in Your Hearing* (Collegeville, MN: Liturgical Press, 2010).

3. *Fulfilled in Your Hearing: The Homily in the Sunday Assembly,* 8.

4. Ibid, 36.

*Knowing and Following Jesus*[5] inspired our creation of this parish course on forming the worshiping community into intentional listeners. We jointly conducted the parish program, "What Makes Preaching Tick? And, How Can I Get More out of It?" in St. Bernadette Catholic Church, Prospect, Kentucky, in the Archdiocese of Louisville. We advertised the course as a vehicle to show parishioners how and why preaching is created and what they can do to deepen their encounter with Christ during the homily. We also found that the formation of more intentional listeners gave the preacher more motivation and assistance to create good preaching.

The five thresholds of conversion Weddell describes in her book formed the foundation for the emphasis on the assembly's transformation into intentional listeners, which in turn lead toward becoming intentional disciples. We believed that if we could inform the listeners about how a homily is crafted, the preaching would catch fire and the assembly would grow into intentional listeners.

A summary of Weddell's thoughts begins with her own description of a problem, 53:

> Genuine Catholic identity flows *from* the experience of discipleship. As the *Lineamenta* notes: " . . . The Gospel can only be transmitted on the basis of 'being' with Jesus and living with Jesus the experience of the Father, in the Spirit; and, in a corresponding way, of 'feeling' compelled to proclaim and share what is lived as a good and something positive and beautiful." If a living relationship with Christ and, therefore, his Father and the Holy Spirit, does not exist, we have not succeeded in "transmitting" the faith.[6]

Wendell goes on to explain how there are five thresholds through which any person must cycle regularly in order to move more deeply into an intentionality with regards to their relationship with Jesus Christ. The five thresholds are: trust, curiosity, openness, seeking, and intentional discipleship.

The *trust* threshold enables a person to move toward a deeper relationship, but does not in itself constitute a relationship. Trust makes the other thresholds possible. As one progresses, the deeper the trust, the more the other thresholds are amplified in their effectiveness. The threshold of trust causes one to lean toward the object or subject of their discipleship.

---

5. Sherry A. Weddell, *Forming Intentional Disciples: The Path to Knowing and Following Jesus* (Huntington, IN: Our Sunday Visitor, Inc., 2012), 53.

6. Ibid, 53.

The *curiosity* threshold, while still a passive stance, moves a person more deeply into an encounter with the object or subject of their discipleship. Curiosity becomes the carrot that entices one to move forward as opposed to only leaning forward, as in the case of the trust threshold.

The *openness* threshold occurs when a person becomes aware of the potential and possibility of change in their perspectives, actions, or experiences. Passing through the openness threshold does not mean that the person will necessarily change, but they have not ruled change out. It is said that the blindest people are those who will not open their eyes. Persons passing through the openness threshold have "opened their eyes."

The *seeker* threshold transitions one from a passive stance to an active one. The seeker, as Weddell describes it, is "dating with purpose." Now the person is engaged in a transformative search for something new, something that could potentially lead to a deeper encounter with the one who is sought.

The *intentional discipleship* threshold occurs when a person commits to the deeper encounter discovered through the completion of the previous thresholds. Here a new plateau is reached in the relationship and one now operates from the new perspective.[7]

We applied Weddell's five thresholds to the listening assembly in the preaching encounter, demonstrating how various aspects of the preaching process can highlight each threshold's presence in a person's preaching encounter with Jesus Christ. Therefore, the course sessions each highlighted a particular threshold that could be shown to be in play. The outlines for the six sessions of the course are presented throughout the following paragraphs.

### Class 1: Introduction

You the Listener

The Five Thresholds of Intentional Discipleship

How Can This Class Help You Progress towards Intentional Discipleship?

What Do You Want to Get out of This Class?

Overview of Future Classes:

- What Is Preaching?
- How Is Preaching Created?
- Exegesis

7. We would note that any would-be-disciple of anything or anyone would go through the same five thresholds in their embrace of whatever or whoever it is they are fixated upon. These thresholds are not unique to disciples of Jesus Christ; many are disciples of various "gods" in our society.

Strategies for Attentive Listening

How Can a Listener Enter More Deeply into the Preaching Event?

### Class 2: What Is Preaching?

Short History of Preaching

Preaching as an Encounter

Curiosity Threshold Relevance

Curiosity kicks in as we find ourselves intrigued by some aspect, perspective, dilemma or witness that causes a tension between what we think we know and what we are now facing. A delivery style, a problem posed, a new perspective explored, or a passionate witness given can predicate a passage through the curiosity threshold.

### Class 3: How Is Preaching Created?

Role of Exegesis (Word/Preacher/Assembly)

Tension = Attention

Structures

Prayer

Openness Threshold Relevance

Openness can occur as one experiences preaching and acknowledges to himself or herself and to God that he or she is open to the possibility of personal and spiritual change. Various preaching structures, such as inductive methods, can bring about an openness in the listener.

### Class 4: Exegesis

Exploration of Various "Criticisms"

Role of Commentaries

Theology Books and Websites

Trust Threshold Relevance

Trust is employed by the preacher in the fact that he or she believes there will be something in the Scripture that needs to be preached into an encounter for the listeners. There is also a preacher's trust in the expertise of the experts one might investigate in study. The listener also exercises some level of trust toward the preacher, that he or she is speaking a valid word, and that this word has been duly explored and prepared.

### Class 5: Strategies for Attentive Listening

Reading

Study of Commentaries

Prayer

*Lectio Divina*

Active Listening Skills

Seeker Threshold Relevance

Seeking as a listener not only engages the mind but also can open the heart, growing out of an expectation of an encounter with God in the preaching event. The listener positions himself or herself for a significant encounter with God by actively seeking insights from the readings prior to the preaching event. Curiosity, trust, and openness have led the listener to this desire of seeking.

### Class 6: How Can A Listener Enter More Deeply Into The Preaching Event?

Summarize Previous Lessons

Four Thresholds Relevance Summary

Intentional Discipleship Threshold Relevance

The fifth threshold of intentional discipleship for a listener of preaching happens as one is shaped by the encounter of preaching and goes forth, committed to particular actions or attitudes as a result.

The completion of the cycle of the thresholds (trust—curiosity—openness—seeking) in the preaching activity each week enhances the preaching encounters and can deepen the listener's relationship with Jesus Christ, thus moving towards intentional discipleship—the subject of our spiritual quest.

The following homework assignments were designed to help participants identify their own movement through the thresholds of discipleship:

- Assignment 1: Initial assessment of your experience of sample homily.
- Assignment 2: Select an upcoming preaching event and note how *curiosity* played a role in your experience of that preaching.

- Assignment 3: Describe how you became more *open* through a preaching encounter in the coming week.

- Assignment 4: Either study a Scripture commentary or go to the SLU liturgy website (liturgy.slu.edu) as a *seeker* prior to an upcoming preaching event; how does this *entrusting* of your time change your preaching event?

- Assignment 5: Study a Scripture and see how you obtain "eyes" to see the Scripture unfold throughout the week prior to its preached encounter. How does this *seeking* change your preaching encounter?

- Assignment 6 (done in class): What are you now getting out of preaching that you were not getting before? What are you now putting into the preaching event that you were not before? In what ways has your relationship with Jesus Christ deepened as a result?

Preaching Encounter Tuesdays were opportunities for the assembly to experience how different preachers create different encounters even though they utilize the same Scripture. Two preachers were selected from a pool of five preachers each week, and the two followed the format below created in the context of a Holy Hour Exposition.

**Lent 2017 Tuesday Evening Preaching Encounter**

(Program runs from 7 PM until 8 PM)

| | | |
|---|---|---|
| 7:00–7:05 | (5m) | Opening prayer to the Holy Spirit |
| 7:05–7:08 | (3m) | Scripture read by Preacher #1 |
| 7:08–7:20 | (12m) | Preaching #1 |
| 7:20–7:25 | (5m) | Silent reflection period |
| 7:25–7:28 | (3m) | Same Scripture read by preacher #2 |
| 7:28–7:40 | (12m) | Preaching #2 |
| 7:40–7:45 | (5m) | Silent reflection period |
| 7:45–8:00 | (15m) | The ordained performs Incensation/ Benediction/Blessing/Reposition of Sacrament |

The sixth class in the parish setting offered the participants the opportunity to share their insights as follows:

### What are you now getting out of preaching that you were not getting before?

Some responses received:

Looking for key words that connect God's word with my life.

Listening for the tension the preacher is creating: Where is the tension? Name the tension.

A new understanding of how much goes into the art of preaching.

A change in my experience of active listening.

Now I look for an understanding of how the preacher prepared.

Anticipating the type of preaching, i.e., Lowry Loop, Wilson Method, etc.

God is calling me to an intentionality of listening.

I am much more attentive to thoughts about zeroing in on one thing.

I have an understanding of the goal of the preacher who has experience, attention, emphasis on what's going on in the world.

I have an appreciation for the insight that a small part of Scripture can result in great meaning.

I have developed new insights into the preacher's sharing of the Good News with children during children's Liturgy of the Word.

### What are you now putting into the preaching event that you were not before?

Some responses:

Attention.

Ownership of my participation in the preaching encounter.

Recognition of the purpose for preaching.

Preparation for the preaching encounter, including time reading before Mass and more desire for the encounter with God.

Intentionality of prayer for the preacher (I hold the preacher in prayer).

Seeking the Holy Spirit in life.

New recognition for the ability to see God's fingerprint in life.

New tools for centering prayer sessions in the parish in preparation for the Sunday Mass.

Being fully present.

Intentionality on the drive to church to become an active listener.

I will take commentaries to choir practice so that we can prepare for the encounter with God through preaching.

## In what ways has your relationship with Jesus Christ deepened as a result?

Some answers that were shared:

Recognizing the most real thing in my life.

A deeper love.

A new spiritual enlightenment.

Happiness in my relationships.

A fresh introspection.

A renewed call to action.

Peacefulness.

God's forgiveness.

A rekindled thirst for God.

It all started with a hunch. Many of our parishioners were hungry for deeper encounters with Christ and seemed open to trying new things. Over the years both of us had heard arguments for adding more training, more preparation, and more accountability to preachers in order to improve the preaching experience of our assemblies. Yet, little was ever proposed for the listeners themselves to do other than perhaps prereading the Scriptures or praying for the preacher or even simply not reading the bulletin or filling out the collection check during the homily. Their hunch was that some formative effort directed at the listener rather than the preacher might yield a rich harvest.

It is easy to focus solely on the preacher when trying to improve the preaching experience. After all, he or she is the one who is creating the encounter through the ordering of words. However, the preaching encounter is only partly created by the preacher; the listener also has an active role in its creation. Our hunch was that an investment in the listener's part might transform the encounter in a way no amount of working with the preacher could affect. This hunch proved true.

Through a six-week course participants explored how discipleship thresholds can be successfully navigated while teaching what preaching is, how it is created, and how a listener can actively become engaged in the preaching encounter. The results indicate that those who participated in our course came away from it feeling more like partners with the preachers in the creation of a preaching encounter, rather than simply passive observers. This element of investment by listeners makes a world of difference in the dividends they take away from a preaching. An investment in the listening assembly can take any preaching encounter to a new level.

The beginning of the Eucharistic Prayer engages the presider and the assembly in a dialogue wherein the presider invites the assembly to "lift up your hearts," and the assembly responds with, "We lift them up to the Lord." As the assembly is formed into intentional listeners, they will also "lift up their hearts" in the preaching event as partners in the preaching, and so deepen their encounter with the Lord.

CHAPTER 14

# The Holy Spirit and Listener Receptivity: Preaching That Soaks in Like Good Butter on Warm Toast

Karla Bellinger

*Come Holy Spirit, fill the hearts of your faithful and kindle in them the fire of your love.*

Let's start with an experiment: one of you be a young man who slouches and looks at the ceiling. Another of you be an elderly man who sits and trims his fingernails. Who'd like to be an eighth grade girl who has her head bent down as though she is looking at something in her lap (a cell phone maybe)? The rest of you could be a toddler who jumps up and down, a mother who tries to quiet him, a man who closes his eyes and looks like he is falling asleep. I will be the speaker who keeps on speaking and speaking and speaking. What is going through my head while all this commotion is going on? I wonder, "Is anybody listening?" Have you been there? You could be a homilist trying to get a message across. You could be a teacher or a parent hoping to say something meaningful. You could be a teenager sharing a witness at a retreat. With me, you may have also wondered, "Is anybody listening?"

When we ponder effectiveness in preaching, what first comes to mind is a "sender-side" perspective—we focus on "here's what to say and here's how to say it." In this chapter, we'll flip that around to a "receiver-side" focus to ask: "How does our preaching land? How are we heard?" In addition, the homily is a relational experience, an interplay between speaker and listener. So there is another player to consider: The Holy Spirit is integral to the interaction of preaching. The Divine Connector hungers for the Good News to be absorbed and vibrantly lived. In this brief chapter, we cannot cover all that is known about the reception of a homiletic message nor the role that the Holy Spirit plays in that. But we can make a start. We focus on expectant hope: we trust that preaching is God's work. Pope Francis says, "Let us renew our confidence in preaching, based on the conviction that it is God who seeks to reach out to others through the preacher, and that he displays his power through human words."[1]

## The Holy Spirit in the Interaction of the Homily

It is both humbling and awe-inspiring to speak on behalf of God. There are no guarantees in preaching: we cannot make anything happen inside of another person; we cannot change hearts; we cannot transform someone else's life. Like the Apostles after the Resurrection of Jesus, we've got nothing to give unless the fire of Pentecost empowers our prayer, our preparation, our delivery, and our hearers' reception of our message. In reflecting upon homiletic effectiveness, we have to concede that there is an element of effectiveness that feels out of our grasp, for it is the Spirit who "effects" change.

Where is the Holy Spirit in the action of preaching? The Holy Spirit shows up in the time that we take to study and pray and discern our message. He is at the core of our preaching, the Divine Connector, the One who bridges the distance between pulpit and pew. Effective preaching is a gift arising from each of these moments: "such preaching means that a bit of Pentecost comes to pass."[2]

We begin with the expectation that the Holy Spirit is with us in our preaching. Let us take a quiet moment and ponder the One in whom we have that confidence: the Holy Spirit is God with us—here, now. In faith, we believe that the Spirit of God is the Almighty One who enfolds us, loves us, and is dynamically involved in this world. As we look at effectiveness in preaching and communicating, then, let us not forget the Effector of effectiveness. We do not minister alone. We trust the Holy Spirit to show up. We pray: "Come Holy Spirit, fill the hearts of your faithful and kindle in them the fire of your love." Then we sing, "Open the eyes of my heart, Lord. I want to see you . . . " For one minute, sit and receive the Holy Spirit. Let the love of God soak into you and fill you up.

## Reception as a Dynamic Action

Receive these words from John chapter 20, verses 19–21:

> On the evening of that day, the first day of the week, when the doors were locked, where the disciples were, for fear of the Jews, Jesus came and

---

1. Pope Francis, Apostolic Exhortation *Evangelii gaudium* (EG), 36.

2. Joseph Ratzinger, *Dogma and Preaching: Applying Christian Doctrine to Daily Life* (San Francisco: Ignatius Press, 2011), 40.

> stood in their midst, and said to them, "Peace, be with you." When he had said this, he showed them his hands and his side. The disciples rejoiced when they saw the Lord. Jesus said to them again, "Peace, be with you. As hthe Father has sent me, so I send you." And when he had said this, he breathed on them and said to them, "Receive the Holy Spirit. Whose sins you forgive are forgiven them, and whose sins you retain are retained."

Listen again to one of the key verbs in that passage: "Receive the Holy Spirit." To "receive" is not passive. The Greek word here is *lambano,* which connotes "take it up and do something with it"—not the passive action of shaking hands in a receiving line, but an active verb that contains within it, "take it in and get going!"

To get going, let's move to the metaphor in our chapter title. The homily is good butter. The hearer is warm toast. But the dynamic action is that of reception, that action of the homily soaking in to the life of the hearer. Imagine it: we may not live on bread alone, but add a bit of butter and heat and you'll find that crunchy homemade cracked wheat bread turns into a sensory delight. In a scientific sense, butter does not change chemically in response to the toast. The melting of butter is a physical response to heat. The warmth emanating from the toast melts the butter so that it soaks in. In the same way, the warmth of the Holy Spirit within the listener (warm toast) is what melts the homily (good butter) so that it soaks in. Sometimes listeners respond in ways that we don't expect. Sometimes, the Holy Spirit moves through us so powerfully that the interaction takes us by surprise. But the goal of our preaching is that soaking-in encounter with God. We know that the experience is ultimately not ours to effect and we trust the Holy Spirit to be active; yet we do have a part to play in creating an environment where encounter is more likely to happen.

## Warming the Toast

Good butter. Warm toast. What memories come to mind for you? At my house, when the timer rings and I grab thick mitts to pull loaves of bread out of the oven, the smell of yeast and flour floats from the kitchen into the living room and up to the bedrooms. A child hops off the couch. A young man hurries down the stairs. My husband opens the door from the garage and leans into the kitchen and says, "Ooh! What's cooking?"

The focus of this book is how to create effective homilies. That's the churning of good butter. Yet no matter how carefully we prepare the butter, there seem to be times when there is little connection. The bread or the toast is dry or stale or cold. Impact also relies on the receptivity of the listener. Some listeners walk into the Sunday liturgy already warm and receptive, as in "ooh, what's cooking" in church today? They may have already read the Scriptures. They may pray often. They are on their way to becoming saints. The toast is hot. No matter how cold and hard your homiletic butter may be, for these folks, it is likely to soak in. This past week, a young lady on my same pew took out a notebook and began to take notes on the homily as Father began to speak. That's *lambano*—ready to pick it up and do something with it.

Not all are so fervent. What can you do as a spiritual leader to "warm the toast"? To be honest, much of a receiver's response is formed before you ever open your mouth to speak.[3] The family dynamics in the car, the hospitality of the parish community, the music at Mass—all of these can warm or cool the "toast." (The slouch of the teenager in the second row may have nothing at all to do with you or your homily.) You may not be able to *make* encounter happen, but by your leadership, you can create a context within which it is likely to happen. Certain conditions foster receptivity. The hard work that you and your lay leaders put into creating an inviting parish and liturgical environment can set the stage for the Holy Spirit to "soak in." The homily does not sit by itself, but within a liturgy in the context of a community.

Additionally, you yourself create pre-impressions—the friendliness that you exude in your opening remarks in the liturgy, the Saturday evening visit with a family at the hospital, and the solidarity that you have created within your staff and with your volunteers—all of this impacts how your folks receive that seven-to-ten-minute string of words from the pulpit. Your holiness matters. You are more effective when a listener feels, "This is a person with whom I am comfortable; one whom I can trust."[4] People listen to someone who they perceive cares for them.

In preparation for this workshop, I asked my two granddaughters about why they listen. Samadhi, age eight, said, "Some people you *have* to listen to . . . like mom." I asked, "Why is that?" "You have to or you get in trouble. Some people you *want* to listen to, like you, Grandma. If you don't, it will make you [Grandma] sad." With a few cultural exceptions, parishioners no longer feel like they *have* to listen to Father or they'll be in trouble. Those days are mostly behind us. People listen best to people whom they care about.

---

3. Robert Cialdini, *Pre-Suasion: A Revolutionary Way to Influence and Persuade* (New York: Simon and Schuster, 2016). See page 4 about the definition of pre-suasion: "the process of arranging for recipients to be receptive to a message before they encounter it."

4. Marianne Gaarden, "Listeners as Authors in Preaching: Empirical and Theoretical Perspectives," *Homiletics* 38:1 (2013), 43, https://ejournals.library.vanderbilt.edu/ojs/index.php/homiletic/article/view/3832.

I asked Sophia, age thirteen, why she listens. She said, "Talk to me respectfully and as an equal, and I will listen." Respect is a key ingredient in being heard in today's culture. As a preacher, the time and care that you put into preparing and delivering your homily is taken as a sign of respect. The warmth of your voice reverences your congregation. Your two-second loving eye contact demonstrates your esteem. As you build your homily with the trust that the Holy Spirit is moving within their lives, your carefully chosen words and images that will reverence the spiritual experience of your community. When asked why she did not listen, Sophie also said, "When someone is not speaking to me respectfully, I will not listen because they are not respecting me. I will find every way to question why they want me to do it." Your parishioners may not push back as obviously as a seventh grader, but internally, they may block you out. Do we reverence the congregation? The finest teachers expect much from their students; the finest preachers expect much from their parishioners and their God.[5]

Lackadaisical homily preparation is frequently received as a sign of disrespect. Pope Francis says:

> Preparation for preaching is so important a task that a prolonged time of study, prayer, reflection and pastoral creativity should be devoted to it. . . . Trust in the Holy Spirit who is at work during the homily is not merely passive but active and creative. It demands that we offer ourselves and all our abilities as instruments (cf. Rom 12:1) which God can use. A preacher who does not prepare is not "spiritual"; he is dishonest and irresponsible with the gifts he has received.[6]

Preparation matters. Spiritual leadership matters. Done with care, it is both a responsibility and a joy to create the conditions conducive to fostering an encounter with the living God. We can do that! In reverencing the holy moment of the homily, we reverence the working of the Holy Spirit. Reverence and respect are nonnegotiable to the warming of the toast.

A few practical points for creating an environment (parish as plugged-in toaster?) where an encounter with God is more likely to flourish:

1. Friendliness matters to receptivity. Keep working on your parish hospitality. Cultures do not change overnight, but with continual focus on welcome and by setting a personally open-hearted example, warmth can grow within a parish. Eat together, engage in communal activities,

---

5. See Kenneth Bain, "What Do They Expect of their Students," chapter 4 in *What the Best College Teachers Do* (Cambridge, MA: Harvard University Press, 2004).

6. EG, 145.

and establish a parish home. The sense of "I am wanted here" opens the heart.

2. In your homilies, initial/concluding remarks, and parish formation and cultural practices, encourage your people to pray at all times. We may not be able to control the quality of our prayer, but we can be regular and constant in prayer, both in church and in everyday life. Prayer and preaching effectiveness walk hand in hand.
3. Within the liturgy, teach your folks to handle silence, to listen to the Spirit. People who are far from regular Mass attendance come (when they come) for prayer and reflection.[7] Foster an atmosphere of respect and contemplation. Many people read "tone" before they hear "words."
4. In your opening comments and preaching, encourage them to enter into liturgy with the joyful hope that God has something to say to me, in this place, on this day. That "speaking" could be through the homily or the songs or the prayers or the sacrament or the interaction of the community. Urge them to be listening. Expect the Holy Spirit to show up!

## Churning Good Butter

As a faith community, we have been addressing how to make "good butter": make one point, preach the Good News, tell stories, design a focus and function statement, speak of the deep things of God, etc. There are many pieces and parts to the "sender-side" of crafting and delivering a homily. From my empirical study on how to connect with young people, it appears that we are shaping academically trained good men in our seminaries; formation in how to preach lags behind that human formation.[8] One of the reasons for this book on effectiveness is to address that gap in homiletic education.

To churn good butter, you stir milk until the solids separate from the liquid whey. Similarly, a homily that is purposefully designed for encounter has to be vigorously stirred. Pour off anything that is extraneous. Let it sit at room temperature for a while. Let it soften; make it easy to spread. Often the words from the pulpit come at the listener as though they came straight out of the freezer—hard and solid words don't soak in easily. Chunky

---

7. Center for Applied Research in the Apostolate (CARA), "Sacraments Today: Belief and Practice among US Catholics," 7, http://www.cara.georgetown.edu/sacramentsreport.pdf.

8. Karla J. Bellinger, *Connecting Pulpit and Pew: Breaking Open the Conversation about Catholic Preaching*, (Collegeville, MN: Liturgical Press, 2014), 63–65.

paragraphs need to be smoothed out. Keep churning so that the structure and the vocabulary of your message flow easily.

As you preach, observe your congregation. You can tell when what you are saying is being heard. There is a certain kind of silence to that "soaking" absorption that we are looking for: shoulders are still, feet do not fidget, eye contact (in western cultures) is focused. Train yourself to be attentive to your listeners' response. Grow in self-awareness and self-evaluation: where was the butter too hard? What did not spread? Where could I deliver this homily more smoothly? Where could I make the words flow more easily? How can I nurture spiritual depth in my people? We are not looking to dumb the Gospel message down. We offer rich theological fare in a soft and spreadable form. By being attentive to the needs of the pew, we are not "selling out" the Gospel. We are caring for our people. We do not want to be saved by ourselves; we want the "others" to come along into this vibrant life with which we have been gifted. We pray that the grace of the Holy Spirit will "soak in."

So keep up your spirits; maintain the blessed assurance that the Holy Spirit wants to speak through you. Here are few practical takeaways for churning smoother, richer butter:

1. Speak slowly. Allow your listeners the time to mentally process what you are saying.
2. After your key points, stop. Use dramatic pause effectively. Allow the Holy Spirit time to "settle." Give them cues within the homily itself—"listen!" If you have prayerfully prepared, you will have important things to say.
3. Speak from your depths. Your prayer life matters. "The greater or lesser degree of the holiness of the minister has a real effect on the proclamation of the word."[9]
4. Vary your tone: be loving, joyful, passionate, enthusiastic, on fire. There is little more deadening to listening than a monotone. Let the Spirit energize you.
5. When you are convinced about your message, you will also be convincing. One student said, "When a preacher 'connects,' they are interested in who you are, and they want to convey an

9. John Paul II, Postsynodal Apostolic Exhortation *Pastores dabo vobis* (25 March 1992), 25.

important message."[10] Leave people glad that they are Christians. Faith is contagious!

6. One editing clue is to read your manuscript aloud really fast; where your tongue gets stuck or you stumble, go back and simplify your words or your sentence structure. You may not preach from this manuscript (it may be a preliminary step in creating an outline or an extemporaneous homily), but running through it at lightning speed will expose any hard chunks which are not readily spreadable.
7. Describe *what* you are about to say in one sentence. If you cannot, clarify your focus. What is the *one* thing that you really want to have "land"?[11] Simple messages stick in the listener's head.
8. Describe to someone *how* you are going to present your one focus in three sentences, as in "this goes to this . . . goes to this . . . goes to this . . . " If you cannot describe the path that your people will follow, refine your structure or form.[12] Clarity of reception is your goal.

## Growing in Grace

Augustine says that our own hearts are restless for God.[13] As ministers of the Gospel, we also have a restless heart for our people to encounter God, so we want to continue to grow in our homiletic abilities. None of us will become perfect in this craft:

> We are not asked to be flawless, but to keep growing and wanting to grow as we advance along the path of the Gospel; our arms must never grow slack. What is essential is that the preacher be certain that God loves him, that Jesus Christ has saved him and that his love has always the last word . . . But by acknowledging his poverty and desiring to grow in his commitment, he will always be able to abandon himself to Christ, saying in the words of Peter: "I have no silver and gold, but what I have I give you" (Acts 3:6). The Lord wants to make use of us as living, free and creative beings who let his word enter their own hearts before then passing it on to others. Christ's message must truly penetrate and possess the preacher,

10. Bellinger, *Connecting Pulpit and Pew*, 100.

11. See Fr. Ed Griswold, "Focus and Function: Kindling the Fire," chapter 11 in this book, and https://www.youtube.com/watch?v=fkq3_ZdL1Fw&feature=youtube.

12. See Rev. Dr. Richard Eslinger, "Plotting a Path to Follow," chapter 9 in this book and https://www.youtube.com/watch?v=9RIjaWZiXdQ&feature=youtu.beyoutube.

13. Augustine of Hippo, *Confessions* 1.1.

> not just intellectually but in his entire being. The Holy Spirit, who inspired the word, "today, just as at the beginning of the Church, acts in every evangelizer who allows himself to be possessed and led by him. The Holy Spirit places on his lips the words which he could not find by himself."[14]

If you and I believe that the Gospel of Jesus Christ helps people to flourish, then the homily is an act of love. We want to keep growing, for preaching is a pastoral practice—there is One who wants us all to thrive. All of the practical elements that comprise effectiveness come together to create good butter that readily soaks in to warm toast. And the Holy Spirit? As we preach, we name the One who gives power to our lives, our preaching, and our ministries. The Holy Spirit is not some amorphous fluffy feeling, but God—the powerful living God—with us, here, now. If we forget the action of the Holy Spirit, we have forgotten the Christian message. The Holy Spirit has not forgotten us. We are not orphans. Just as we wait in joyful hope for the coming of our Savior Jesus Christ, we also live in expectation that the Spirit of Pentecost will empower our preaching. Let us pray for a renewal of our youthful confidence in the power of the Holy Spirit to work through preaching. You who bring us from darkness to light, from death to life, from despair to hope, come! We need you, Lord our God. You who effect effectiveness, come!

*St. Augustine's Prayer to the Holy Spirit*

*Breathe in me, O Holy Spirit,*
*that my thoughts may all be holy.*
*Act in me, O Holy Spirit, that my work, too, may be holy.*
*Draw my heart, O Holy Spirit, that I love but what is holy.*
*Strengthen me, O Holy Spirit, to defend all that is holy.*
*Guard me, then, O Holy Spirit, that I always may be holy.*
*Amen.*

14. EG, 151.

CHAPTER 15

# If You're Not Real, I'm Not Coming

Peter McCormick, CSC

## Introduction

Preaching to young people requires more than faith. While the Good News of the Gospel has not changed, the vehicle has been modified. For students to listen and take to heart the message, preachers must establish an understanding of what young people are going through, demonstrate one's own authentic living of the Gospel, and offer homilies that express some personal vulnerability.

## Defining of Terms

Throughout this chapter, "young people" should be taken to mean college-age undergraduates (eighteen to twenty-two) and early professionals in the work place. It assumes that the overwhelming portion of this population is single and still working to find their place in society at large.

There has been much written about young people as more and more millennials not only enter the work force, but begin to assume leadership responsibilities as well. To clarify my assumptions, I'll list several tendencies that I have noticed over the years.

## Strive for Perfection

The quest for perfection can take multiple forms: academic, social, athletic, etc. This quest for perfection is often rooted in something that is all too common in people across the generations: comparison. While people throughout the ages have engaged in all types of comparison—just think of what happened to Joseph when his brothers became tired of the perceived affection that his father had for him in Genesis 37—this generation has a new tool at their disposal. You guessed it, social media. This web of interconnected devices, which provides live updates, filter settings, and the capacity to package life in a way that is entirely tailored to one's own personal brand, has a downside.

Said simply, social media often leaves those receiving the content to conclude that everyone else's life is a highlight reel and theirs is a blooper reel. Why? Because any person who is honest with themselves knows that life is far from the perfect reality presented on a four-inch screen. Yet, when people look around for assurances that others are challenged by this same aspect of our humanity, all they see is perfection.

## Overly Committed

Building off the quest for perfection is the need to remain constantly busy. With a belief that one's dignity is enough to merit love and respect, this generation of young people seeks approval from being involved. The praise that comes from taking fifteen credits, serving as the senior class president, vice president of the chess club or secretary of the American studies club provides not only status, but a sense of worth. What's even better? Be engaged in all four at the same time. Such a blinding array of responsibilities affords the overly committed person to talk about how busy they are, but don't be fooled. Busy is really code for the following, "I'm a passionate person, with many talents, but uncertain of what I bring to this world. So, I will be engaged in as much as possible to prove to others and to myself that my existence matters." As a result, young people travel the journey of life with increased amounts of stress and anxiety. They report feeling alone, isolated, and overly committed.

## Religion Equals Good

"Remember to say please and thank you." That's what my mom would say to me almost every time I got out of the car on my way to a friend's house. It was a reminder then, as it is now, that civility and respect matter. This generation of young people often see religious training as an opportunity to learn the same lessons. Noted University of Notre Dame professor and sociologist Christian Smith wrote the following in his book *Souls in Transition*:

> The best thing about religion is that it helps people to be good, to make good choices, to behave well. For this reason, it can be a good thing for children to be raised in a religious congregation, since they need to be taught the basics of morality. At the same time, once youth learn what it means to be good, there is no real need to continue being involved in a religious congregation. The time comes to "graduate" and move on.[1]

1. Christian Smith, *Souls in Transition* (Oxford University Press, 2009).

## Multiple Opportunities for Community

The movie *Concussion*,[2] starring Will Smith, which chronicles the challenges NFL players face in the context of a high impact sport, offers the following quote: "The NFL owns a day of the week. The same day the Church used to own. Now it's theirs." In many ways, this quote sums up the reality we face as preachers. There was a time in an earlier generation when the faithful not only came to be spiritually fed, but also to be a part of a community. The spiritual and communal served to deepen people's ties to the parish. Today, there are multiple opportunities for forming such communities, typically around specific areas of interest. There is no longer the perceived need to deal with people that may be different. Couple the splintering of community with the fact that less and less young people have a habit of attending Mass every Sunday and the divide only gets wider. The connection back to parish communities gets less and less.

## Cautious about Institutions

Young people today have looked on as major institutions have failed. From the sexual abuse crisis to the 2008 market collapse, institutions have seemingly proven themselves to be fraught with infighting, quests for power, and abuse of that very same power when attained. While we as preachers hope to communicate the integrity of the message, which Christ intended when he said to St. Peter "and upon this rock I shall build my Church" (Matthew 16:18), young people today feel that it's easier to go their own way: to be spiritual, but not religious. There is seemingly far less baggage that way.

## Baptized, but Searching

The Catholic author Sherry Weddell is fond of saying, "never accept a label in place of a story."[3] How many times have we asked a young person "Are you baptized?" Upon answering yes, we draw a series of conclusions about what they believe, what they know, and how they live. Yet, the fact of the matter is that this could not be farther from the truth. This generation of young people, many of which have been baptized, have grown up in an era where Mass attendance was balanced with other commitments to extracurricular activities that are far too numerous to name here. It is more likely that when

---

2. *Concussion*, directed by Peter Landesman (2015).

3. Sherry Weddell, *Forming Intentional Disciples: The Path to Knowing and Following Jesus*. (Huntington, IN: Our Sunday Visitor, 2012).

a young person answers affirmatively to having been baptized, it should be taken to mean he or she is baptized, has some basic understanding of Christianity, but is still very much on the fence about how faith fits into the wider narrative of life.

## What Is Real?

"If You're Not Real, I'm Not Coming." It's a fun title for a preaching conference: a pithy assessment of a far wider reality for preachers today. I hardly believe that preachers are entering the pulpit with the intent of being dishonest, unreal, or fraudulent. So, what is real? Before proceeding, I have one editor's note to offer. The collective understanding of "real" will not be from the vantage point of the preacher; rather, from those that we wish to reach. What is real?

## We Want Relationships

When you read this subheading, I hope you responded with "So, what else is new?" It is a common human desire to be in relationship, but how do we as preachers begin to foster that connection? First, accept that the era of "Father knows best" has come to an end. It's dead! At best, young people will initially view those who represent the Church as individuals who have insights about a life well lived. Here is the good news. Young people have a complete openness to relationships with authority, but we first must earn their trust. They want to encounter real people, not someone who stands from the sanctuary and utters doctrinal vagaries. Young people today value mentorship from individuals that they believe have lived life, done so authentically, and embrace their own failings. Said differently, they want to know you as a person first.

With so much written about young people today, the temptation can be to assume that we know their life, but that would be a mistake. Rather, the surest way to fostering a human connection is through our own humanity. In prayer, speech and certainly preaching, the more in touch we are with what makes us human, the better the message will resonate in the ears of those young people listening.

## Challenge Me, Please!

It was a chance encounter. I was walking back from Mass late one Sunday evening in the spring semester when I saw a group of four students huddled together chatting. As I passed by and said hello, one of the students said, "Fr. Pete, we were just talking about you." Curious, I simply asked "About what?" They then went on to talk about their desire to be challenged. Specifically, they wanted to move beyond the chapel to literally go and announce the Gospel of the Lord. Yet, the path seemed unclear. It felt more like people were being sent back to the normalcy of their daily lives. They wanted more.

Young people today have a delightful sensitivity for justice and those on the margins. They see a world so desperately in need of love and mercy, but grow frustrated when communities of faith are inactive and not working toward a solution. It's imperative that we understand that young people will not get angry at the Church when they perceive inaction. Rather, they'll simply leave in the form of a silent migration actively seeking out other groups that are engaged in building a more just society.

## What Did Jesus Do?

A question to ponder. When preaching, how often do you speak about the Church and how often do you speak about Jesus? How often do you say things like "The Church asks us to abstain from meat on Fridays" or "The Church believes in the inherent dignity of the human person"? We can all too often slip into speaking about the institutional reality of our faith lives. While I cannot speak for all generations, I can tell you with certainty that the phrase "the Church" does not inspire young people. It feels removed from one's lived experience of life. Now this does not mean that you should never preach about the Church and her teachings, but we do have an opportunity here. Start with Jesus.

I often think about the call of the Apostles. What made Jesus so compelling that Peter and his brother Andrew left their nets to follow the Lord? Was the invitation, "Come after me, and I will make you fishers of men" (Matthew 4:19), that persuasive? If so, why? If Jesus could invite grown men with adult commitments to leave everything and follow him, why not explore the attractiveness of that offer to its depths through our preaching? We have an opportunity to frame everything that the Church does through the lens of responding to Jesus' offer to come after him.

Let's look at the Church's firm stance on human dignity as an example. Instead of repeating over and over that the Church affirms the dignity of the human person, what would it look like to draw from the examples of what we encounter from Jesus in the Gospels? Perhaps you might consider using the parable of the good Samaritan from Luke. Conversely, you may work to unpack John's recounting of the Samaritan woman at the well. Both instances provide a rich narrative where those listening are afforded the opportunity to enter themselves into the scene. In doing so, one's imagination is engaged in a new way, people begin to see as Jesus sees, to encounter love and respect. From that firm foundation, young people are inspired as the early followers of Jesus were inspired. Come after me.

## The Fine Print

There is a curious element to all advertising in the United States. The attractive aspects of the product, which a company wants us to know, are presented in large font with splashy photos to help make the intended association. However, invariably down below are a series of lines in barely legible print, which have far greater influence over whether the customer will be able to possess the item of their desire. If we had such an ad for preachers the photo would be of a congregation rapt with attention, a preacher firmly ensconced in the pulpit, with a Bible in hand and a word of hope flowing forth. But down below in the fine print it would read "Homiletic preparation and a willingness to be courageous are critical components for a preacher dedicated to proclaiming the word of God."

## What Holds Me Back and Perhaps You As Well?

The main thing is to keep the main thing the main thing. It's a line that I repeat to myself when trying to remain focused on the essential and non-essential parts of life. If your experience is anything like mine, preaching is not the only responsibility you have. While the list can be varied, we end up balancing our days with a docket of pastoral conversations, planning sessions, supervision, weekly emergencies, and the desire to have some sense of an integrated personal life. So, when do you find time to prepare your homily?

A homiletics professor at Notre Dame once said, "Homiletic preparation is much more like a crockpot than a microwave." Yet, often I find myself in the final hours before Mass working on a homily that needs to be done no matter how imperfect it presently stands. Ding! In those moments, I ask myself the same questions.

- How did prayer have the chance to influence this homily?
- How am I able to reflect upon the subtleties of Jesus' call to discipleship with sophistication, if I'm organizing my homily in the last minute?

The good news is that the Holy Spirit needs very little time and space to work. The bad news is that repeated failure to prepare in a meaningful way leads most often to a repetition of themes that rarely go beyond surface deep.

## Finding the Courage

Offering a challenging homily is difficult. Time is spent choosing each word, laboring over turns of phrase and hoping to blend the right portion of pastoral care with cultural critique. Invariably, someone will be offended and either make that offense known after Mass or in a crafted email designed for maximum impact.

There are times when I actively choose to back down from difficult subject matter. Why? It requires more time than I typically have available, the risk of offense, and the complexity of the topic. As a result, I end up preaching on topics that are safer and routine. The Scriptures address such behavior, "I know your works; I know that you are neither cold nor hot. I wish you were cold or hot. So, because you are lukewarm, neither cold or hot, I will spit you out of my mouth" (Revelation 3:15–16).

Courageous preaching will come with some form of the cross. However, we have not been left abandoned! The following reflection from the *Constitutions of the Congregation of Holy Cross* offers a perspective of hope that comes from embracing the cross encountered as a disciple of Jesus Christ.

> But we do not grieve as men without hope, for Christ the Lord has risen to die no more. He has taken us into the mystery and the grace of this life that springs up from death. If we, like Him, encounter and accept suffering in our discipleship, we will move without awkwardness among others who suffer. We must be men with hope to bring. There is no failure the Lord's love cannot reverse, no humiliation He cannot exchange for blessing, no anger He cannot dissolve, no routine He cannot transfigure. All is swallowed up in victory. He has nothing but gifts to offer. It remains only for us to find how even the cross can be borne as a gift.[4]

## Preaching: The Heart of the Matter

St. Anselm summarized humanity's deepest longing to know and understand God as "faith seeking understanding."[5] Said differently, what we are drawn to in faith, can be sought after and more wholly understood. Gratitude for the generosity of God draws humanity more deeply into the mystery of love that plays out in the sacred texts of the Gospels. With any number of options to choose from, perhaps the most iconic example is John 3:16, "For God so loved the world that he gave his only Son, so that everyone who believes in him might

4. *Constitutions of the Congregation of Holy Cross*, para. 118.
5. St. Anselm, *Proslogion* (11th century).

not perish but might have eternal life." God, who always acts as the first mover, demonstrates his love for humanity by sending his Son. Jesus further demonstrates the depth of that love through his life, death and Resurrection. Each gesture is an act of self-gift, one that models for all humanity how far God will go to remind us of our inherent dignity and wider vocational calling. Warning: If you preach in this style to young people, you will fail.

## Lenses

Faith seeking understanding is a powerful reminder of our call as Christians. However, young people are not asking the same types of questions St. Anselm once asked. St. Anselm longed to go deeper, to understand more fully the mystery of faith. The questions young people are asking today look and feel very different. One such question stands out above the rest: "What is the meaning of my life?"

In the world that makes few claims about truth, young people today end up drifting in and out of meaning making. They look for sources of wisdom throughout the created world as opposed to primarily coming to the Church. Interiorly, they frequently wonder if they are making the right decisions: choosing the correct major, marrying the right person, etc., as they drift along looking for meaning.

From the perspective of a preacher, we often feel that the greatest need they have is catechesis. If they only knew more! We hope to get them caught up, back on the track of faith seeking understanding. For a portion of young people the catechetical approach will work, but only a portion.

How do we get young people to faith seeking understanding? Straight through their own experience. When writing a homily, refrain from using overly theological language; rather, draw young people into the very mystery of their own lives. Repeatedly preach on themes such as these: vulnerability, empathy, suffering, beauty, acceptance, forgiveness, and gratitude. While belief in God may seem like a choice to young people, each person encounters these elemental realities of a life lived. The challenge is to begin helping young people to detect an element of the divine within their own experience.

Many years ago, I was speaking with a colleague who said that he thought the FedEx logo may be the most creative logo he had ever seen because of the arrow placed between the E and the X. I had no idea what he was talking about, until I looked at the logo once again. With a second look and a new lens from which to gaze, I saw a distinctive arrow neatly tucked between the E and the X. Now that's all I look for! As preachers, we have the chance to draw people into their own lived experiences and allow them to see what had been there all along, but not observed.

Admittedly, such an approach will feel like a half step back from time to time. Yet, giving young people an understanding of how to use their experience as a mediator for God, will go a long way towards deepening their faith and guiding their understanding.

## Practices

In fifth grade I discovered one of the great joys of my life: basketball. I love everything about the sport from the fluidity of the game to the way your sneakers sound when striking the court. In the early stages of what would amount to a great love affair with the game of hoops, I needed to learn how to dribble without looking at the ball. To help develop this skill my coach recommended dribble goggles. Like any other goggles, they are designed to be worn over your eyes with one considerable difference. The entire bottom half of the goggles have a one-inch ledge protruding forth, which prevents the wearer from looking down with ease. Upon purchasing the goggles, I was told to wear them for thirty minutes a day and dribble with my right and left hand; I was not to work on any fancy dribbling (between the legs or behind the back). Just the basics.

We have an opportunity to provide young people with tangible ways to practice living a life of faith in our preaching. Pope Francis serves as a wonderful example of what it means to embody the joy of following Jesus when he writes:

> Jesus' whole life, his way of dealing with the poor, his actions, his integrity, his simple daily acts of generosity, and finally his complete self-giving, is precious and reveals the mystery of his divine life. Whenever we encounter this anew, we become convinced that it is exactly what others need, even though they may not recognize it: "What therefore you worship as unknown, this I proclaim to you" (Acts 17:23).[6]

Once a young person has begun to encounter the divine through their own experience they can't help but be drawn in more fully, to seek greater understanding, and order their life appropriately. As a fifth grader I walked around in dribble googles for thirty minutes a day for the better part of the summer because I loved the game of basketball. Imagine if we help our young people to realize that they are loved by God and invited to have a relationship with him. That relationship will then set them forth to feed the hungry,

6. Pope Francis, *Evangelii gaudium* (2014), 265.

clothe the naked, bury the dead, forgive offenses, and console the afflicted. Just to name a few.

## Evangelization (Confirmation)

The word evangelization should conjure in our minds some of the great biblical figures who boldly proclaimed the faith. One such example is St. John the Baptist. With clothing made from camel's hair and an appetite for wild locusts and honey, John the Baptist drew people away from the comforts of their lives to contemplate the truth of who they were. There was need of reform, there was an opportunity for repentance, and they should begin to look for another who will baptize with the Holy Spirit. Today, the same word often invokes in our minds the concept of a TV evangelist. With their hair glistening from too much styling product and their cheekbones overly rosy from too much makeup, they too have a message: salvation can be yours for just $49.99.

As the theological one-liner goes, the Church is not a mausoleum for saints, but a field hospital for sinners. Young people today need to know that they are loved and accepted for who they are. So often those we seek to reach are trapped in the politics of the day, which often leads to inaction or worse, movement away from faith. To effectively preach the Gospel we must see as our primary role to evangelize with the same fervor witnessed in John the Baptist, Mother Theresa, Augustine, Juan Diego, and Thérèse of Lisieux.

> We cannot forget that evangelization is first and foremost about preaching the Gospel to those who do not know Jesus Christ or who have always rejected him. Many of them are quietly seeking God, led by a yearning to see his face, even in countries of ancient Christian tradition. All of them have a right to receive the Gospel.[7]

Through words, actions, and deeds we hope to demonstrate the unexpected beauty of what the Church professes. It is through beauty that we will attract, it is through attraction that we will teach, and it is through learning that their hearts will be set on fire.

## Conclusion

It has been my hope to emphasize that what young people today are looking for is *not* an individual who knows the way, but rather a fellow traveler who has been drawn in by Jesus' invitation to come after him and desires to share that vocation authentically.

---

7. Ibid., 15.

■ CHAPTER 16

# If Our Hearts Are on Fire, What Are Our Bodies Doing?

Suzanne Nawrocki

My hope is to examine how we can bring our people (and ourselves) to a closer encounter with God. Toward that end, this chapter will discuss the concept of embodied communication, with the hope that those entrusted with the charism of preaching will have a better understanding of how our bodies are integrally involved in the preaching event. As a result of full integration of our word and our body, our congregants will not merely observe and understand us, but be engaged enough to experience and respond to the Word.

Augustine, who is credited with writing the first homiletic textbook in the fourth century, argued for the use of the secular discipline of rhetoric in preaching. When challenged by his contemporaries, he asked: "Why should we be disadvantaged in proclaiming truth?"[1] Today, preachers can draw from social science to preach as effectively as possible. We communicate truth through the lens of faith—using all available tools—in a way that makes what we say cogent, logical, and persuasive. Embodied communication is one of those tools.

## Overview

This chapter will give general background information about the following embodied communication categories: physical display, proxemics, oculesics, and paralanguage. I will explore the benefits of using the social sciences applied to these categories for preachers and the receivers. The term "receiver" is used with great intentionality, and helps remind us that congregants are not just listeners; they are also observers. Next, comes a deeper look at another important part of embodied communication: gestures. The use of gestures can be one of the most convincing aspects of embodied communication.

1. Lucy Hogan, "Rhetorical Approaches to Preaching," in *A Handbook for Catholic Preaching*, ed. Edward Foley (Collegeville, MN: Liturgical Press, 2016), 200.

References of clips and pictures will further demonstrate the theory I am explaining.

I will take a quick look at four categories of embodied communication, and then a longer look at the category of gesture. All categories of embodied communication are useful for our particular task: to further effective preaching.

## Types of Embodied Communication

### Physical Display

Physical display is what our body is saying even before our lips are moving. Display goes far beyond one's healthy vigilance on grooming—although that is important, of course. What is your demeanor as you walk down the aisle in your vestments? What can a parishioner see as they observe you in the presider chair as the deacon is preaching? Are you drumming the arms in your chair? Are you looking around? Your body language is available for all to see. "Unlike verbal expression, physical display is always available and inviting judgment, since a characteristic of embodied communication is that most of the senses (visual, auditory, tactile, and olfactory) are always at work in a social setting."[2]

Physical display plays a key role in first impressions, and first impressions matter. Consider the primacy-recency effect. This theory suggests that the initial information collected is given greater weight than future information. If more information is collected, resistance ensues if it contradicts the first impressions.[3]

Alternatively, consider the concept of congruence, which occurs when your body and words align. Incongruence is when they don't, and incongruence can hobble preaching. Saying "Jesus forgives" or "Jesus loves you" with an angry intonation and forceful, hostile body movements is not convincing. Or again, a preacher will not ring authentic if quoting "do not fear, for I am with you" (Isaiah 41:10) while wearing a deer-in-the-headlights look.

An interesting fact about incongruence: When body and word do not align, research shows the vote of confidence goes to communication from the body. Anecdotally, we probably know that it is harder to deceive with one's body

2. M. Patterson, "Nonverbal Communication," in *Encyclopedia of Human Behavior,* ed. Vilayanur S. Ramachandran, 2nd ed. (Atlanta: Academic Press, 2012), 731. Also available in Suzanne Scheiber Nawrocki, "Every Body Helps the Preacher: The Impact of Embodied Communication" (thesis, Aquinas Institute of Theology, St. Louis, MO, 2013), 74.

3. Joseph A. DeVito, *The Interpersonal Communication Book,* 10th ed. (Boston: Pearson, 2004), 99.

than with one's words, and we have all heard someone saying, "you can be read like a book." Nonverbals are "less subject to control and therefore presumably more honest."[4]

We do not need to simply rely on anecdotal evidence, however. Mehrabian's studies from the 1960s have shown that a message can be misconstrued if the physical display and the words are not in harmony with each other.[5] Arguments continue over the methodologies to use in investigating this phenomenon, but the conclusion remains unchallenged. For effective preaching, our bodies and our words must be congruent.

## Proxemics

Proxemics is the category of embodied communication that deals with physical distance between speaker and audience—or for our purposes, the distance between preacher and congregation. What social science has determined is this: the closer you are to receivers, the more they can feel that they know you. The more they know you, the more they trust you. And the more they trust you, the more persuasive you can be.[6]

The *General Instruction of the Roman Missal* (2002) gives some latitude about where one can preach: the ambo, the presider's chair, or when appropriate, another suitable location (n. 136). Implicit in this latitude is a prodding to consider not only what to say, but the place from which preaching is most effective.[7]

Movement closer to the congregation should be done with intentionality. Once in place, further movement can be beneficial as you seek to include different areas of space, but that movement should be related to content. Movement grabs attention, so meandering unanchored to content or form can be distracting. Plan your movement with your thoughts. There will be more benefits to be gained from bodily movement and gesture presented below.

---

4. Geoffrey Beattie, *Visible Thought: The New Psychology of Body Language* (London: Routledge, 2003), 22.

5. Carmine Gallo, *Talk like TED: The 9 Public-Speaking Secrets of the World's Top Minds* (New York: St. Martin's Press, 2015).

6. Researchers have identified twenty-two different categories of embodied communication that influence persuasiveness. To learn which categories are most effective, see Judee K. Burgoon, Thomas Birk, and Michael Pfau, "Nonverbal Behavior, Persuasion and Credibility," *Human Communication Research* 17, no. 1:140–169, 1990.

7. Edward Foley, Nathan Mitchell, and Joanne Pierce, eds., *A Commentary on the General Instruction of the Roman Missal* (Collegeville, MN: Pueblo Books, 2007), 243.

## Oculesics

Oculesics is the category of embodied communication that deals with eye contact. In the American culture—but not all cultures—directly looking at people is a sign of honesty and forthrightness, which are key attributes of effective preachers. Making eye contact with as many receivers as you can, while avoiding looking over their heads or at the floor, is important. Moving your gaze around the space might be harder for introverts than extroverts—and might take practice—but it will help you connect with those to whom you are speaking, and help them to trust your message.

As you look out at your congregants while you are preaching, you might think that they are frequently not paying attention. That is not necessarily so. Receivers look away from speakers twice as often as speakers look away from receivers.[8] Receivers—your congregants—could just be taking a momentary break, or framing their internal response before they return attention back to the speaker. Preachers, however, are not allowed such luxury.

Of course, looking away can be an intentional technique, for emphasis or for character reenactment. An example of the latter will help. John 9:6 is the miracle story of Jesus curing the blind man with spittle. While preaching, your gaze could change from looking out, to looking at your hands as your hands are in the act of curing the man's blindness. Your gaze will direct others. "Depictions reference what is known, but not necessarily what is seen or present at the moment. Such gestures are highly enmeshed with the context of the setting and situation. Minimal configuration of hand movements can easily be translated into something known through a shared understanding of the world around us—our common ground."[9]

## Paralanguage

Paralanguage is everything but the word itself—how you say something, not what you say. Paralanguage comprises pitch, tone, tempo, amplitude, fluency, voice quality, and more. Two sub-categories of paralanguage stand out in their importance for preaching.

Chronemics is a category that focuses on how we perceive, structure, and use time as communication.[10] Studies reveal that 150 to 160 words per minute is the ideal rate of speech for audio books. Because this statistic is

---

8. Michael Argyle, "Non-Verbal Communication in Human Social Interaction," in *Non-Verbal Communication*, ed. Robert Hinde (London: Cambridge University Press, 1972), 250.

9. Nawrocki, "Every Body Helps the Preacher," 53–54.

10. Judee K. Burgoon, Laura Guerrero, and Kory Floyd, *Nonverbal Communication* (London: Routledge, 2010), 186.

based on audio listening, we can assume that in a preaching context, the pace of words per minute can be increased slightly, since your receivers have the additional advantage of cues from your body.[11]

How fast do you talk when you are preaching? Speed might be conditioned by attempting to abide by Pope Francis' suggestions to be "brief" and "measured in length" (*Evangelii gaudium*, 138). If you feel the compulsion to speak quickly to keep the balance and rhythm of the liturgy that Francis suggests, consider instead shortening the content and slowing the delivery.

Timing can also be affected by the tone required of a topic, navigating a cumbersome accent, or struggles with second language issues. In addition, if you are a manuscript preacher, you will likely deliver a faster-paced homily since your words are predetermined. Non-manuscript preachers, even well-prepared ones, will be selecting words from their large lexicon bank, and thus likely be slower.

Timing of delivery can be used to garner attention. If you are windmilling your arms, a still countenance will call attention to yourself. The converse is true: if you are deadpan in your delivery, the preacher who suddenly becomes animated will draw attention to themselves. Knowing your normal pacing is best understood by watching videos of yourself; however, that input alone is not enough information to determine if you need to adjust your deportment. Do not be reticent to ask for feedback.

Vocalics are the acoustical properties of the voice. Much of this is determined by biology, but not all. Some vocalic characteristics are culturally determined. Accents are readily learned from those you interact with as you learn to speak. Experts also note that vocal properties are efficient at relaying the state of the mind. Think about an excited voice, high and loud; or a dominant voice, low and loud.[12]

## Gestures: An Important Type of Embodied Communication

The big impact of gestures on successful preaching demands examination of this aspect of embodied communication in a bit more detail.

---

11. Carmine Gallo, *Talk like TED: The 9 Public-Speaking Secrets of the World's Top Minds* (New York: St. Martin's Press, 2015), 82. Also, watch lawyer Bryan Stevenson perform a TED Talk on YouTube: https://www.youtube.com/watch?v=c2tOp7OxyQ8. Gallo suggests Stevenson is the "Goldilocks" model for speaking tempo (82–83). What do you think of the tempo?

12. Burgoon, et al., *Nonverbal Communication,* 72.

## Gestures Are Synchronous with Speech

Words and gestures are synchronous—together they "co-express" what the speaker is trying to say. "Gestures can be deliberate or unconscious modalities of expression, but are almost always synchronous with the part of speech in which they are co-expressive. This synchrony reflects the mind simultaneously performing dual tasks. The co-expressive nature of gesture/speech is usually not redundant, but rather overlapping—additional information is provided using a specific modality of expression.[13] Gestures are valuable assets for adding substantive information to the speech act."[14]

Though most likely unaware of it, receivers too are affected by this synchrony: they hear the words and see the gestures as one act of communication. "It is not clearly understood how the integrated system of gesture and speech during spontaneous expression occurs. However, despite the lack of a complete explanation, the integrity of the synchrony is not disputed. The integration is so complete that when, after a short delay, receivers are asked to identify which piece of information was generated from which modality, they cannot."[15]

Realizing that words and gestures are synchronous can help preachers locked in less successful communication habits. Change is the key to regaining the attention of your regular listeners. If you usually windmill your arms, a still body will call new attention to your words. The converse is also true: If you are usually still in your delivery, becoming animated will draw new attention to your words. Knowing your normal approach to gesture is best understood by watching videos of yourself.

## Gestures and Ideas, Emotions, and Images

As Pope Francis has written:

> An attractive image makes the message seem familiar, close to home, practical and related to everyday life. A successful image can make people savor the message, awaken a desire and move the will toward the Gospel. A good homily, an old teacher once told me, should have an idea, a sentiment, an image. (*Evangelii gaudium*, 157)

---

13. David McNeill, *Gesture and Thought* (Chicago: University of Chicago Press, 2005), 22–24.

14. Quoted in Nawrocki, 43.

15. David McNeill and Susan Duncan, "Growth Points in Thinking-for-Speaking," in *Language and Gesture*, ed. David McNeill (Cambridge: Cambridge University Press, 2000), 141–161. Quoted in Nawrocki, "Every Body Helps the Preacher," 43.

In addition to our words, how can our gestures help preachers communicate in the three modalities Pope Francis suggests: an idea (or information), an emotion, and an image?

For example, envision preaching these three sentences with great emotion: "As Jesus stood on the hillside, and looked out at the bustling city, what did he see? He saw the segregation, the divisiveness, the hostility, the anger. He wept."

An idea or piece of information can be communicated through gesture. When you say that Jesus "looked out," for instance, you could literally look out. With a turn of your head and your gaze, you could create virtual space that correlates with your words. Your gestures help your receivers see the city that Jesus sees.

An emotion, the second suggestion on Pope Francis' "must-have" list, can also be heightened through gesture. Expressive gestures, gestures that deliver emotion are the most telling on the face. Faces are unique but culturally and familiarly influenced. Receivers do not just observe faces, they observe posture. In our example, a preacher can stand erect as Jesus looks out over the hillside, and then shrink back and lower and slow the voice when Jesus weeps. The gesture pulls the listener into the sorrow. It is not just the facial expressions; postures too can emote.

Image is the third component suggested by Francis. When preached well a vivid image of Jesus can emerge from the preaching. One that starts with a tall Jesus looking out—the previous pericope was the triumphant entry in the city—and then a Jesus diminished by what he sees.

## Gestures as Regulators

Gestures used to delineate key points are helpful to receivers—much like bullet points in a memo. For example, the key points can be counted on fingers. When exercising recall, receivers might not stop until they too can reach the appointed number. The gesture is obviously not the important part of the content but simply regulates the delivery.

Gestures can help delineate the different characters in a story. A simple move to one side of the ambo or the other can imply a change in character. Movement does not have to be large to be effective. Movement can be as subtle as shifting your weight from one foot to the other.

A gesture can be a simple open flat hand as if to offer an idea. Or, an open flat hand can represent that you have an empty set. Imagine using that gesture when saying, "I cannot explain the acute suffering that is devastating us today."

A common gesture of Pope Francis is one that indicates precision: the index finger and thumb pressing together to make an "o."

Simply changing the movement of this "o" gesture changes its meaning. When the "o" gesture moves up and down, sometimes both hands together, it often insinuates that you are quoting someone precisely. Quoting someone is also executed with the second and third bent fingers drawing quotation marks. Changing the finger configuration can also change its meaning. For example, if the "o" fingers release, the meaning again changes to signify letting go or an ending.

## Gestures Help with Memory

Experimentation has shown that gesturing while speaking increased memory on the part of the listeners. The increased memory might be explained by the additional storing of motor coding. If paired speech and gesture encodes speech more deeply in memory than speech alone, it is easy to ascertain how this might be helpful in preaching preparation.[16]

When practicing, preachers can delineate their text into key points to prompt memory upon delivery and sharpen their thoughts. Thoughtful planning and practicing using gestures, like regulators, will help with memory during delivery. This is a simple tip for preachers who want to successfully transition from being a manuscript preacher to those preaching without a script.

## Gestures as Beats

Often gestures are used in tandem with syllables or words for emphasis. Beat gestures are repetitive and can add a sense of unity and intensity to what you are saying. When the topic changes, the beat is dropped. Beat gestures can be used alone or combined, for example, with the "o" gesture. They can be performed with more than just your hands. An example will be helpful. In Mark 8, Jesus becomes aware the disciples are muttering: they have forgotten to bring the bread. Jesus is exasperated that the disciples still do not understand despite having witnessed previous miracle feedings. Imagine using beat gestures as Jesus rapidly fire questions:

> Do you still not perceive or understand?
> Are your hearts hardened?
> Do you have eyes, and fail to see?

---

16. Susan Cook, Terina Kuan YiYip, and Susan Goldin-Meadow, "Gesturing Makes Memories Last," *Journal of Memory and Language* 63, no. 4, 2010:465–476. Quoted in Nawrocki, 67–68.

Do you have ears, and fail to hear?
And, do you not remember? (Mark 8:17b–18)

Adding beat gestures to your proclamation of this Marcan text will add emphasis to reveal Jesus' frustration. Jesus' disciples still do not understand!

### Gestures as Emblems

Emblems are predetermined gestures that have established meaning. They can substitute for verbal language. If you change the configuration, you abolish the meaning. Because emblems are tied with language, different cultures can have different meaning for the same emblem.

Emblems are often extremely coveted signs of esprit de corps. Since preachers prepare with the newspaper in one hand and the Bible in the other, using an emblem that reflects what is current in pop culture is a quick way to connect yourself to your receivers. For example, if you are preaching in a town that had an impending sports event, working an emblem into the text can be an easy way to ingratiate yourself to the receivers. You too are rooting for the team! The "thumbs up" gesture can be such an emblem.

### Gestures as Noise Factors

Not all gestures are helpful. Constant nervous throat clearing, hair adjusting, or pushing up your glasses are annoying and distracting gestures—and most likely nonsynchronous with your words. In our germ-conscious culture, some might object to gestures that could suggest contamination, such as touching your face or coughing in your hands.

## Conclusion

This was a quick, wild ride through the fascinating world of embodied communication. We do not want parishioners just to watch and wonder, but to engage and to experience God's endless love permeating their lives, here and now. In seeking to preach with greater awareness of embodied communication, your movements may seem awkward and over-stated in the beginning. You may be self-conscious or fearful of what your receivers will think. Give it time and some practice and it will become natural. Embodied communication is contagious. Using your body can offer subtle liveliness to your preaching, so give it a try!

■ CHAPTER 17

# Fired Up—Burned Out

Richard Stern

For the public are accustomed to listen not for profit but for pleasure, sitting like critics of tragedies, and of musical entertainments, and that facility of speech against which I declaimed just now, in this case becomes desirable, even more than in the case of barristers, where they are obliged to contend against one another. A preacher then should have loftiness of mind, that he may correct this disorderly and unprofitable pleasure on the part of the multitude, and be able to lead them over to a more useful way of hearing, that his people may follow and yield to him, and that he may not be led away by their own humors, and this is not possible to arrive at, except by two means: indifference to their praise, and the power of preaching well.

—*St. John Chrysostom*[1]

I realize that some priests find preaching intimidating, tedious, or even futile. It's a grind to put together regular weekly effort into preparing a homily when the fruits of preaching seem so meager: people do not pay attention, they are critical, or they do not offer any response at all.

—*Peter John Cameron,* OP[2]

We know that the faithful attach great importance to [preaching], and that both they and their ordained ministers suffer because of homilies: the laity from having to listen to them and the clergy from having to preach them!

—*Pope Francis*[3]

There is, perhaps, no greater hardship at present inflicted on mankind in civilised and free countries, than the necessity of listening to sermons.

—*Anthony Trollope, Barchester Towers*[4]

---

1. St. John Chrysostrom, *Treatise Concerning the Priesthood.*
2. Peter John Cameron, *Why Preach* (San Francisco: Ignatius Press, 2009), 9.
3. Pope Francis, *The Joy of the Gospel: Evangelii gaudium* (Frederick, MD: The Word among Us, 2013), 135.
4. Anthony Trollope, *Barchester Towers* (Oxford: Oxford University Press, 1980), 52.

## Section 1. What: Definitions and Overview

These four quotations cover a significant span of Christian preaching history, yet with remarkably (or unfortunately) similar views. All recognize a problem: the status of preaching and, perhaps by implication, the status of *preachers*.

Before I dive in, however, a little survey. First, when you think of good preaching, what are the qualities or characteristics that come to mind? Second, then the qualities or characteristics of preaching that are not so good. We will come back to these at the end of the chapter.

When Fr. Mike Connors invited me to lead a workshop for the biennial preaching conference at the University of Notre Dame, he left the topic open. The title of the conference is, of course, "To Set the Earth on Fire: Effective Catholic Preaching." I started noodling around the word "fire." When "fired up" popped into consciousness, another phrase emerged *immediately*. That phrase is "burned out." There was my title: "Fired Up—Burned Out." My first inkling was that they were closely connected and not distinctly separate stages or conditions, but two sides of the same coin. But first I needed to examine the issue of burnout in general and then burnout among clergy in a broader way, whether short or long term. Finally, then, we look at what might be done to minimize the chances of burnout and remain fired up for preaching.

In the March 27, 2017, issue of *Bloomberg Business Week* (pp. 68–69), there is an article entitled "Feel the Burnout," an obvious play on a phrase or image that athletes use, "feel the burn," to justify the inordinate pain and suffering they experience in developing their athletic ability, particularly in building stronger muscles.[5] The "burn" is the buildup of lactic acid in muscles after strenuous exercise. In short: no pain, no gain. The author, Kayleen Schaefer, claims the concept originated with psychologist Herbert Freudenberger in the 1970s and refers to drug users who would blankly watch their cigarettes burn down without actually smoking them, entranced by the glow of the cigarette and the pattern of the rising smoke. In 1980 Freudenberger wrote a book entitled *Burnout: The High Cost of Achievement.*[6] Other origins for the word/concept refer to a term that is used in rocketry.[7] When a rocket is launched, the job of the first stage is to get the rocket up and off the launch platform. When it has done its work, that is, when it has exhausted all of its fuel, it drops off and falls back to earth as a spent shell. I prefer the athletic and rocketry versions to the drug user

5. Kayleen Schaefer, "Feel the Burnout," in *Bloomberg Business Week*, March 27–April 2, 2017, 68–69.

6. Herbert Freudenberger, *Burnout: The High Cost of Achievement* (New York: Anchor Press, 1980).

7. William H. Willimon, *Clergy and Laity Burnout* (Nashville: Abingdon Press, 1989), 21.

version. Applied to people, however, "burnout" implies a negative condition; the "fuel" necessary to complete a given task, a job, a life, has been used up prematurely or possibly was never present in adequate amounts in the first place for the task, such as agreeing to do a presentation on a topic you actually know nothing about. In either case, there is a miscalculation in the amount of fuel or energy or dedication that is required in order to move the task to completion.

There is then a complex of physical, emotional, and spiritual symptoms that may come into play. It is more a name given to a *pattern* than a single-symptom malady. Professor Christina Maslach notes three factors that can lead to burnout: "exhaustion, cynicism, and low professional efficacy—the feeling that nothing you do matters."[8] Defining and describing burnout is difficult because it takes different forms for different people. Whatever its symptoms, "burnout generally leads to a progressive loss of ambition, idealism, energy, calling, and purpose."[9] In a world in which technological advances were supposed to make work *easier,* they have often resulted in more work: longer hours, less free time, less privacy, and more pressure to produce. Our contemporary culture puts significant pressure and value on people to perform and success based on a performance that is better than the performance of others. Multitasking is seen as a great virtue, even though there really seems to be no such a thing. Rather we practice a "permanent partial attention." This perspective plays right into the hands of factors leading to burnout, the importance of being everything to everyone. I think we tragically misread St. Paul, who claims in 1 Corinthians that he has become "all things to all people" (9:22). It seems to me that Paul is talking there about *communication,* adapting to his various audiences, recognizing their diversity, trying to achieve, as Kenneth Burke labeled it, "consubstantiation."[10] Burke used it not in any religious way but to describe what good communicators need to do to achieve the fullest communication: common ground, shared substance. He is writing of the need to adapt to the frames of reference of those with whom he is preaching and evangelizing. Actually trying to be all things to all people is bound to reveal the inevitable "gap

8. Quoted in David J. Schaefer, *Surviving the Sermon: A Guide to Preaching for Those Who Have to Listen* (Cambridge, MA: Cowley, 1992), 68.

9. G. Lloyd Redinger, *Coping with Clergy Burnout* (Valley Forge: Judson Press), 138.

10. Stephen Littlejohn, *Theories of Human Communication,* 2nd ed. (Belmont, CA: Wadsworth, 1983), 57–58. See also Kenneth Burke, *A Rhetoric of Motives* (Berkeley: University of California Press, 1969), 20–27.

between expectations and achievement" that often yields "disillusionment, the apparent loss of a dream."[11]

How then does the idea of burnout apply to clergy? There is a mountain of literature on the topic of clergy burnout. I discovered that it is by no means a new problem. Apparently it can happen in any denomination. It can happen to the newly ordained and the veteran alike, although one to five years following ordination is a critical time in deciding whether one can stay with it. As Archibald Hart notes, "What sets the ministry apart . . . is the fact that new pastors and Christian workers tend to have a higher level of idealism than other new professionals; the possibility of disillusionment is therefore greater."[12] That initial bloom of idealism and enthusiasm begins to wear thin in the light of actuality. Indeed, because of changes in cultural values and priorities and because of clergy shortages in many denominations, the problem may well get worse with fewer clergy in fewer parishes with fewer resources. In other words, too much work for too few people. With some local exceptions, that seems to be the prognosis for the institutional church in the United States and elsewhere. Old Testament scholar Walter Brueggemann writes of preaching in this time as "preaching among exiles,"[13] that is, to a community increasingly marginalized with regard to impact or influence on the larger cultural conversations about values, direction, and policy.

Being severely stressed is not necessarily the same as burnout. "Often removing a person from a stressful situation produces immediate signs of recovery. This is not true for the burned-out person."[14] In the literature, burnout is often connected to depression. Depression is more than being depressed *about* something in particular; it is an overall malaise that impacts multiple layers of one's life.

My initial suspicion was that burnout, whether of a momentary or a long-standing nature, is common in the so-called helping professions, including among clergy. When I was a pastor, back in the 1980s, I attended a monthly meeting of deanery clergy during which a therapist from the local county health agency talked about burnout. Nearly everyone in the room was a candidate. But, as William Willimon notes, "many of us *like* to present ourselves as being under constant stress, suffering from jobs that are

---

11. Archibald D. Hart, *Coping with Depression in the Ministry and Other Helping Professions* (Waco, TX: Word Books, 1984). 4.

12. Hart, *Coping with Depression in the Ministry*, 124.

13. Walter Brueggemann, *Cadences of Home: Preaching among Exiles* (Louisville: Westminster John Knox, 1997).

14. Redinger, *Coping with Clergy Burnout*, 19.

demanding and overwhelming."[15] Yet Willimon wonders, with reference to research by John Sanford, whether burnout might be less about *time* for work than about the *meaningfulness* of the work being done.[16] People appear to burn out in the church, Willimon speculates, "not necessarily because they are overworked, but because they are overburdened with the trivial and the unimportant."[17] "When we no longer find meaning in what we do, even the smallest action drains us."[18] He cites fifteen factors he believes relevant to work in the church that can lead to burnout, including the following. See if any of these sound familiar.

- "The work of the church is never done."
- "The church doesn't give us a clear picture of the expectations and tasks we are supposed to fill."
- "Ministry tends to be repetitive."
- Further, persons in ministry often are required to adopt a persona that might conflict with their inner feelings and perceptions, appearing to be in control and compassionate at all times and in all places.
- "Church people may be exhausted by failure."

Where does one look for metrics to assure clergy and church staff that they are making progress as ministers? Time management issues abound. Pastors often spend significant time on the aspect of ministry they like the least: administration. This shows up in national studies as well as in my own study, more among priest respondents than with deacons. This difference between priests and deacons could well be because the deacons are somewhat less involved in administration or that *fewer* are as heavily involved in parish administration. Finally, clergy are expected and indeed pledge to be in harmony with their institution's values and policies.[19] This can be a difficult place to be on occasion as people change, as culture changes, as administrations change.

Factors leading to burnout can be related to personal dynamics or to institutional dynamics, policies, and practices, and in some cases a

15. William H. Willimon, *Clergy and Laity Burnout* (Nashville: Abingdon Press, 1989), 21.
16. Willimon, *Clergy and Laity Burnout*, 25.
17. Ibid.
18. Ibid., 26.
19. Ibid., 31–51.

combination of the two. In my own study of Saint Meinrad Seminary graduates and those who completed our Permanent Deacon Formation program between the years 1993 and 2016, this same issue was borne out.[20] Priests ranked their tasks according to importance in four categories: pastoral care, preparing to preach the weekend homily, personal spiritual practices, and administration. That was also the order of importance for priests. Note preparing to preach was second. Fourth was administration. When asked to rank the same categories according to time spent, administration moved to first; the others then slid down one place.

Among permanent deacons, there was a slightly different order. As far as order of importance or preference, the sequence went: pastoral care, personal spiritual practices, preparing to preach the weekend homily, and administration. The same ranking held for assessment of time consumed. It is not too hard to speculate about the difference between the priest and deacon respondents. Their roles in the parish differ, perhaps dramatically so.

In an essay entitled, "The Maceration of the Minister," Joseph Sittler describes one of the symptoms of impending burnout as "the exchange of honesty for sincerity."[21] This is the shadow side of trying to become all things to all people. One not only recognizes the diversity one must engage in ministry, but deeply believes it is the expectation put on one by others and by oneself. This soon conflicts with the realization of the impossibility of meeting those expectations. This is called am*biv*alence—trying to live between two conflicting sets of values: in this case, internal and external.

Focusing more narrowly on preaching, how does preaching indicate or even become a contributing factor to burnout? In my survey I asked priests and deacons how often they experienced some version of burnout or spiritual dryness related to preaching. While it varied some depending on how long one had been ordained, and between priests and deacons, it seems not to have reached anything like a major crisis in the Church. Yet it has to be of concern, if only because preaching is one of the top two reasons Catholics value participating in Mass. Permanent deacons as a group said they either periodically or seldom experienced spiritual dryness for a combined total of 67.5 percent. For priests, as a group, it was 86.6 percent. The statistics varied slightly depending upon the group, but the most common answer was "seldom," with "periodically" next in line.

---

20. My thanks to Dr. Thomas and Rita Walters for their enormous help in putting the survey together.

21. Joseph A. Sittler, "Maceration of the Minister," in *Grace Notes and Other Fragments* (Philadelphia: Fortress Press, 1981), 57–68.

Some general responses from my survey in relation to the question include many, many respondents' comments, from both priests and deacons, about the lack of time to give to proper preparation of preaching. For some it is lack of time to prepare for preaching but others observe that a lack of adequate time to give to prayer and spiritual health can transfer to their preaching—a "general spiritual dryness," as one priest put it. Relatedly, others comment about a lack of time "spent in prayer with the Scripture readings." "The three to four hours a week that I give never seems enough to prepare a well-crafted homily." According to the Carrell study, Catholic priests spend an average of three hours compared to Protestants who spend ten hours to prepare for a Sunday sermon or homily. Other studies come up with slightly different averages, although the basic outcome is the same. We can, of course, come up with reasons why that might be so, but the difference is telling nevertheless. It is telling especially because other studies suggest that for many in the assembly, the most meaningful portion of the Mass is the homily! One priest observes that "spiritual dryness in preaching often leads to a feeling of disconnect to God as well as feelings of disconnect from the people." Feelings of inadequacy plague some preachers. Another said this "usually happens when I am overwhelmed with some administration problem." Or, preaching can come to feel "like another task."

What is easily overlooked in all this are the needs and desires of those who preach, as well as those of the assembly. Fr. James Wallace, in his excellent book about preaching at the rites, feasts, and saints, entitled *Preaching to the Hungers of the Heart,* notes that all people experience three basic hungers: hunger for meaning, hunger for wholeness, and hunger for belonging. He explains how the rites, feasts, and saints can address each of those hungers. But how easy it is to forget that the preacher lives with the same hungers. Obvious? Yes. Overlooked or neglected? Quite possibly. How then does the preacher satisfy these basic hungers?

## Section 2. So What?

How does it relate to preaching? In my personal experience as a *listener,* when a preacher drifts more and more into telling me what to do or explaining more and more what Paul or Matthew *meant,* those are signs of frustration, if not burnout. If we only understood better what Paul meant, and did that, things would be good. If I feel browbeaten at the end of the homily, that, to me, is a sign of the preacher's frustration, if not impending burnout. I am talking here about a chronic and evolving pattern, not any particular homily.

In the relevant literature, one of the potential causes of stress or eventual burnout out is the repetitive nature of some work. What is more repetitive than preaching? What can I say this Easter or Christmas that I haven't already said? By the time Christmas has arrived, I am generally out of gas trying not to preach about Christmas but about Advent. Christmas comes, and I am pooped. An impending sign of my own near burnout was an Advent homily I did at a deanery mass. I mentioned that it seemed to me that I enjoyed Christmas less every year since I had been ordained. I thought it was a mighty risky statement to make, but I thought I might as well be honest. I saw a number of nodding heads and later heard appreciative comments.

## Section 3. Now What?

Thankfully, it does not end there. Respondents to my survey and other research projects have come to some important, though in some ways not terribly surprising, ways of dealing with, forestalling, or coping with spiritual dryness or, in its worse forms, burnout. I wish I could just list all of the responses for you, even if just from my own survey. There is a lot of wisdom there, which coincides quite closely with much larger studies.

G. Lloyd Redinger notes, "We tend to leave clergy . . . to their own resources until there is a problem."[22] The recent document from Rome *The Gift of the Priestly Vocation* bears this out. It talks about, as do other earlier documents, the importance of ongoing formation. At various places within the document it encourages the formation of small groups to be supportive of the individual in various stages of formation. This is commendable. However, the responsibility for this ongoing formation seems to resort to the priest's personal initiative. "Ongoing formation must be concrete, that is to say incarnate in priestly reality, so that all priests can undertake it effectively; after all, it is the priest himself who is principally and primarily responsible for his own ongoing formation."[23] True enough, but a little "soft paternalism" might be just the thing needed for the sake of the preachers and for their parishioners.

*Working on your own.* One cause of burnout is insufficient skills or training for the job at hand. How then does one begin to improve one's preaching? Ongoing formation. First, improvement of any lasting value calls

---

22. Redinger, *Coping with Clergy Burnout*, 51.

23. Congregation for the Clergy, *The Gift of the Priestly Vocation* (Vatican City: L'Osservatore, 2016), 35–36.

for three steps: awareness, intentionality, and implementation. Some improvements can be achieved on one's own.

Preaching can be a lonely enterprise. But does it have to be? One way of starting is to assess, what is your initial question? What sets preparation in motion? Are there ways of distributing the responsibility or sharing some parts of it, bringing in, as it were, additional conversation partners? In my own experience, a simple change in questions has made an enormous difference. I don't recall any emphasis in my seminary classes on reckoning with the particular assembly: who was there and who was not there. When I was in seminary and for the years I was in the parish, the operative question was, "What am I going to say on Sunday?" The problem with this question is that it puts the entire burden on the preacher's shoulders. I have, however, learned to rephrase that question to, "What do I hear being said here? What do I hear from the lectionary readings, from the news, from my parishioners, from the Holy Spirit? What am I bringing to the texts?" Lots more voices to listen to, voices that may have important things to contribute to the interpretation of the lectionary readings and their subsequent proclamation.

Another helpful tool is *lectio divina,* a great help in slowing down the process in order to let the readings do their work. Even prior to or as part of *lectio,* try reading the texts *aloud.* It is too easy to skim read through the readings without really letting them speak when we read to ourselves. When I read out loud, I hear what words I emphasize and which words I let go unemphasized. Where do I pause? Reading out loud makes more obvious how I interpret the passage. Read it again with different inflections. And again.

When you look at the Scripture readings, what do you read for? Authors Paul Scott Wilson and Eugene Lowry both suggest looking for trouble, in the text and in you as you read the text.[24] I would expand the word trouble, however, to include the idea of resistance or tension in the text but also in you as you engage the text. Do you find any trouble, resistance, or tension in you as you read that 1 Kings passage?

Another exercise preachers can do on their own is freewriting, a writing practice intended to break the log jam of ideas that is also known as writer's block. This log jam can come because I have too many things I want to cover but also because I can't see any ideas; they are all stuck in a clot, locked up in an inaccessible corner of my imagination. The idea for this is from Natalie

24. Paul Scott Wilson, *The Four Pages of the Sermon* (Nashville: Abingdon, 1999) and Eugene Lowry, *The Homiletical Plot,* expanded ed. (Louisville: Westminster John Knox, 2001).

Goldberg in a book entitled *Writing Down the Bones*.[25] There are several rules to freewriting:

1. Keep your hand moving.
2. Don't cross out.
3. Don't worry about spelling, punctuation, and grammar.
4. Lose control.
5. Don't think.
6. Go for the jugular.

One additional important area to work on in order to improve your preaching, whether alone or with others, is to strengthen your prayer or spiritual practice. The major studies I looked at noted this with regard to ministry in general and also for preaching. I am particularly indebted here to the work of Dr. Lori Carrell, who has done some important research into preaching, interviewing some 30,000 people, Catholics and Protestants, pastors and parishioners, about preaching. The results of her research are found in two books: the first from 2000, *The Great American Sermon Survey*, and an expansion in 2013, *Preaching That Matters: Reflective Practices for Transforming Sermons*.[26] Dr. Carrell also gave the 25th Annual John S. and Virginia Marten Lecture in Homiletics at Saint Meinrad Seminary and School of Theology in 2015. Dr. Carrell notes that in the research she did with preachers and parishioners who worked together she discovered, without prompting from the researchers, that as the preacher's spiritual life got stronger, so did the preaching. In a major study of priests conducted by Dean Hoge, he concludes, "Both priests who have stayed and those who have left assert the need to have a solid prayer life based on strong faith in Jesus' mission for the Church."[27] My own survey draws the same conclusion. Over and over, when asked to provide advice to others about avoiding or coping with spiritual dryness or even burnout, respondents mentioned the importance of prayer and spiritual direction.

*Working with others.* Referring again to the research by Dr. Carrell, the other significant tactic she reported was to begin to talk with others about

---

25. Natalie Goldberg, *Writing Down the Bones* (Boston: Shambala, 1986), 8.

26. Lori J. Carrell, *The Great American Sermon Survey* (Wheaton, IL: Mainstay Church Resources, 2000); Lori J. Carrell, *Preaching That Matters: Reflective Practices for Transforming Sermons* (Herndon, VA: Alban Institute, 2013).

27. Dean Hoge, *The First Five Years of Priesthood: A Study of Newly Ordained Priests* (Collegeville, MN: Liturgical Press, 2002), 106.

preaching, that is, getting preachers and parishioners talking about preaching—together. Again, this was not prompted by the researchers. Various groups figured it out on their own with quite positive results. "How good it is when priests, deacons and the laity gather periodically to discover resources which can make preaching more attractive!"[28]

But it rarely happens. In my own survey, only 6.5 percent of the priests reported working with small groups (staff, parishioners, and/or other clergy). They also reported working with ecumenical groups 0.8 percent for a total of 7.3 percent. For deacons the numbers were similarly underwhelming: 6.7 percent and 1.3 percent respectively for a total of 8 percent. Between my experience and the research we have read about and conducted at Saint Meinrad, we have installed this as a standard part of every preaching assignment: to work with a small group to test out ideas prior to their actual preaching. The preaching is also recorded on video and reviewed with the student preacher. Students report the value of such an enterprise. It may take a while for this to develop some momentum in a parish setting. Parishioners are probably not used to offering feedback, nor preachers in getting it directly.

I gave up some years ago on the idea of trying to generate interest in three-to-five-day workshops on preaching. We moved to a completely different mode. The mode is called "supervision" or by its more current designation, "reflective practice." The word "supervision" unfortunately evokes a number of unfortunate images that are not especially helpful in talking about the process, terms evocative of factory work or of Clinical Pastoral Education (CPE). Saint Meinrad Seminary and School of Theology has had a two-track program that trains people to be reflective practitioners for those ministering in pastoral care, or in homiletics. Several have fulfilled requirements for both tracks.

The supervisor's role is to enable the other to form goals for improved practice. These sessions often begin with the person wanting to improve various skills related to pastoral care or preaching. The goals are determined not by the guide/practitioner but by the person desiring to improve his or her practice. Equally and ultimately more important is to clarify and develop the person's *identity* as, in our case, a preacher. The practitioner can certainly help the person come to clarity on the goals but the goals are the person's goals, not what the practitioner thinks the person should work on.

---

28. Pope Francis, *The Joy of the Gospel*, 159.

Reflective practice or supervision starts from a different premise, than, for example, mentors or coaches. Supervision can be done one-to-one or in small groups. The goal is to develop the supervisee's goals as a preacher. This often starts when someone wants to improve delivery skills. But it does not stop there. The larger goal is to develop the supervisee's self-image or identity as a preacher. But who is the person as a preacher? This has become an important part of my work as a teacher in a seminary. I ask every class of seminarians and also permanent deacon candidates why they entered a program leading to ordination. How many did so because they wanted to be preachers? Never more than 10 percent.

## Conclusion

We come back to that little survey we did at the beginning about qualities that characterize good preaching. Most preachers are certainly capable of working toward those good characteristics. It takes awareness of areas to work on, a desire to work on them, and actually implementing some sort of action: experimenting, trying something different, getting feedback, etc. Two activities that seem likely to lead to improvement are maintaining or developing a good spiritual life and talking with others about preaching. Ironically, these are two activities with which the ordained are identified, yet the ones most easily compromised.

CHAPTER 18

# Spirituality: Preaching's Catalyst[1]

Fred A. Baumer and Patricia Hughes Baumer

It is a ritual of spring. There is warmth, light, and waiting. Red tinted nectar as an enticement. The feeder is hung outside the breakfast nook window.

Yet there are so many distractions, principally the coffee and the morning paper. If we do not look up, we will not see. If we are sitting in different chairs, we will not be facing the right window. If we are preoccupied with the demands of a day crammed with doing, we will be rushing to be up and out, made captive by a too-tight schedule. We will not see. But in a contemplative pause, we watch, we see. Suddenly there is a fluttering, a hovering of a tiny one. The hummingbirds have found their way home.

Why do we watch and rejoice? Because we are preachers. The job description requires that we *notice*: needs and beauty, seasons and homecomings of the birds of the field. Our spirituality is centered on *noticing*.

Ah . . . there is that word: *spirituality*. The focus of the fairly new discipline of spirituality is the entirety of lived faith.[2] Roger Haight defines spirituality as "the fundamental organization of a person's life. It is the center of gravity that supplies coherence to the sum total of one's behavior."[3] This chapter will reflect on the relationship between spirituality and preaching, specifically the spirituality of the one who preaches. How does the preacher's spirituality become a catalyst for preaching so that it is experienced as an opportunity to plunge into an encounter with God, an encounter that is compelling enough to merit the breaking of silence?

This chapter will discuss two spirituality constructs that have arisen from our work as teachers of preaching for over thirty years. We call them

1. A catalyst is an "event that causes change or action." This paper probes the relationship between preaching and spirituality. The organizing question: How does the preaching event affect the spirituality of the preacher? On the other hand, how does a preacher's spirituality shape the preaching event?

2. Elizabeth A. Dreyer and Mark S. Burrows, eds., *Minding the Spirit: The Study of Christian Spirituality* (Baltimore: Johns Hopkins University Press, 2005). Definition: The material object of the discipline is "the lived Christian faith," 5.

3. Roger Haight, *Christian Spirituality for Seekers* (Maryknoll, NY: Orbis, 2012), xx.

"study spirituality" and "sidewalk spirituality." Our premise is that preaching is a catalyst or change agent for our spirituality, and that our spirituality changes how we preach.

As an organizing guide, we call upon the work of rhetorical theorist Kenneth Burke (1897–1993), who devised the "dramatistic pentad" as a model for analyzing speeches or writings.[4] A homily or collection of homilies can be analyzed by identifying their "scene, act, agency, agent, and purpose." Burke's analysis is the basis for one tool we have used to analyze homiletic preaching. Listing a preacher's greatest strength as one and numbering to five, the weakest of the five dynamics, reveals something about the spirituality of the preacher.

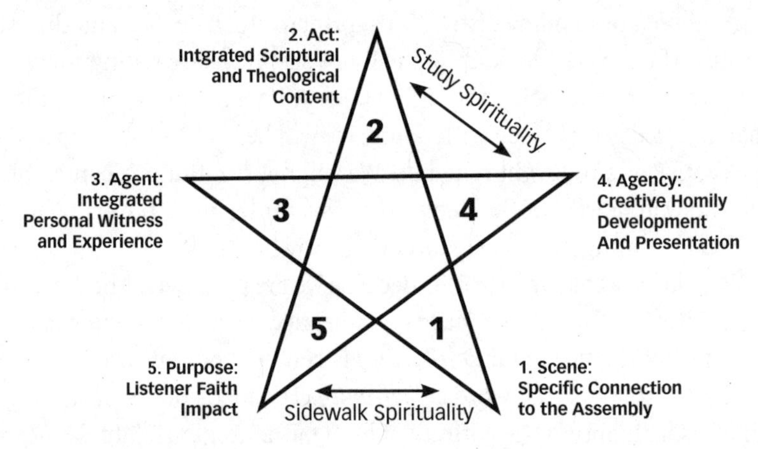


Figure 1. The Dramatistic Pentad

1. Specific connection to the assembly ("scene"—the existential need of this assembly in this time and place). The preaching is immediately relevant to and addresses the needs of the listeners in this time and place.

2. Integrated scriptural and theological content ("act"—the organizing principles of the preaching). The preaching is directly connected to scriptural/liturgical texts, demonstrating exegetical knowledge and theological insight.

3. Integrated personal witness and experience ("agent"—the self-understanding of the preacher). The preacher demonstrates

4. The dramatistic pentad arises out of Burke's larger philosophy of language developed in his writings over a fifty-year period, 1931–1983: *Counter-Statement* (1931); *Permanence and Change* (1935); *Attitudes toward History* (1937); *The Philosophy of Literary Form* (1941); *A Grammar of Motives* (1945); *A Rhetoric of Motives* (1950); *Rhetoric of Religion* (1961); *Language as Symbolic Action* (1966).

a spirituality that communicates with passion, speaking as a person of faith who has experienced the "so what" of the message in his/her own life.

4. Creative homily development and presentation ("agency" —the unique style characteristics of the preaching). The preacher uses imaginative speech, a variety of forms and stylistic elements and communication skills such as articulation, phrasing, rate, tone, pitch, and gesture that hold attention.

5. Listener Faith Impact ("purpose"—why the preaching is being given and what it hopes to achieve in the listeners). Listeners say how the preaching opened their minds/hearts, leading to an encounter with grace that has impact on their daily lives.[5]

Burke argued that any collection of speeches, or each individual speech, could be analyzed using his pentad, visualized as a five pointed star. He also suggested that focusing on the relationship between two of these five elements would evidence a worldview.[6] We suggest that a homily or collection of homilies analyzed through this model elicits a preacher's worldview—their "center of gravity" or "lived faith."

Most homilies given by preachers in the 1982–1985 NOCERCC[7] diocesan workshops centered on the "integrated Scripture/theology" (act) and "creative development" (agency). They evidenced study spirituality. By contrast, the 1982 USCCB document *Fulfilled in Your Hearing: The Homily in the Sunday Assembly* reinforced a "specific assembly" (scene) and "faith impact" (purpose) relationship. Homilies from this perspective evidenced sidewalk spirituality.

---

5. The focus on the liturgical context of preaching or "homiletic" was reinforced in the Vatican II Council documents and subsequent writings on preaching.

6. Fred A. Baumer, *Toward the Development of Homiletic as a Rhetorical Genre: A Critical Study of Roman Catholic Preaching in the United States since Vatican II* (PhD dissertation, Northwestern University, 1985). In this study, I use Burke's dramatistic pentad to highlight the ratios of four distinct preaching genres: evangelization, catechesis, theological argument, and homiletic.

7. NOCERCC, National Organization for the Continuing Education of the Roman Catholic Clergy, is a network of diocesan and religious directors of presbyteral continuing education/formation that attempts to educate and motivate clergy for more effective ministry in the Church. The document of the Bishops' Committee on Priestly Life and Ministry, *Fulfilled in Your Hearing: The Homily in the Sunday Assembly* (Washington, DC: USCCB, 1982) became the centerpiece for a NOCERCC four-day priests' preachers retreat. From 1982–1985 some forty dioceses sponsored these retreats, which included presentations on hermeneutics, ritual, spirituality, and communication skills, along with peer-preaching workshops. Along with St. John's of Collegeville's William Skudlarek, the primary author of *Fulfilled in Your Hearing*, Chicago's Gerry Broccolo, Notre Dame's John Gallen, and Fred Baumer participated in giving these retreats. This document was the subject of a commentary in 2010: James Wallace, ed., *Preaching in the Sunday Assembly, A Commentary on Fulfilled in Your Hearing* (Collegeville, MN: Liturgical Press, 2010).

## Study Spirituality

While in the office, we study the scriptural/liturgical texts for a meaning that will relate to the people of our time. We think through and find the messages that become an apologetic for the faith tradition and our communal belief systems.

Figure 2. "Arbor picta," *Manual for Curates*

Many times sermons with a predominant focus of scriptural/theological content creatively developed are structured according to a mnemonic device used in the Middle Ages, called the "arbor picta." This 1506 *Manual for Curates* lays out considerations for preachers, and pictures the sermon as a tree with three branches and a crown of leaves. At the base of the tree is the word "thema," suggesting the preacher first state the theme of the preaching; second, greet the people, "salutatio populi"; then restate the theme, "thematis resumptio." Then the manual suggests the preacher divide the "ratio," the reason or content of the sermon, into three parts (the three branches of the tree) and "amplification," amplifying each of these three parts (the leaves), before drawing to a "conclusion." We may know this model of preaching as "three parts and a poem."[8]

The focus of this style of preaching is on thematic content. Many times the sermon reinforces a specific theological truth, church doctrine, or catechetical message. The creative phraseology and linguistic energy of the preacher brings the message home by suggesting that the thematic content will be treated in three ways with clear examples. The sermon concludes with a poetic encouraging word to live by the message.

Guerric DeBona, in his 2015 Marten Lecture, described the dynamism of this form of preaching in the Evidence Guild, a preaching movement in the late 1920s and early 1930s that addressed growing anti-Catholicism in the United States. In parishes, retreats, and classrooms, the preachers

8. Johann Ulrich Surgant, *Manuale curatorum predicandi prebens modum tam latino quae vulagri sermone practice illuminatum* (Strassburg: J. Pruss, 1506). In the authors' private collection.

reinforced Catholic beliefs on such topics as "Why Catholics honor Mary," and "Why priests don't marry."[9]

One consequence of study spirituality is the potential separation of the preachers' prayer from the preparation of their weekly preaching. During the four-day NOCERCC workshops in the 1980s, many priests shared how praying the breviary, recitation of daily Mass, time before the Blessed Sacrament, and the yearly retreat were the lynchpins of their spirituality. Coming to an understanding that the very preparation of their Sunday preaching could be a new center of gravity for their spirituality was an exciting new thought for some of them. And furthermore, the recommendation that the preparation of their preaching would cause a prayerful encounter with God for themselves each week was, for many, a new way to think about their preaching.

Several years ago we had the opportunity to interview at length eight priests, ordained between 1963 and 1973, who had preached in inner city and suburban parishes, universities and South American missions. We got their names from people who regarded them as homilists who connected with their listeners. When asked what they had learned about preaching as a catalyst for their own spirituality they all shared how their spirituality had changed, but how it had begun as study spirituality.

- "I knew a lot about sin, salvation, incarnation, God three-in-one, church doctrine, the virtues—all in my head, and it all came out of my head in preaching without much of an effect on my own life."
- "I came out of seminary somehow believing I was a gift to the congregation because of my theological training. I could teach the faith."
- "We didn't get a lot of preaching practice in the seminary, and preaching was a chore for me early on. My prayer was the Mass; preaching was something I struggled with."
- "The pulpit was a pedestal for me early on."

One downside of a study spirituality is that the preacher can often come across as academic, disconnected from the specific community, and not describing an encounter with God, either for the preacher or the listeners.

Two examples. On January 21–22, 2017, the presidential inauguration weekend and the women's march across the nation, the reading from Paul

9. Guerric DeBona, OSB, "Recovering Our Voice: Reflections on Catholic Preaching before the Second Vatican Council" (John S. Marten Program in Homiletics and Liturgics, Notre Dame, Indiana, 2015), https://www.youtube.com/watch?v=_OFjProbR_w.

(1 Corinthians 1:10, 17) decried the divisions in the community in which some were claiming that they belonged to Cephas, others to Apollos, and yet others to Paul. The Gospel was from Matthew (4:12–23), Jesus calling the fisherman from their nets to be his disciples.

The preacher we heard gave a carefully crafted homily on discipleship using the metaphor of the net as the call to each of us on how to bring people into a relationship with God. There was no reference to what was happening across the nation. Our community itself, like the nation, was a collection of allegiances, marching that inauguration weekend for many different reasons. The theological understanding of discipleship (act) was developed through a well-thought-out, imaginative, and creative use of language (agency). The preaching had no direct connection to our particular congregation in which it was preached, nor any connection to how the preacher had experienced the national weekend upheaval.

Several weeks later on the Sunday before Valentine's Day, a perennial high holy day for sweethearts of all ages, the Gospel was Matthew's christological view of how Jesus does not come to abolish the Law, but brings it to completion (Matthew 5:17–37). The preacher explained the Gospel, how Jesus' teaching did not abolish the earlier law, but went beyond it. The preacher suggested that each Mosaic command needed to include an understanding of a "right relationship with God, a relationship of love." The command against murder required looking into anger with one's brothers and sisters. The command to give sacrifice at the altar can only come after reconciling with one's brothers and sisters. The preacher reinforced that the new commandment of right relationship with God and with others was the command of love. Love became the central theme and focus . . . yet Valentine's Day was never mentioned, nor were there any examples of how the members of this specific community or the preacher would be living out this commandment.

## Sidewalk Spirituality

Now back to the interviewed seventy-year-old lifetime preachers—who transitioned from study spirituality to sidewalk spirituality. Each of them told a story about an experience with parishioners, or in a workshop, or on a sabbatical that moved them from focusing less on the theological content (Burke's act) to focusing more on the context (Burke's scene) in which they were saying it. For one it was the elders of the inner-city parish who took him aside to say: "We hear you talkin' but you aren't talkin' to us." For another it was the matriarch of his first small Louisiana parish who said to him after Mass: "I'm so sorry you didn't have enough time to prepare your sermon specifically for us this morning." For another, it was starting "Tuesdays with Tim" in a parish where a small group met for coffee and shared their thoughts about next Sunday's readings. For another it was a storytelling workshop in which he found that fairytales and children's fables all connected emotionally to him in a deeper way, and he began to read Scripture looking for the same emotional bond.

Their experiences echoed what Paul Tillich preached in a sermon entitled "The New Being."[10] "We want only to communicate to you an experience we have had, that here and there in the world and now and then in ourselves is a New Creation." A sidewalk spirituality makes the preaching event a new creation within the preacher based on the experience of grace that emerged here and there in the world in which the preacher is living, and/or now and then within the preacher's own prayer and daily life. This is the essence of a sidewalk spirituality, whose ratio is "the specific community—faith impact" (scene-purpose). The preachers with sidewalk spirituality often find themselves as bystanders in the dark waiting for someone to come by and wipe God's grace like mud on their blind eyes.[11]

They find themselves in relation to their community and to the scriptural text as listeners and watchers hoping to notice how God is acting *here and there, now and then*. What are sidewalk spirituality preachers looking and listening for? They are looking at and listening to their lives in its day-to-day reality. They know that Mystery is there, in boredom, in pain, in loneliness, in excitement and gladness and joy. Every moment has a possible encounter with God within it, waiting only to be noticed. *Fulfilled in Your Hearing* described the preacher's goal as "not to interpret the text of the Bible, as much as to draw upon the texts of the Bible to interpret people's lives."[12]

For what purpose are preachers doing this? They do it for the purpose of enabling encounter—of experiencing a new creation—first in themselves, and then in the preaching event. Simply put, the sidewalk spirituality preachers are able to give an answer to the "so what?" They know that before they stand before their communities they must answer the question: "So what experience of God's grace did I have as a result of my preparation?" This

---

10. Paul Tillich, *The New Being* (New York: Scribner and Sons, 1955). Fred Buechner expands on this quote encouraging preachers and novelists to "listen to your life" throughout his autobiographical book *Now and Then* (New York: Harper and Row, 1987).

11. John Shea, *Stories of Faith* (Chicago: Thomas More Press. 1980). Shea poetically narrates the story of the man born blind using the image of "Jesus smearing mud on the eyes of the man born blind."

12. *Fulfilled in Your Hearing*, 52.

is the new creation that is sought for themselves and for the community of listeners.[13]

Returning to our initial image of noticing the arrival of a hummingbird outside the breakfast room window, we would suggest that the Scriptures position us in the ideal direction, much like we choose a seat from which we can see the birdfeeder. But what we attend to, what we focus on, is not the place where we sit, but rather the view beyond the window. Nor do we focus on the windowsill or the framing. When we experience ourselves as members of the faith community in which we preach, we share awareness of what the windowpane reveals as this community's human life. Very seldom is the community's life preoccupied with steeples or stained glass. If we can't see the focus from here, then it doesn't pass muster as an effective focus for this week's preaching.

The narrowing technique is straightforward. The preacher shares the viewpoint of the listeners. What is said is not so much an expansion of the vision, as a deepening of it. The preacher's spirituality is noticing what is hidden in plain sight. How is God being disclosed? Can we name that God, and give praise and thanks?

We are not discounting the significance of serious exegesis of the day's Scriptures, or the time spent studying to allow ourselves to feel what resonates in our hearts. It is humbling to yield to the realization that in God's grace, we are designated by this community of faith to preach on this day, in this place. The resonance of our hearts matters or else someone else would be preaching.

When asked the question as to how their preaching changed over decades, the homilists we interviewed were frank and clear:

- "The biggest change I've made after I've written my homily is that I take a walk and ask 'so what?' So what difference does this passage mean in my life? Because if I can't answer that for myself, I can't preach it. How does this homily give me life?"

- "I realized somewhat late in my preaching career that there was good news in the Scripture, not academic good news, but good news for me, the preacher, and I had to experience it before I could preach it."

- "I learned from the people of Cuernavaca, where I spent a couple of years as pastor, that these struggling people always found application

---

13. Thomas J. Scirghi, *Longing to See Your Face: Preaching in a Secular Age* (Collegeville, MN: Liturgical Press, 2017), 55. Scirghi reinforces this question several times throughout this manual for preachers.

to their daily lives with Scriptures written centuries ago. They didn't go to theology classes; they just reflected and found God talking with them. I could do that too."

- "I changed from doing only historical-critical exegesis and included a reader-response method where I got inside the Scriptures to feel its emotions and intentions . . . not so much what the passage meant when it was written, but how the passage feels when it speaks its truth."

Here are two examples of homilies that manifest sidewalk spirituality. On the Sixth Sunday of Easter, the Gospel spoke of the disciples asking for and receiving the Spirit. "I will not leave you orphans, but I will come to you" (John 14:15–21). The preacher began by sharing a story of volunteering to paint the exterior of a Habitat House for an Ethiopian immigrant mother and her four children. But weather intervened, and on-site, instead of being handed a brush and paint, the preacher was tasked with wearing a breathing mask and scraping the old lead paint from the hundred-year-old structure. The day wasn't what the preacher had signed up for. The preacher grumbled and sulked all morning long.

At lunch time the Ethiopian home owner came out to the sweaty group with a pitcher of apple tea that she had brewed and a tray of the most exquisite and delicate hand-painted teacups and saucers. She insisted the dust-covered hands of the volunteers use these rather than the convenient disposable cups. In that moment the preacher noticed and felt the grace of Jesus' promise: "In a little while the world will no longer see me, but you will see me." The preacher felt the Spirit's grace in this encounter with someone sharing the most precious possession she had. Because of her selfless gift the preacher's afternoon was filled with a new energy.

Let's return to the metaphor that we have been using for the process of preaching preparation. The preacher watches and waits for some movement beyond the windowpane that signals the arrival of a hummingbird. Being attentive, noticing, the preacher is at last aware of something moving, the flutter of an "aha!" that becomes the focus of the preaching. Unearned, this experience leads to praise, a spontaneous offering of recognition of the holy. Gratitude follows in its wake, because there is a moment of light breaking in without the preacher's laboring for it.

The practice of sidewalk spirituality is the practice of watching and waiting for the insight for preaching, noticing the movement beyond the window. Making connections that enflesh faith in human actions, words, and emotions. Noticing is at the heart of this form of spirituality, and becomes the catalyst for preaching.

One preacher who modeled noticing and the sidewalk spirituality approach was Bishop Ken Untener. He preached the weekend of 9/11 in the Saginaw Cathedral, the Gospel of the day being Luke 15:1–32: the parable of the lost sheep, lost coin, and prodigal son. The preaching is worth quoting in its entirety, because it does not deny the reality of the 9/11 context as it peers through the lens of the Scriptures of the day to impact faith. Bishop Untener's intent was to give the listening community, including the bishop himself, an encounter with God's grace, a new creation.[14]

> When Jesus and his disciples left the Last Supper table and were walking to the Garden of Gethsemane, Jesus said to them, "This night you will have your faith in me shaken." Peter and the rest of the disciples responded that this would never happen. Well, it did.
>
> This past week we've had our faith shaken. We wonder how God could let a thing like this happen. And sometimes in a tiny millisecond, the thought flits across our minds: "I wonder if there is a God."
>
> At a time like this, a preacher might think of changing the Sunday Scripture readings to find passages in the Bible that bear more directly on what has just happened. There's something to be said for that. On the other hand, instead of looking for something that we *want* God to say, it may be better to listen to what God has to say through the readings that are already there, and listen to them with fresh ears.
>
> When we listen to the Scriptures in the light of whatever is going on in our lives, we sometimes hear some things we didn't expect to hear. I can tell you that I have never listened to the words of this Gospel in quite the same way before. I heard it with fresh ears.
>
> Our normal thoughts when we read the parable about the lost sheep, the lost coin, and the lost son are almost predictable. They weren't predictable this time. We all heard it "live," the words colored by the feelings and thoughts that are in us.
>
> The Scriptures read at liturgy are always "live." They are always contemporary, addressed to us here and now. We believe that when the Scripture is read at liturgy, God is especially present in the words, speaking "live" to us. What do we hear this morning?

---

14. Bishop Kenneth Untener, "Sermon for the Twenty-Fourth Sunday in Ordinary Time, Year C" (September 16, 2011). All of Bishop Untener's homilies can be found at www.visitationnorth.org.

This section in Luke's Gospel is about loss—the lost sheep, the lost coin, the lost son. Last Tuesday, we all experienced loss. Each of us lost peace of mind. New York lost its firemen. Families lost fathers, mothers, brothers, sisters, daughters, and sons. The whole world lost its sense of security. In each of these three parables, someone takes the initiative to find what is lost. It was the shepherd who went out to find the lost sheep. It was the woman who lit the lamp and swept the house to find the lost coin. It was the father who ran down the road to embrace and kiss his lost son. The shepherd represents God. The woman represents God. The father represents God.

People ask, "What do we do at a time like this?" What we do is let God find us. What we do is open ourselves up to God who is taking the initiative right now to reach out to each of us. We admit that without God we are lost, in the dark. What we do is turn to God with a new realization that we depend upon God. We recognize that our ultimate security lies in God, who is all-powerful. And we find God—or rather—when we let God find us—we let God comfort us. And we listen to what God has to say, and resolve to do what God tells us to do.

It was eight years almost to the day when there took place in Chicago an unusual event. Some 6000 people from around the world, representing 125 faiths—all major world religions—gathered for an eight-day event call the "Parliament of the World's Religions." The last time something like that happened was in 1893. They prayed together, listened to talks by religious leaders, and near the end of the conference 250 representatives of these religions signed a document called "the declaration of a Global Ethic." It stated fundamental principles shared by the world's great religions as a framework for dealing with problems in the world.

It was more a statement of basic human values than a religious document, and it invited all men and women, whether religious or not, to commit themselves to this.

Among the things it said, "In particular, we condemn aggression and hatred in the name of religion." It also said, "We are interdependent. Each of us depends on the well-being of the whole, and so we have respect for the whole community of living beings—for people, animals, and plants, and for the preservation of earth, air, water, and soil. We must treat others as we wish others to treat us."

At the very end it said: "We invite all men and women, whether religious or not, to do the same." Each of us represented by the lost sheep, the lost coin, the lost son, may hear God saying words like that to us. They sound like something God would say. Perhaps this awful time in our history is a new opportunity in our history. I call myself and I call all of us to let God speak to us.

Keep in mind that in the parable of the lost son, the older son argues with his father. There's part of that older son in all of us. We shouldn't be surprised if part of us wants to argue with God. God's ways are not always our ways.

I close with this. Yesterday I baptized two children. You couldn't help but think, "Who would want to bring a baby into this world?" Well God would. God did! God's son was born into the world—God made flesh. And the Lord promised never to leave this world. His last words in Matthew's Gospel are, "I am with you always, even to the end of the age." So take heart. The Lord is with us, especially in these days, when we feel very, very lost.

# ABOUT THE CONTRIBUTORS

Fr. Ron Rolheiser, OMI, is a well-known speaker and author of innumerable books and the recipient of many Catholic book awards. He currently serves as president of the Oblate School of Theology in San Antonio, Texas.

Fr. Michael Connors, CSC is director of the John S. Marten Program for Homiletics and Liturgics at the University of Notre Dame. He has edited three books of preaching: *We Preach Christ Crucified* (Liturgical Press, 2014), *To All the World: Preaching and the New Evangelization* (Liturgical Press, 2016), and *What We Have Heard and Seen: Fostering Baptismal Witness in the World* (Wipf and Stock, 2017). He is also the author of *Preaching for Discipleship: Preparing Homilies for Christian Initiation* (Liturgy Training Publications, 2018).

Ann Garrido, DMIN, is associate professor of homiletics at Aquinas Institute in St. Louis, Missouri, and a consultant with Triad Consulting Group, a conflict mediation and communications team. She is the author of six books and numerous articles in the field of Church leadership and ministry, including *Mustard Seed Preaching* (Liturgy Training Publications, 2007).

Bishop Sylvester Ryan is the retired bishop of the Diocese of Monterey, California, and coauthor of *Preaching Matters: A Praxis for, Preaching* (Paul Bechtold Library Publications, Catholic Theological Union, 2015).

Fr. Joseph Juknialis is a priest of the Archdiocese of Milwaukee. Now retired from teaching homiletics, he still teaches homiletics for the archdiocese's permanent diaconate program. With Bishop Richard Sklba, Fr. Juknialis coauthored *Easter Fire: Fire Starters for the Easter Weekday Homily* (Liturgical Press).

Fr. Guerric DeBona, OSB, is professor of homiletics at Saint Meinrad Seminary, as well as subprior and novice/junior master for Saint Meinrad Archabbey. He is the author of the series *Between the Ambo and the Altar: Biblical Preaching and The Roman Missal* (Liturgical Press, 2013, 2014, 2015, Years A, B, and C), *Preaching Effectively, Revitalizing Your Church* (Paulist Press, 2009), *Rites of Passage: Preaching Baptisms, Weddings and Funerals* (Liturgical Press, 2018), and *Fulfilled in Our Hearing: History and Method of Christian Preaching* (Paulist Press, 2005).

Dr. Alyce McKenzie is the LeVan Professor of Preaching and Worship and director of the Center for Preaching Excellence at Perkins School of Theology at Southern Methodist University. She is the author of at least eight books on preaching and for many years wrote the *Knack for Noticing* blog on the Patheos website.

John (Jack) Shea is a theologian and storyteller who lectures nationally on storytelling. Jack has published twenty-five books on theology and spirituality, three works of fiction, and three books of poetry.

Dr. Dick Eslinger is emeritus professor of homiletics and worship at United Theological Seminary in Dayton, Ohio. He is the author of *A New Hearing: Living Options in Homiletic Method* (Abindon Press, 1987) as well as numerous other books and articles on preaching.

Deborah Wilhelm, DMin, is adjunct professor of homiletics at Aquinas Institute of Theology, St. Louis, Missouri, and coauthor of *Preaching Matters: A Praxis for Preaching* (Paul Bechtold Library Publications, Catholic Theological Union, 2015).

Fr. Ed Griswold, DMin, is the Henry J. and Marion I. Knott Professor of Homiletics, associate professor of pastoral theology, and vice-rector at Saint Mary's Seminary in Baltimore, Maryland.

Deacon David Shea, DMin, is associate professor of homiletics at the Athenaeum of Ohio. He is the author of *Unfulfilled in Their Hearing: Critical Issues in the Sunday Homily* (St. Anthony Messenger Press, 2010).

Sharon Schuhmann, DMin, is the Pastoral Associate for Intentional Discipleship at St. Bernadette parish in Louisville, Kentucky.

Fr. Jeff Nicolas, DMin, is the pastor of St. Bernadette parish in the Archdiocese of Louisville.

Karla Bellinger, DMin, is associate director of the John S. Marten Program for Homiletics and Liturgics at the University of Notre Dame. She is the author of *Connecting Pulpit and Pew: Breaking Open the Conversation about Catholic Preaching* (Liturgical Press, 2014) as well as numerous other articles and publications.

Fr. Peter McCormick, CSC, is a much beloved preacher on the campus of the University of Notre Dame and currently serves as its director of campus ministry. He is also the chaplain for the Notre Dame men's basketball team.

Suzanne Nawrocki, DMin, is adjunct professor of homiletics at Aquinas Institute of Theology, St. Louis, Missouri. Her specialty within the field of homiletics is the use of the body. Nawrocki presents on embodiment in preaching at conferences and workshops nationally.

Dr. David Stern is professor emeritus of homiletics at Saint Meinrad Seminary and School of Theology, Saint Meinrad, Indiana. He has produced a six-part video series, *Preaching for Today . . . and Tomorrow*, as well as many other articles and papers. He writes a column regularly for *Deacon Digest*.

Fred A. Baumer, PhD, business consultant, and Patricia Hughes Baumer, MDiv, executive director and founder of Partners in Preaching, have trained clergy and lay preachers in dioceses, parishes, and theology schools since 1991. Fred was on the committee that authored the USCCB 1982 document *Fulfilled in Your Hearing*. Among other publications, Fred and Patricia have authored articles for *PREACH* magazine and the commentary on the three lectionary cycles in the *Workbook for Lectors, Gospel Readers, and Proclaimers of the Word* (Liturgy Training Publications). They published *Pocket Prayers for Marriage* in 2015.

# INDEX


active listening, 149, 151
Aquinas, St. Thomas, 26
Augustine, St., 23, 114n, 133–138, 143, 163, 175
  *Confessions,* 162n
  *De doctrina christiana,* 23, 114n, 157, 183

Bain, Kenneth, 159n
Bellinger, Karla, 21, 28n, 112, 155, 160, 162n
Benedict XVI, Pope, 18, 99
Bloom, Allan, 3
Brown, Raymond E., 107n
Brueggemann, Walter, 55–58, 188
Buechner, Frederick, 53n
Burgoon, Judy K., 177n, 178n, 179n
Burke, Kenneth, 187 198–199, 202
Buttrick, David, 24 68–69, 104, 107, 108n, 125

Cameron, Peter John, OP, 19, 140, 185
Carrell, Lori J., 72–73 191, 194
Cialdini, Robert, 158
*Confessions*, 162n
  see also Augustine, St.
congruence, concept of, 239
Connors, Michael E., CSC, 72, 112, 186
Cook, Susan, 182n
Craddock, Fred B., 17n, 23, 68, 86, 125

DeBona, Guerric, OSB, 63, 64n, 101n, 130, 200, 201n
*De doctrina christiana*, 23, 114n, 157, 183
  see also Augustine, St.

editing (sermons), 112, 114–116, 119, 121,126, 162
effective preaching obstacles, 15, 72, 115
embodied communication, 54, 175–179, 183
  categories of, 176–179
  oculesics, 175, 178
  physical display, 175, 176, 177
  proxemics, 175
  paralanguage, 173, 178
    chronemics, 178
    vocalics, 179
*Evangelii gaudium (Joy of the Gospel),* 19, 21, 24, 50, 64, 105, 125–126, 150, 173, 174
experiences told in story form, 91, 94, 96

Farley, Edward, 102n
Ferris, Theodore Parker, 77
Fisher, Roger, 34
focus and function, 123–132, 160
homily/sermon preparation, 27, 30, 43, 51, 67, 89, 93, 95, 107, 117, 123, 125, 132, 145, 151–152, 156, 159, 170, 182, 191, 193, 203, 205

focus sentence, 67–68, 72
Foley, Edward, 47, 175n, 177n
*Forming Intentional Disciples*, 145, 146n, 167n
  see also Weddell, Sherry
Francis, Pope, v, vii, 19, 21, 24, 49, 50
*Fulfilled in Your Hearing,* 17–18, 24, 27, 64, 100, 145

Gaarden, Marianne, 158n
*Gaudium et spes,* 24n, 69
Gaughan, Thomas, csc, 136
*General Instruction of the Roman Missal* (GIRM), 17, 48, 17
gestures, 19, 138–139, 175, 178–183
*Gift of the Priestly Vocation, The,* 192
Gilkey, Langdon, 56
Goldberg, Natalie, 194
Goldin-Meadow, Susan, 182n

Good News/Gospel, 15, 19–22, 26, 28, 155, 160, 165
Getting the Gospel Heard model, 17
Getting the Gospel Said model, 17
*Great American Sermon Survey, The,* 194
see Carrell, Lori J.

Hardy, Barbara, 54
Heath, Chip and Dan, 21, 70
Heen, Sheila, 32n, 39
Heille, Gregory, 105n
Hillman, James, 3
Hoge, Dean, 194
*First Five Years of the Priesthood, The,* 194
Holy Spirit and preaching, 51–52, 117, 146, 155–163
homiletic reassessment
tools for, 72, 125
homiletic method, 68–69, 101
homilies
liturgical, 99, 101
and inductive narration, 69
as a sacrament of the Word, 69
globalized, 70–71
unified, 66–68
Honigsbaum, Mark, 36
Hopkins, Gerard Manley, SJ, 45

Intentional Listeners, 145–153
internal voice of congregants, 38
intentional discipleship
five thresholds of, 146–147, 149

Jensen, Richard J., 54n
John Paul II, St. Pope, 64, 161n
kataphatic dimension, 25
Keating, James, 33

language
archetypal, 11
biblical, 24
body, 11, 176, 177n
of critical thought, 12
religious, 4–6, 11–12
of the soul, 4, 12
of spirituality, 25
tool, 89

*lectio divina*, 65, 113, 116, 149, 193
listening assembly, 73, 145, 147, 153
Long, Thomas G., 123, 124n, 125–132
Lowry, Eugene, 68–69, 151, 193

McNeill, David, 180n,
Mitchell, Nathan, 177n
Moriarty, John, 1–2
Morneau, Robert, 52
mother tongue, 1–2, 4–7, 9–12
mystagogy
see sacramental imagination

narrative homiletics, 68
Nawrocki, Suzanne, 112, 176, 178n, 180n
new evangelization, 47n, 48n, 64, 65, 69, 133n

O'Connor, Michael Dominic, 133n, 134n
O'Malley, Timothy P., 47n, 48
*On the Art of Writing: Lectures Delivered in the University of Cambridge, 1913–1914*, 114n

parable, 82, 101–106, 169, 206–208
definition of, 82
Paschal Mystery, 12, 26, 45, 104, 107
Pastores dabo vobis, 161
Patterson, M., 176n
Patton, Bruce, 32n, 34n
Pierce, Joanne, 177n
Pontifical Biblical Commission, 18
postmodern era, 53, 55, 57
preaching
and being heard, 30, 161
and emotional interests, 34
and spirituality, 197
as a communal experience, 30
as an encounter with Christ, 18, 135, 138, 146
as dialogue, 19, 27, 50–51, 67–69, 85, 93, 100, 106, 140
as encounter, 18–20, 24, 28, 64, 67, 112, 138, 143, 145, 146–150, 153, 199, 201, 203
as negotiation, 31–32, 34, 36, 38–39
burnout, 186–194
doctrinal, 57 143n
feedback, 20, 27, 38, 38–39, 72, 195

from the table of the Word, 65–66
moralizing, 21
mystagogical, 25
oxytocin effect, 36n, 37, 40
personal authenticity, 22
personal theology of, 64–65
*Preaching the Mystery of Faith*, 28, 47, 65
primacy-recency effect, 176
purpose of, vi, 16, 18, 47, 49, 53, 56, 58, 89, 91, 114, 138, 141, 198–199, 203
qualities of, 20
the Paschal Mystery, 26, 104, 107
to postmodern believers, 55–57
to the Sunday assembly, 17, 18n, 145, 199n
to young people, 160, 165–174

Radcliffe, Timothy, OP, 15, 47
Redinger. G. Lloyd, 187n, 188n, 192
Rieff, Philip, 3
Rite of Christian Initiation of Adults (RCIA), 17
Rolheiser, Ronald, OMI, 1, 112
Ryan, Sylvester, 43, 48n, 112, 114

sacramental imagination
mystagogy, 25
*Sacrosanctum concilium*, vi 16, 64
Sancken, Joni S., 108n
sermons
see editing
scene crafting, 83, 87
Schaefer, Kayleen, 186
Scirghi, Thomas J., 204n
Shapiro, Daniel, 34
Shea, David, 133, 134n
Shea, John, 113, 203n
sidewalk spirituality, 198–199, 202–203, 205–206
Sittler, Joseph, 190
Smith, Christian, 166
Smith, J. Perry, 136, 137
spiritual teaching stories, 89, 91, 96
Stone, Douglas, 32n, 39
strategies for attentive listening, 149

Taylor, Barbara Brown, 16, 50
Thomas, Frank A., 86n
Toohey, William, CSC, Notre Dame Preaching Academy, 73

Untener, Ken, 51, 66, 68, 131, 206
Ury, William, 34n

*Verbum domini,* 99n

Wallace, James A., 133n, 140, 141, 145n, 191, 199n
Weddell, Sherry, 145–147, 167
Wilhelm, Deborah, 48n, 111, 114n
Willimon, William H., 186n, 189n
Wilson, Paul Scott, 69, 86, 125, 151, 193